Finding Faith

in the

FURY

One Soldier's faith challenging journey through
OPERATION IRAQI FREEDOM

Frank Selden

Published by

VMI PUBLISHERS

Partnering With Christian Authors, Publishing Christian and Inspirational Books

a division of VMI Publishers
Sisters, Oregon
www.vmipublishers.com

ISBN: 1933204257

Library of Congress Control Number: 2006929965

Author Contact: http://home.comcast.net/~frankselden

Printed in the United States of America

Cover photo courtesy of CPT. David Kalamen

Cover design by Joe Bailen

Dedication
To my wife and best friend,
Philese
Whose love and support from halfway
around the world helped me
find the energy and inspiration to keep writing.

Marian + Neil,

Thanks so much

for your support!

Jack Joblen

CONTENTS

ACKNOWLEDGEMENTS

I would not have had the time, energy and mental focus to write anything in Iraq without the incredible support I received from my beautiful bride, Philese Selden. Thanks to her I did not need to worry about anything at home leaving me free to concentrate on my military duties and my writing. I wish all married soldiers received the same degree of support from home. Sadly I spent numerous hours listening to stories about letters or phone calls by soldiers who did not. A top secret "Thank you darling" for everything you did to make this book a reality.

My daughter Rhea first voiced the idea to break my leg so I would not have to go to Iraq. My other children devised additional clever, and painful, schemes to help me avoid deployment. Once deployed, however, I received incredible encouragement from each of them. They especially provided a huge motivation to return home safe. Hugs and kisses to Rhea, Melissa, Joshua, Richard, Victoria and Layne. You all are turning out to be amazing individuals despite the short-comings of your dad / step-dad.

Some say that faith comes by hearing. I also know that faith comes by watching. Indeed, if we speak faith but never live it successive generations will not learn faith's most valuable lessons. If I am able to pass on any lessons about faith in this book it is because I am blessed to be my mother's son. My mother, Delores Koole, continues to be a source of positive influence for everyone who knows her. Thanks are not enough, but thanks mom! Your example helped me help dozens of others in Iraq.

I am also blessed to be one of few men who can appreciate his mother-in-law. Lee Schulstad supported her daughter on a daily basis without once, so I am told, complaining about me at all. Thank you Lee for not only raising a delightful daughter but for standing with all of us during my deployment and recovery.

A commander needs a special kind of fortitude to have a writer - lawyer - politician - thrill seeker in his unit. Lt. Col. Michael Hefty should have received a medal just for continuously putting up with questions such as "Could I have a day off to go on a fact finding mission in Baghdad?" As far as I noticed he only rolled his eyes once. Although he always placed safety and the mission first, he also allowed some latitude for writing and excursions. I am especially grateful for his permission to accompany convoys to the Turkey border and various northern villages.

Although I deployed and redeployed as a solo soldier, I have a special place in my heart for the soldiers of the 116th RAOC. They are one of the most professional units in the military, a true credit to the Armed Forces and the United States. Still, I hope to never deploy with any of you again. Here's to peace and staying home.

Our unit received boxes and boxes and boxes of support. Most of them arrived thanks to the compassion of Lois Gustafson. She rallied support from numerous businesses and individuals, primarily the Eastside Republican Club. Most of the school donations I delivered arrived via Lois' army of supporters. They also contributed to holiday meals and Christmas stockings, late night snacks and DVD movies. We certainly enjoyed our tour of duty more thanks to her generous reinforcements.

We also received many packages from Nadine Gulit and Terry Harder of Operation Support Our Troops and Amy Oxford of Operation Yellow Ribbon. Thank you for your countless hours in support of deployed soldiers and their families at home. If you can support either of these worthy causes please do so. They continue to help soldiers around the world.

Many friends pitched in to help with household chores and home repairs during my absence. Although not a direct aid in writing the book, your help indirectly made this tome possible as my mind could focus on the task at hand knowing home remained in good hands. Special kudos, in no particular order, to Charlie Klinge, Don Ege, Mark Isaacs, Greg Manciagli, Tricia Richards, Ted Brandstetter and David Gustafson. I am leaving out dozens of people in this category because they performed most of their work without telling me they did it. May you all receive abundant blessings for the way you continue to bless others.

There are two groups of people I want to thank whose names I do not know. First, a huge thank you to all of the medical staff in Iraq, Germany, Fort Lewis and the Seattle VA who helped me progress step by painful step. You kept your cool even when I didn't, you never lost sight of the healing process, and you also helped me overcome the more difficult obstacle of bureaucratic paperwork. I am still in awe of the results you achieve with wounded soldiers and vets. God bless every single one of you! Second, I want to thank the people of Dallas and

Fort Worth who take time to meet returning soldiers at the airport. While flying home on leave I was one of the first to ascend the international tunnel at Dallas-Ft. Worth airport. You started applauding, cheering and handing out souvenirs and water. I spoke to a few of you, many of whom are Vietnam vets. You remember all too well what it was like for you to step off the plane. I too will remember. You will always be in my heart. Thank you so much!

Finally, huge thanks to the staff at VMI Publishing. Without you this dream would not be a reality. From the day I first received a phone call from publisher Bill Carmicheal until receiving my initial copy you helped me feel at ease with the process and excited about the results. Special kudos to editor Mike Valentino. I pictured editors as the worst nightmare for a high-school English teacher only older; bespectacled, frizzy-haired, chain-smoking grammatical fanatics who maintain a permanent scowl, a disdain for writers and three drawrers full of red pens to prove their superiority. I still picture editors this way, but now I know they can also be pleasant to work with and worth listening to.

PREFACE

This book integrates three types of articles. The groups were originally different collections: news, opinions about the new and reflections about making sense of the chaos through the eyes of faith. This book weaves current events, poignant essays on contemporary issues, and faith lessons into a chronological story.

This book is not easy to read; at least I hope it isn't. I do not want readers to simply sit back, relax and enjoy the ride. I want you to feel the struggle, ponder the perplexities and question how real your faith is to you. This book is not a novel and not the result of an author carefully engineering events to enhance character development or reveal a surprising plot twist. Life can be stranger than fiction and this journey in Iraq certainly fits that description.

The "News from the Front" articles began as weekly e-mails to family and friends. I wrote home about events as I witnessed and experienced them in northern Iraq during Operation Iraqi Freedom II. Recipients forwarded them to other people eager to hear news of the troops not discussed in the media. The "News from the Front" segments tell the story of our activities in Iraq beginning April 24, 2004 (4-24-04), more than five months after my National Guard unit first received activation orders.

Beginning with the first week of activation I started writing a journal of my thoughts and reactions more to maintain my sanity than because of any desire to share my reflections. Most of those op-ed essays comprise the bulk of this book. Some of them cover fun subjects, others delve into serious topics and all of them open up the world that is duty in Iraq for our troops.

The news articles and opinion pieces were not enough for me to put a book together. I decided after several months stateside that I would also include the faith struggles I endured. The articles that begin "Faith Focus" are, to me, the most important part of the story. Many books already written describe the military endeavors and humanitarian efforts of Operation Iraqi Freedom. My focus is not what happened or why it happened. Instead, it centers on my beliefs about God, and myself and the world around me after living through the experience.

Many people believe that there are no atheists in the foxhole. I found that proverb false. More soldiers struggled with their faith as a result of our experiences than chose to believe in God. This struggle is not unique to Iraq.

Faith is coming under fire from numerous parapets. People who preach tolerance often practice it in favor of anyone but people of faith. Faith to some is the root of all evil as it breeds intolerance for their sinful lifestyles. Many of our top universities, some of them formerly private, religious institutions, do not allow faith concepts to be taught in certain scientific disciplines. People of faith need to bridge the gap. We must learn to exercise our faith in such a way that others will recognize faith for what it is: God's gift to a disadvantaged world. Our faith can meet people in their needs. Faith is timely, relevant, and active. Our faith includes answers to the most challenging problems facing our generation. Now, more than ever, this world demands that we live by faith, in Iraq, in the United States, and in every country on our globe.

11-17-03 * ACTIVATED

This year I activated credit cards with a phone call, on-line accounts with e-mail responses, and contracts with a signature. Now, with a terse phone call, I myself am activated. Not unexpected, considering world events, but still surreal. The sergeant delivered his news quickly over the phone and moved on to notify other National Guard soldiers. After he hung up I felt as disconnected from my life as I am from the caller.

The decision makers do not know the impact this will have on my family and me. They also do not care whether I respond to the call with the prescribed action. The consequences for failing to do so are sever enough to deter all but the fully determined. The decision makers, those chosen few with vast powers of delegation, speak, and the Army's Mordor-like furnaces rumble to create an incredible, if not invincible, army.

Am I merely the result of clever military programming? I shudder at the thought. Charles Bronson, in the 1977 action thriller *Telefon*, tracked a renegade Russian agent activating long-dormant terrorist cells. He triggered the activation with a Robert Frost line coincidentally the title of a book depicting Jackie Pflug's survival of a terrorist hijacking. Dean Koontz's psychotic psychologist, in False Memory, programmed patients to perform his atrocities when activated by a haiku. Finally, here I am, ready to spring into action from a cryptic phone call. I like to think that there are significant differences between these frightening fictional characters and me.

Each day of my nine years in the Guard contained the realization that I was only a phone call away from activation. Donning my uniform every drill weekend reminded me of the duties I swore to uphold. Requesting a regulation haircut always reminded me that I did not enjoy freedoms ordinary civilians take for granted. The phone call did not turn me into a mentally and emotionally detached android. I serve willingly and proudly. To be completely honest, I often found part-time soldiering inconvenient. This switch to an all expense paid 18-month vacation in Iraq is definitely not coming at a good time.

Three days ago I took my oath of admission into the Washington State bar.

I want to live my life that has been on hold during four intense years of school. I want my vacations, holidays, time with family and friends. However, I am not the only one today with a life on hold. Every Guard soldier has a civilian life bound by a military leash. Activation, like diarrhea, is inconvenient at any time.

I called my family and close friends to tell them about my upcoming deployment. The more I spoke to them about the mission the more excitement I felt about actually participating in events in Iraq. Despite the inconvenience, I want to go! I want to participate in creating a foundation for democracy amidst the ashes of Saddam's brutal regime. I want to fully see for myself the transformation Iraqis will develop with their new freedom. I am activated today, but I do not report for two weeks. I want to get rolling! It is, after all, what I have been programmed to do.

Many people wonder about why I am excited to go to Iraq. If they think about their question at all they usually mean why I would want to go to a hostile fire zone. After all, who wouldn't want to visit Iraq in peaceful conditions? Some of humankind's most ancient history is in Iraq. Early Bible stories occurred there. Iraq is the land of the Tigris and Euphrates, Babylon, Nineveh. Although I explored most of North America, this will be my first time off of the continent.

The adventure of Iraq aside, they continue, why do I want to go to combat? Fortunately our particular mission is not about combat. We are not at war with the people of Iraq; in fact we are helping them recreate their country. Saddam is out of power thanks to our combat troops. They set the stage for our mission and our success.

Won't I miss my wife and kids? Yes, I believe I will. I will miss Christmas, our anniversary, birthdays, school plays, family meals or movie nights, hugs, kisses and all the growing up kids do in a year. Philese and I do almost everything together. She is my best friend and I have never grown tired of spending time with her. It is difficult for me to state that I want to go to Iraq knowing that it means we need to be apart for over one year.

Often life presents us with choices, alternatives that we want yet cannot come true at the same time. We want our kids to grow up successfully yet we are afraid to let go. We want a new car or house, yet we do not want the payments. We want love without the pain of losing it, good health while eating and drinking our way into an early grave, or the blessings of God without the responsibility of living as His creation. I both want to go to Iraq and I do not want to be away from my family.

A few people ask how I feel in my spirit about heading to Iraq. I do not see a clear or full picture, yet I believe that there is a personal spiritual component to this mission. God has something specific for me to do in Iraq. That, for me, settles all the other questions. Probably not a missionary journey, more likely a bridge building or faith strengthening mission. I expect this will become clear shortly after our arrival.

Philese and I wanted to get away from anything to do with the mobilization. Spending my final week of freedom in Las Vegas seemed a good solution. We were married in Las Vegas on Valentine's Day and returned on one of our four anniversaries. Las Vegas seemed an ideal location to avoid thoughts of leaving and concentrate on our relationship. Little did I realize how a simple chain of events would instead vividly remind me of the entire conflict in less than twenty-four hours.

I decided to take a money order I received in the mail rather than stop by the bank to cash it, even though we had enough time before our flight. It was a Western Union money order drawn on an east coast 7-11. What could be easier to cash? Or so I thought. Our hotel would not cash it. Neither would the strip's Western Union office. We didn't need the cash but I felt obsessed. Not even my wife's smiling suggestion to focus on our vacation deterred me from my goal. I figured a local 7-11 would be my best hope. A hotel employee thought the closest one lay roughly two miles east along Tropicana Ave.

I dressed in sweats to counter the brisk early morning air. Philese's soft voice from across the room reminded that the cold air might aggravate my lung condition. I did not realize at the time that she might have her own subtle reasons for wanting me to stay. I kissed my wife on her cheek, promising a hasty return.

The fifty-degree temperature instantly chilled me. Reminding myself that I went polar bear swimming in colder temperatures than this, I started jogging. Within minutes breathing grew more difficult. I continued past McCarran airport. My lungs felt hot. As I passed the southern end of the UNLV campus, I started coughing congestion from my chest. When I reached the 7-11, I coughed on the decorator rocks along side the store. I felt guilty about coming here to ask a favor, then doing disgusting things to their rocks. I waited outside until I could talk without sounding as if I wanted someone to call 911 on my behalf.

The cashier explained that she could not cash the money order since it was not made out by that particular store. Evidentially one downside of 7-11's low cost money order issuance system is the lack of system-wide verification. If I

could just come back in three hours when the manager arrived? Come back?!
She had no idea what I went through to get there just once! Disheartened, I
sauntered out of the store. This money order seemed harder to get rid of than the
bronchitis. Another coughing attack. This time I went to the rocks in the front
of the store, and I didn't feel guilty.

I slowly jogged and staggered toward the hotel. Doubts surfaced about my
ability to accomplish a mission in Iraq. If I couldn't handle a short run in Vegas,
what made me think I could survive a year in Iraq? Part of my fear centered on
the fact that so far no consistent explanation surfaced about why I periodically
suffered from these symptoms. Lots of possibilities, numerous suggestions from
people who went through similar experiences, offers of products sure to help,
frequent prayers, but no lasting solutions. Would this erupt again in Iraq to the
detriment of me, my unit or the military?

The doubts slowed me down more than the labored breathing. I paused on
the sidewalk about halfway back to the hotel hands on my knees trying to relax
and get more air. I stayed that way for several minutes. A significantly older
gentleman jogged by. "You can do it! Keep going!" he declared, sounding very
cheerful for an early hour on a dreary day. I lifted my head, smiled at him, and
watched him disappear around a corner as he turned north.

Rising to my feet I determined to complete the remaining distance to the
hotel without stopping. A small segment of the landscape froze me in my tracks
before I took my first step. Two towers from the New York New York hotel rose
above the MGM Grand. Those towers were the only part of the New York New
York visible to me at the moment. In an instant I realized that this part of the
Las Vegas skyline was the one part of the real New York skyline no longer visible
in that great city.

News reports mentioned that several of the terrorists visited Las Vegas before their fateful flight that changed the world. I wondered if they looked at
the New York New York towers with any sense of foreboding. I wondered if
they laughed, pointed, perhaps even made comments that people who met them
could have recognized as premonitions. The sight of the two New York towers in
Las Vegas spurred me into action. I vowed to do everything I could to participate
in Iraq beginning with finishing this run.

12-01-03 * PEACEMAKER RESERVATIONS

Report day. My waiting is over and the adventure begins. My one-hour drive gave me too much time for reflection. I would rather spend my mental energy looking forward, but I do not know anything about my future other than generalities and rumors. Instead, I spent my entire drive thinking of an e-mail I received. A good friend of mine, a Quaker and ardent peace advocate, suggested I should disobey my orders.

He challenged me to live consistent with the teachings of Jesus who promised, "Blessed are the peacemakers, for they will be called sons of God" (Matt. 5:9). He reminded me that God hates those who sow discord and stir up trouble (see Prov. 6:19) and wants us "If it is possible, as far as it depends on you, live at peace with everyone" (Rom. 12:18). His comments resonated with my soul, stirred my mind into deep contemplation. I want to live in peace. The challenge is how to bring it about when other parties do not want to live in peace and are willing to kill themselves and others to prove it.

Peace is not created by legislative fiat, UN resolution, or dictatorial edict. Peace is more than a mere truce between striving neighbors. Evading issues that create conflict brings quiet, but not peace. Ignoring truth can help people pretend peace exists, a state many of us lived in prior to 9/11, but real peace requires foundation based on truth. How can we have peace if people or nations we deal with smile, pledge their support, shake our hands, but secretly plan our demise?

I thought of two heroes in the peace movement I admire, Dr. King and Gandhi. Dr. King preached and practiced nonviolence. As I understand Dr. King, nonviolence seeks reconciliation, not defeat of an adversary. Nonviolence is directed at eliminating evil, not destroying an evil-doer. Nonviolence includes a willingness to accept suffering for the cause, but never to inflict it. Most importantly, Dr. King taught a strict refusal to commit physical violence. Gandhi expanded the principles of nonviolence into its spiritual culmination; Satyagraha. Satyagraha literally means insistence on truth. An insistence so resolute it will never resort to falsehood to pursue truth, or violence of any kind (not even cursing) to accomplish peace. Satyagraha is a weapon, spiritual, never physical. What course of action would Jesus, Dr. King and Gandhi recommend? They would not recommend that I remain passive, but that I collaborate with others to raise a strong, collective voice against all violence.

Some people argue that Mohammed is a great moral teacher, on par with or surpassing the three previously mentioned. What would Mohammed say about this conflict? If I understand him correctly, I deserve to die. Any Muslim who kills me is doing the will of God and if he dies in the process he will be absolved from all sin and rewarded above all non-martyrs. Mohammed would recommend that I convert to Islam, that only by converting to Islam can I achieve peace. I disagree that Mohammed is a great prophet. He does not speak for any God I know. I believe people should have the freedom in the United States to practice Islam if they so chose. Yet why do some members of the Islamic faith, acting on the words of their prophet, not accord me the same freedom?

We do not live in peace in the United States. Peace, however, is a goal most Americans share. I want to be a peacemaker. However, I disagree with Dr. King and Gandhi on one point. There are steps we can take that will get us closer to peace. Right now, I think one of those steps is to ensure our national security. I strongly disagree with blowing up innocent civilians to make a statement to others. Terrorist acts are a type of evil I find hard fathom. Defending my family or my country against these evildoers is not a moral equivalent to terrorism. In our defense of liberty, however, we should not become terrorists ourselves.

At the end of all things I will stand alone in the eternal judgment of my life. My friend will stand for his. I think that eternity will judge us each of us as taking a stand for right. But then, Islamic terrorists believe the same thing about themselves.

It ended as quickly as it began. A decision by a general in Iraq, a stamp by a major in Ft. Lewis and I am on my way home. Prior to deployment National Guard troops endure a multi-day vigil referred to officially as the MOB station and unofficially with words unfit to print. The MOB station consists of numerous workstations that each support a distinct paperwork function. One station processes individual orders, another verifies background checks, and another ensures soldiers have a will and other necessary legal documents. Each station has its own line. Its own long, boring, move-up-one-chair-at-a-time line. A ten-hour day in the MOB station typically includes an hour for lunch, an hour of actual processing, and eight hours of waiting. I abhor waiting.

Our orders specifically conditioned our activation on passing a medical certification. The medic station is tasked with certifying that every soldier meets or exceeds the minimal medical qualifications for the mission at hand. The requirements may, at the decision of the mission command, surpass the Department of Defense minimums. The Iraq Theatre Commander issued a directive for MOB medics to screen for respiratory conditions.

The medical questionnaire directed us to list all current medications. An open prescription for Advair sits on the upper shelf in my bathroom medicine cabinet. I have yet to finish my first purple thirty-day dial since receiving it 10 months ago. An emergency inhaler and nebulizer lie in my top dresser drawer even though my wife and doctor suggest I should have it with me at all times just in case. I planned to take the inhaler, and a spare, to Iraq.

On active duty orders, the military issues a 90-day supply of current prescriptions with virtually no out-of-pocket expense. All I needed to do was record the prescription in the proper box. I listed "Advair" under current medications and waited in line.

A doctor read my form. He stopped when he came to the prescription section.

"Why are you taking Advair?" he asked, setting down the form and peering at me over his glasses. I described my lung condition, hoping to make it sound trivial. He nodded, stamped my form, and then circled the words "No Go."

"You need to take this form through that door to get your new profile..." he began, assuming I knew what his actions meant and wanting to move the line along. I froze, not accepting the papers he held out to me. He paused, a reassuring smile crossed his face and compassion softened his voice.

"You can't go, son. The theater commander refuses to accept any more soldiers with respiratory conditions. He's sending too many of them home. The air quality is particularly bad over there." He extended the paperwork further in my direction. I still refused to accept it.

"I don't have a respiratory problem, sir. I just have a prescription for Advair. In fact," I argued, "I don't need it!" I wanted to submit a new form, without listing the prescription. As if he could read my mind, the doctor stopped my idea faster than a Barbara Streisand refusal to perform at the Bush ranch.

"If you lie about your condition, and you have any challenges in Iraq, you will be sent stateside and discharged from the Army."

"But I can pass a PT test! I can do anything that needs to be done! My unit needs me!"

"If something happens and you can't get the attention you need, then you become a liability to your unit. Is that what you want?"

"No, sir."

"I realize you are disappointed. You are not being discharged here. You can be mobilized to Bosnia, Macedonia, in fact anywhere but the Iraq theatre. I can't override the commander's decision, and it's for your own good." Once again he held out my paperwork. "You need to take this through those doors."

This time I accepted the forms and walked slowly toward the exit. I felt shocked, my emotional presence so overwhelmed it seemed like my brain had been replaced by a training video on how to act like a zombie. I want to go to Iraq! Others might look at this as a blessing. I felt like a football player who had to sit on the bench with an injury while his team played in the Super Bowl.

"I want to go to Iraq!" I screamed inside. "Why? Why did I list the prescription? Why once again am I so close to a goal only to have a door slammed in my face?"

The question continued with increased intensity. No answers, other than the obvious. It did not matter that I postponed applying for legal positions in anticipation of an Iraq mission and had no job to fall back on. It did not matter that I trained for and focused exclusively on going to Iraq ever since the initial phone call. It did not matter whether my unit actually needed me or wanted me. The extent of my condition was irrelevant and immaterial.

I reached the door of doom. The doctor inside read the previous doctor's decision. "I'll be back in a minute with your profile," he said, rising to his feet.

"Can I appeal? Can I request a review board? Is there anything I can do?" I squeaked, my vocal chords already as tense as the rest of my body.

"Yes, you can appeal, but it won't do any good."

A divine proclamation or prophetic revelation signed by God Himself declaring that I would return from Iraq incident free would not change the minds of these doctors.

I appealed and included my commander in the process. Two lieutenant-colonels discussed my fate as I prayed for an opportunity to continue on with the mission.

12-10-03 * FAITH FOCUS—
DEALING WITH DISAPPOINTMENT

I'm not going. Me, the most excited person in the unit about going to Iraq. Why am I the only one staying behind? I feel frustrated, disappointed, jealous, and angry. But angry at whom? The General, for creating the order refusing any soldiers with level two or greater breathing problems? No, he made a good decision in the best interests of the military and the soldiers. The doctor, for deciding that I fit the level two pulmonary category? No, he is likewise doing his duty, exactly what the military and his country expect of him. God, for creating me with a disposition to such illnesses?

Amazing how often human beings rationalize that humans are not to blame for events we face in life so it must be God's fault. An "Act of God", although not to the hurricane or other natural disaster degree. In the midst of my swirling emotions I note that I also believe this will work out for the best of all concerned. That belief gives me peace, calms the emotional storm, helps me lift my head and open my eyes to the possibilities on the horizon rather than swamping my life-raft with huge waves of despair.

People who do not understand faith say believers are nothing more than blind, Pollyanna robots who fail to deal with painful emotions. I strongly disagree. My anger, frustration and disappointment settle quickly not because my faith dictates that I stuff them into the recesses of my mind but specifically because my faith gives me an effective way of dealing with emotional pain. I reject the notion that dealing with emotional pain requires a specific number of sessions with a psychologist who entered the profession in the first place because he couldn't handle his own problems.

Not every Christian or person of faith develops this same attitude. I find most people who endure tragedy wrestle with questions about faith and God. Some of the most important lessons we can learn are only found in the crucible of painful situations. I am fully at peace (spiritually... not there emotionally yet) knowing that God can work all things related to this medical decision to work together for good. Besides, God did not say no, only a doctor said no. A doctor closed the door. Okay, an Army doctor with a lot of rank, backed by the theatre's commanding general and pages of Army regulations. Still, Jesus said that one can observe the Spirit as one observes the wind. Evidence of the wind is everywhere even though we can't see it. Right now I feel a spiritual wind. God is working in Iraq.

America wrestles with the question of whether our involvement in Iraq is the right thing to do. Some believe we need to take out Saddam as a matter of national and international security, others adamantly oppose the entire campaign. I am not crusading for the Congressional decision to go to war with Iraq. However, I strongly believe that those of us who volunteered and vowed to uphold our dutieobligations as soldiers have a duty to fulfill our vows as long as we wear this uniform. I also believe that God needs a few good men (and women) in Iraq. His mission is radically different from the military's mission.

I reject the concept that the United States is or should be a Christian nation or that we are one nation under God. I am not even convinced God is on our side in this campaign to the extent He led Joshua and the Israelites through battles for their Holy Land. There is no cheering section of angels in heaven waving the American flag or spiritual warriors fighting with us for our national cause. God is involved in this fight because God cares about people and about His church. God cares about the Iraqis and even the terrorists. I want to participate in Iraq because one of the greatest spiritual battles in the world today is taking place there and I want to be part of it. The battle is not U.S. versus evil. No, the battle is for each of us to understand who is God and God's role in human events. Will God's identity and role be as clear to the world after this campaign ends as it was when Elijah prayed and God answered with fire from heaven? (Read 1 Kings chapter 18). I doubt it, especially if we continue to characterize this war as good versus evil.

I do not have even rudimentary answers today. I want to understand these events from a spiritual perspective and that is the primary reason I believe I need to go to Iraq.

12-12-03 * CHANGE IN PLANS NUMBER 1,483

My activation orders were cancelled as if they never existed in the first place. Master Sergeant Johnson asked me to consider working for the State operation center, a joint task force in charge of certain anti-terrorism tasks in Washington State. Several National Guard soldiers working full-time in the office received deployment orders. MSG Johnson, one of the Operation center deployed soldiers, arranged for an interview with the Colonel in charge. Although I could have simply resigned myself to life in the civilian world with duty one weekend per month, I decided to do my part by working for the military stateside during the length of my unit's deployment.

The most wonderful part of this new plan is working close to home. Most days, though, I do not feel wonderful. I feel guilty thinking about the soldiers in my unit absent from their families for over a year while I drive home every night. I feel displeased about not serving in Iraq, frustrated with my less than perfect health and angry about how the actions of a few people I never heard of could set in motion events that threw my life into this turmoil.

As a result of 9/11, I spent almost half of my second and third years of law school on military assignments. Changes keep coming on almost a weekly basis. I worked for three years as a representative of BarBri, a bar review prep course, to earn a seat in the review class, yet missed my graduation and the review class for training at Fort Bragg. BarBri went beyond their agreed duties by providing me with everything I needed to study on my own. I took two days of leave prior to the bar and reported for duty the day after. With all of the deployments and other types of duties calling soldiers to action I also missed the third year interview process and probably my best shot at landing a decent firm position. Not at all the experience I wanted or envisioned from law school.

I once listened to someone teaching a time management course brag that he knew when he would be taking bathroom breaks five years in the future. I found his assertion so ridiculous I tuned out the remainder of his speech. I am not against planning our future, In fact, as a result of that incident, I wrote a 50-minute time management seminar of my own. Yet, life is so full of change that I do not take serious anyone who thinks they have that much control over their own future.

Maybe I am just jealous. Some people do seem to have that amount of control over their own lives. Sheltered by money or political power, they seem able to shape events to further their own causes. Lacking both, I feel no more significant than flotsam floating on the tides with a law degree. Actually, I feel more like jetsam, tossed aside by the military after devoting the past two years to creating stability in the chaos of 9/11 terrorism. Jetsam washed up on the shore of jobs left over for the non-deployable.

Watching ship debris floating ashore does not readily hint at whether the wreckage is flotsam or jetsam, hence the tendency for the majority of people who know the terms to treat them as synonyms. The two words, however, represent very different concepts. If a wooden ship crashed into pieces against a rock, the debris found floating in the water would be called flotsam. The term also refers to people who live on the margins of society, such as vagrants, the homeless, or the destitute. No, I am not flotsam, even though I am carried uncontrollably by the tides of change.

Jetsam, on the other hand, is cargo or equipment that either sinks or is washed ashore after being thrown overboard to lighten the load of a ship in distress. In the modern context it represents things that have been discarded as useless or unwanted. Things like me. True, the military does want me to play a stateside role in this operation, but I look at the ship carrying my unit to Iraq and come to no other conclusion than Army regulations required them to toss me over the side, whether they wanted to or not, so the unit could stay fit for the mission.

Some people tell me I should count my blessings and get on with life. "Play the cards you have been dealt"… "Look on the bright side"… "Cheer up, things could be worse." The next time someone spouts off with such Pollyanna rhetoric I think I will take the largest positive thinking book within reach and bonk him with it.

For most of my life I subscribed to the philosophy that change came from God. All change, for better or for worse, whether sickness or health, God controlled it and therefore must have willed it to happen. That theology resulted, at least for me, in a life tossed by the winds of circumstance. Changing direction and location every few years resulted in continued poverty and a lack of depth in my friendships and careers.

I discovered that positive change begins within. The key is knowing what to change, what to develop and what to discard. For me the most challenging part of Saint Francis' prayer turned out to be developing the "wisdom to know the difference."

Step by step I began to recognize changes I could make to improve my spirituality, my family, and my finances. I now believe that a fortified obstacle in my path does not necessarily mean God wants me to change course. It might mean I need to remove the obstacle and blaze a trail for others to follow.

I am still not experiencing serenity or acceptance that the mobilization doctor's opinion is the last word on my deployment status. In the meantime, I am making the most of the opportunities presented to me. I am now a member of joint operation center coordinating military assets to help with local anti-terrorism efforts. I am also moving forward on my direct commission application to become a JAG (Judge Advocate General) officer. I feel that I do not have the power to choose between these three options: Iraq, anti-terrorism and JAG. The military seems to control the decision-making process at this point. What can I change? What do I need to accept? I don't see the difference. When I do, I believe I will display the courage to make the necessary changes.

Two thoughts continue to perturb me. First, I firmly believe that the doctor did not correctly catalogue my health challenges. I do not actually fit the profile of soldiers who should not serve in the Iraq region for health reasons. I am a false positive on the mobilization screening radar. If the doctor had made the correct judgment I would now be in training for Iraq with my unit. That knowledge, coupled with the second persistent belief that I have a personal mission to perform in Iraq, leave me in a state of less than full acceptance of my current situation.

I can accept that right now I am not in charge of the decision process. I can accept that right now I have a stateside duty station. Wisdom tells me that God is not yet finished with this situation. For me, that makes all the difference.

02-14-04 * A Tougher Kind of Valentine

I do not remember the first Valentine's Day cards I gave or received. In the first elementary school I attended, where my mother taught third and fourth grade, and my father taught fifth through seventh grades while doubling as the principle, the students exchanged Valentine cards with each member of the class. Each student usually brought one card for the teacher as well, a card typically bigger than the ones given to other students.

In that small, rural school we exchanged notes of love with everyone regardless of gender. Perhaps we found that an easy task because we did not really have to mean what we wrote. Telling people we loved them was an assignment. It did not have to come from the heart. I did not really want 30 kids to "Be Mine" on Valentine's Day any more than I wanted an arrow really shot through my heart.

In the seventh grade, at the budding age of 12, I experienced my first crush. My first real brush with love, longing and other Valentine's Day sentiments. I chose the most special card from my manufactured box of assorted cards wrote a short note and signed my name. The card I received from her seemed normal, as if I was just some other guy in the class. I kept my feelings to myself, never telling her how I really felt about her.

When I asked my mother why the incident literally hurt inside she explained I was the type of person to show love by actions more than words. She told me that I wore my heart on my sleeve although I am sure at the time I had no idea what she meant. Some people emphasize love as a noun, others experience love as a verb. Love is perhaps the most complicated word in the English language.

I grew into a person who did not say "I love you" even when asked, even if I did feel that way, even if I showed it in actions instead. The words would not come out of my mouth. At the time I thought I was the only person in the universe with this inability to articulate the love I felt for people. The stronger the emotion, the more impossible to express. I studied love for several years, albeit by reading books such as C.S. Lewis' *Four Loves* and *Love* by Leo Buscaglia rather than experiencing relationships.

Telling a stranger "I love you" proved easier than telling my family. I practiced on people I did not know, accepting their disdain, apathy or kindness. One day I told myself that I would say "I Love You" to every member of my family, beginning with my mother. I called her. We shared current events for several minutes. I planned to say "I love you, mom" as my parting comment. We said good-bye; I paused, and then hung up. Failure. A few days later I tried again.

The next phone call I moved my problematic phrase to the forefront as the reason for my call.

"I love you, mom."

"I love you too, Frank."

An incredible elation followed. In some sense, like the experience of Dr. Seuss' Grinch, I changed that day. I next worked on telling my sisters, my brothers, and then other people I cared about. I began to realize that I wanted to hear those words as much as I felt the desire to share them with others. I would prefer to be in a relationship with people who do not say they love me but act on it rather than with someone who says "I love you" all the time but does not live accordingly. However, I firmly believe that verbalizing the thoughts and emotions of love adds an entirely new dimension to life we do not experience with just our actions.

Now I am surrounded by love on a daily basis. Philese and I married on Valentine's Day. We built our relationship on a foundation of love. We speak love, we share love in the things we do for each other, and we continue to learn about the intricate concepts of love's kaleidoscope. Love lives in our home. It binds us closer together, eliminates our fears, and moves us to reconciliation.

Some people say that the United States is partially responsible for the 9/11 terrorist attacks. The reason, if I understand them correctly, is that we Americans do not tell the rest of the world we love them. If we would only reach out to understand and build relationships the terrorists would not be so mad at us. If only we would share more of our wealth, assimilate more of their problems, tolerate their customs or embrace their ideals the terrorists would realize that we are good people. The process I experienced, they say, will work on a macro-cultural level as well as it does for individuals.

I understand the argument. I personally live the values and believe in them, yet I disagree with the conclusion. The United States is already the most generous nation in the world. We already invite other nations to send us their poor and tired who yearn for freedom. We open our schools to foreign students so they can take our collective wisdom back to their countries. We helped secure freedom for millions around the world. We stand against tyranny in other countries even if it costs American lives. What other country says and acts on "I love you" on a universal scale more than the United States? Yet, despite all our efforts, we are the number one target for terrorists.

What Valentine's Day message should we send terrorists to get them to like us and leave us alone? Is it even possible? "Dear Terrorist: We want to live in peaceful co-existence. We do not want to harm you. We will, however, defend ourselves to the fullest extent possible if attacked. For your sakes, and the peace of the entire world, please cease your attacks against us. Love always, the U.S." A few former Presidents left out, by their own lack of retaliatory action, the part about defending ourselves. That message did not work. In fact, if we do hold any responsibility for 9/11 it is partly because of our unwillingness to defend ourselves in the past.

In my opinion the reason terrorists target the United States is that we, above all nations, will not do the one thing they demand: submit. They want us to submit our will to theirs. They want control of our schools, our religions, and our government. They do not necessarily want to control all of our institutions personally, but at least force us to make our decisions by seeking out their advice on what we should do and then follow their dictates.

How many people want to be in a relationship with someone who wants full control, wants to dictate all of the decisions and actions? Are we so desperate for terrorists to leave us alone that we become willing to establish this international relationship hell? I, for one, am not. The terrorists have no right to demand this of us as a term of peace. I will not submit my will, my beliefs, my leadership, my individuality to any group of thugs who believe they have a mandate from God to destroy anyone who does not submit.

Love is not the only issue at stake. I love them, by which I mean I wish them happiness and success in this life and the next. Not success or happiness in destroying me, rather, in relationships, in family, in productive labor and strong community. Do they return my love? No. In word and in deed they tell me I must die. Because I do not love them? No. Because I do not submit to their version of God's will for my life.

We can send Valentine's Day messages of love to the terrorists every day of the year. It will not matter. They will still hate us. Let us not naively think that, without submission, they will ever revere us as good people and leave us alone. Our messages need to be more than our willingness to live peacefully in this world. We need to forcefully impress upon them that we will not tolerate their acts of terrorism. We might not create true peace but it is our best chance for at least an absence of terrorism.

Even though I was born and raised in Canada, I registered for the Selective Service at the age of 18. I moved to the United States shortly after the U.S. elected Ronald Reagan to a second term as President and Canada elected Pierre Trudeau to his fifth span as Prime Minister. On the basis of the election results I surmised numerable characteristics about Canadians and Americans, most of which proved overly simplistic since then. Never receiving a request from the Selective Service to serve in the military of my adopted home country, at the age of 32 I decided to join the Army National Guard as an officer. A recruiting officer informed me that my scant college experience left me 10 credits short of the minimum requirements to apply as an officer. The good news, he told me, was that I had enough credits to transfer to Officer Candidate School (OCS) as an enlisted soldier. He signed me up as a Private First Class, E-3.

Two months later all of the enlisted soldiers in our unit were obliged to listen to an OCS sales pitch. I expressed a desire to attend OCS. The unit commander told me that I owed him one year as an enlisted soldier before he would allow me to transfer. Although I could not find that obligation in any of the regulations or in my contract, the transfer did require his signature. I fulfilled my year of enlisted duty, beginning with attending boot camp at age 33. True to his word, he signed my OCS application the following year.

Two months into OCS I received word that the OCS commander needed to see me immediately. I knocked on the door of the Lieutenant Colonel, the highest-ranking officer I had met in my short service. He informed me that I exceeded the maximum age for OCS by six months. He further reported that he attempted to obtain a waiver for me but that waiver was denied. He had no choice but to drop me from the OCS program. I explained to him that I applied the year before only to be told I needed to complete a year of enlisted duty. That extra year cost me my commission. The Lt. Col. scowled, and then added that the one year enlisted duty was a company commander decision. The OCS age requirement, however, was an Army regulation and his hands were tied.

The only other option available to become an officer was a direct commission, a process open to enlisted personnel who hold a four-year college degree. Already attending college during the evening to complete my bachelor's, I decided to try again when I earned my BA in psychology. Philese and I graduated together from the University of Washington in the spring of 2000. Within a few days I once again presented myself to officer recruiting.

"What branch do you want?"

"JAG," I replied, meaning the Judge Advocate General Corp. "I am attending law school in the fall."

"I recommend, then, that you wait until you finish law school because you need the law degree to be a JAG officer." He dismissed me. Wait? Again? I left officer recruiting for the third time even more disgruntled than before.

In the summer of 2003, law degree in hand, I once again contacted officer recruiting.

"I am sorry," the recruiter concluded after reviewing my application, not looking apologetic at all. "You are too old. If you had only applied for the direct commission when you received your bachelor's degree we could have commissioned you to another branch and transferred you to JAG now that you finished law school."

Restraining the anger I felt bubbling to the surface faster than a Texas artesian well I described how another recruiter in that very office told me three years earlier to wait until I finished law school.

"I really am sorry." This time the recruiter looked and sounded genuinely sympathetic. "The age waiver can only be granted by someone at the D.C. level and that is just not happening right now. We have so many people signing up since 9/11 that they do not need the older officer candidates." For the fourth time, and final time I told myself, I slowly walked out of the officer recruiting office.

While meditating on how to best structure my stay at home military I spent many hours dwelling on my ten-year struggle to become an officer in the military. I felt bitter, angry, frustrated. I honestly felt like quitting the military. Why was the officer goal so important to me? The answer did not matter. It was my goal! I did not need to justify it to anyone. The military said no. Four times!

"Why stay?" I asked myself numerous times each day. "They do not want me for Iraq. They will not offer me the position I want. Why stay?" One phrase, however, kept nagging me – "granted by someone at the D.C. level". I decided in January to ask for the waiver and find the right people who could make it happen.

I now faced an obstacle even tougher to overcome than my age. The doctor's analysis at the mobilization station resulted in a permanent physical profile lower than the officer application required. No exceptions and no waivers exist for this condition. I not only needed an age waiver but I also needed a more conclusive medical evaluation that would restore my previously perfect health ranking.

I pressed for, and was allowed to take a series of tests to confirm or deny the presence of asthma. A specialty respiratory clinic in Seattle conducted a series of tests including x-rays, spirometry, an exercise related peak expiratory flow test, and a challenge test consisting of breathing in increasing amounts of an asthma-inducing chemical until asthma symptoms become apparent.

After increasing the chemical level six times, the technician stopped the testing. "You are at a level right now where, if you had asthma, you would be dead. And your breathing output is still above normal!" He pointed to the chart of my test results. I nodded as if I understood the lines and graphs. "You definitely do not have asthma," he muttered repeatedly as he signed the lab report.

I took the results to the doctor in charge of my officer application physical. He upgraded my physical condition to its previous "fully mission capable" level. Two weeks ago the officer recruiting staff submitted my completed packet to D.C. for an age waiver. Today I received a phone call.

"Get packed. You report for duty to Iraq on Monday." Changing the profile also placed me back on the list of soldiers eligible to report for duty in Iraq. The combination of my unit's mobilization, the inability of the military to fill my position with someone else both available and qualified and my renewed eligibility to join them equals an all-expenses paid vacation in Iraq. I placed my goal to become an officer on hold again but I get to go to Iraq!

I periodically struggle adopting the concept of acceptance. Occasionally someone will remind me that, "when God gives any man wealth and possessions, and enables him to enjoy them, to accept his lot and be happy in his work – this is a gift of God" (Eccles. 5:19). Sometimes when I am in a rambunctious mood I reply that God did not give me the gift of wealth and possessions. Why, then, I am I still told to accept my lot in life and be happy with it?

Our forefathers, most of whom expressed a belief in God, built our nation in a spirit of refusal to accept their lot in life. I did not accept that milking cows would be my life journey and frequently expressed discontentment with my agrarian surroundings. I always believed God had other plans in store for me. Today I believe and accept that I am now where God wants me and I am very happy with the work I do. The journey required a refusal to accept anything else as my destiny in life and a refusal to accept the word of believers who told me to accept my lot in life and walk in acceptance and satisfaction. Who displays the greater faith: the one who happily accepts or the one who looks forward to a future vastly different from the present? After years spent in pursuit of happiness and my place in the kingdom I now believe that these concepts are not mutually exclusive.

On a daily basis I should express gratitude for God's abundant gifts to me. I thank God for my health, my family, the work before me and the ability to enjoy the fruit of my labor with people I love. At the same time, if God is leading me to a different path, I work with God to prepare myself for the changes heading my way. The key is whether the source of the dissatisfaction is my greed or God's grace.

Dissatisfaction itself can be a gift from God. Dissatisfaction in spirit with our lot in life could suggest that God wants us to move elsewhere. Dissatisfaction provides part of the motivation and can lead to setting goals for our future, another powerful source of motivation. Dissatisfaction moves people to open their eyes to look for signs of God moving in a different direction. I think it is possible to be satisfied with our dissatisfaction, to accept our refusal of the destiny laid before us.

I discovered that I struggled not as much with acceptance as with confidence in my ability to follow God's leading. I struggle with a lack of faith. When I began to see by faith that God held a different future and purpose for me, when I believed that God's power could overcome all the obstacles, then I could rejoice. God showed me a future not in heaven but here on Earth where He would fulfill the dreams I felt stirring my soul. God kept his promise more abundantly than I ever imagined.

God also helped me think differently about the Christians who cared about me enough to comment on my dissatisfaction. In the past I viewed them as part of the problem. I now realize that they did sense something in me that needed correction. The problem, however, was not dissatisfaction but my discouragement and lack of faith. When I mentor younger people who exhibit a passionate drive for goals beyond their given lot in life I do not squash their dreams with exhortations of how they should be satisfied with their lot in life but I focus on their faith. Do they believe God will fulfill His promises to them? Are they participating with God's plan for them? Or, are they defeating God's purpose for them through disbelief?

I wanted to serve in Iraq. I fully believed God's will for my life included our military mission in Iraq. The doors slammed in my face. The windows were barred. Warnings signs reminded me of dangers awaiting those who crossed the line from lawfully challenging military decisions to disobeying command decisions. More people encouraged me to accept this course of events as my lot than any other situation in my life. "Why place yourself in danger?" they asked. Why risk not coming home to my wife and children? Why risk jeopardizing the investment of time and money spent pursuing a legal career? Look at the closed doors. The decision was made, all possible appeals followed, and I should just accept that decision with happiness. I listened to their wisdom but still felt that God wanted me in Iraq.

Since the military would not discuss a medical evaluation for the purposes of overturning the medical fitness for duty decision, I asked for a medical exam for the one reason left open – my direct commission. I ran the risk of having the path to that dream closed as well if the exam resulted in a confirmation of anything less than a "1" in every category. I prayed that I would receive the report I wanted and also prayed that I could accept the results regardless of the findings.

Within days of posting the medical evaluation I received a phone call to begin training for duty in Iraq. The doors reopened specifically as a result of my unwillingness to accept the original doctor's and appeal board's decisions as final. An unwillingness born in the faith that God's plan for my life specifically included a mission in Iraq. Messengers of God from Martin Luther to Martin Luther King, Jr. preached a type of civil disobedience as a Christian duty. I believe that this concept of civil or Christian dissatisfaction is part of that duty, although not as eloquently expressed.

04-12-04 * AN ARMY OF ONE

An Army of One." Not just a motto, today it became a reality. The rear detachment First Sergeant asked me if I wanted a send-off ceremony before departing. I asked if the governor would attend as he did the observance of the 81st Brigade's exodus at a Tacoma Do me extravaganza. "No," he told me, perhaps rolling his eyes, "the governor will not be attending." In fact, my send-off would be little more than the officer of the day giving impromptu comments on staying safe followed by a few handshakes from whoever happened to be in the area. I opted to spend my final day with my family.

My daughters and I quacked ourselves silly on Seattle's Ride the Ducks tour. That night we played Cranium and U-Dubopoly disregarding even the most lenient bedtimes. I wanted to reserve the late-night airport trip just for Philese and my 200 pounds of baggage. I hoped for at least an hour with her at the airport, just to talk and reminisce, but our allotment soon dissolved in returning for forgotten items, traffic snarls, and FCC regulation paperwork for my crated M-16. At the ticket counter I discovered that the complexities of mobilizing an individual soldier continued to haunt me. The flight voucher I handed the clerk did not mention the excess weight allowed by my orders. The infamous "they", the administrators of all things Army, had infected my life again. I paid $185 to check baggage the government and fifteen months of living required, vowing to correct this injustice as soon as possible.

We had less than ten minutes for our bon voyage kiss. Since we first met, my wife and I have never said good-bye to each other. Upon parting, or concluding a phone call, we say, "See you soon" or "Ciao". That night was not going to break our tradition. I kissed Philese. She held me tight and did not want to let go. I looked into her watery eyes, her tears a mixture of emotional pain at our separation and an attempt to be brave in front of me.

We talked for a few minutes about our pain. We vowed from the beginning of our relationship that we would never intentionally create pain for each other. Had I in fact done the opposite of what I promised her? This present sorrow, she reassured me, was not created in betrayal or neglect or the myriad of other ways couples can hurt each other. She just did not want to spend fifteen months apart from her best friend. Neither did I, although I guess I showed it differently.

"I need to go," I whispered.

"I know," she replied, holding me closer. She bit her lower lip as it trembled, then confided something that still rings in my ears.

"This is the hardest thing I have ever had to do!" She choked back a torrent of tears that would erupt when she could no longer see me walking down the terminal C concourse. I have often listened to stories of the challenges in her life, admiring her courage and willingness to continue on under intense emotional pain. For her to state that this was the hardest spoke volumes of her love for me. She later told a friend with pride that I had been a true soldier to the end, focused on my mission, not even shedding a tear at our departure. She missed one. One tear, representing thousands held inside, would escape the corner of my eye after I rounded the final corner.

"See you soon!" I announced, now holding only her hands.

"I love you!" she sobbed.

"I love you, too!" I let go.

Sometimes people who go through a personal tragedy come to a position where they are at peace with themselves, their God, their life. If given the opportunity to go back in time and avoid that tragedy, they say they wouldn't because of the incredible place the path through that pain brought them. They might even comment that they now understand why God caused that to happen. I do not personally believe that God does cause all things, but I passionately advocate that God can work all things for the good of those who believe. No matter what happens in life, no matter how stupid the decisions made by people with the power to choose, God can create a plan that works out for the good of His faithful.

Growing up in a church founded on the teachings of John Calvin, I am frequently asked to comment on the debate between free will and predestination. To those of the free-will camp I point out that will is no freer than people are independent. From the day we are born we are interdependent. Shoppers in Washington complain when the price of bananas goes up a few cents per pound, yet few of them realize, since bananas are not native to our state, that literally thousands of people are involved in the process of getting bananas from other countries to our corner grocery. We are not capable of making a truly free choice, not even when we muse whether to buy bananas versus apples at Safeway.

When discussing faith with someone who believes in predestination, I caution them against adding more to their doctrine than what the Bible states. Yes, names written in the Lamb's book of life were preordained before the foundation of the world, but that scripture verse does not include the "logical extensions" fostered upon it by centuries of well-intended theological debates. God is not the author of evil in this world. We are. People make bad choices.

A doctor closed the door to my mobilization. His decision was not a bad or evil decision. I do not fault him at all, yet I challenged that decision for two reasons. First, I believe that I do not have a medical condition that meets the criteria specified in the General's order. The military does not burden me with the duty of challenging the doctor's decision. I could honorably fulfill my duty to my country on U.S. soil. The military is not letting me out of deployment, just deploying me 45 miles away from home at Ft. Lewis rather than in Iraq. And I get to go home at nights and on weekends. However, the second reason I challenged the decision is that I believe I have a mission to do in Iraq. Maybe not the military's mission, but the military is paying the bill. If only every person who felt called for an overseas mission could procure such funding!

There are, of course, several strings attached, as there is anytime the government funds anything. In exchange for my salary and lodging I am expected to be a soldier first, foremost, at all times. Even if I am not able to devote any off-duty time to other endeavors, I can at least get by on one less hour of sleep that the government allots me. That means 365 hours of mission-related time available I would not have without this mission. Some people think I am making a weird choice. I feel like I am predestined for such a time as this.

A nalysts are trained to spot trends, so it did not take me long to figure out I am in for long-term frustration. With two hours in the Açores I could have seen a significant portion of the 16-square mile island we landed on, but we were not allowed to leave the security hangar. Another two hour layover in Frankfurt, but again confined to the military terminal rather than allowed even a cursory tour of the city. Then, two days in a Kuwait base not even large enough to be a Boy Scout camp back home, but no freedom to visit Kuwait City or the ocean clearly visible a few miles past the fence. If security and safety concerns prevented me from traveling outside peaceful locations, I doubted an occasional weekend at the Iraq base would find me exploring the ruins of Nineveh or bartering with shop-owners in a Mosul bazaar.

I boarded a C-130, another personal first, for the four-hour flight to Mosul. The accommodations or lack thereof, made me wonder whether those who jump from these planes do so because of where they want to go or what they want to leave. The flight attendants are surly airmen who bark orders and never smile. No safety lecture about oxygen masks or life vests, no overhead lighting or air vents, no in-flight meals or beverage service. No pillows, blankets, or call buttons. No lavatories, armrests or window seats. Leg room? As unavailable as space for a carry-on. Those we stored either on our laps or in the back of the HMMWV accompanying us. We sat opposite each other in rows of sling seats so close together the aisles resembled a tight weave of upper thighs. No FCC concerns here about leaving aisle ways clear.

Although we flew at night, and I felt exhausted, I could not sleep. Another unique aspect of a C-130 flight is the ability to loudly hear every moving part of the plane even through the mandatory earplugs. The crew extinguished the cabin lights since we flew over a combat zone. Dark, loud, crowded, with none of the amenities of home. And I had called this "The adventure of a lifetime!"

The airstrip in Mosul is within the base run by my unit. Although larger than the base I stayed at in Kuwait, it is still less than 2 square miles. As one soldier told me, "it gets very small, very fast." The U.S. has three small bases in this city of over 1.7 million people. The Alamo had better odds than this! Fortunately, we are not at war with the entire city, only the sparse terrorist cells operating here. Still, the terrorists are effective enough that, as I already feared in Kuwait, we are confined to base. Only trips to other U.S. bases for official business are authorized. The security requirements are so stringent that few official trips materialize, certainly none for tourist purposes.

Some soldiers feel satisfied even relieved, to remain on base. Not me. I like to explore whenever I visit a new location. True, previous trips did not include cities where I had a price on my head, but safety warnings had not stopped me from walking through New York's Central Park at night, or navigating back roads of Mexican villages. Mosul is full of such interesting people, culture and history! On our office's large aerial photo of the city I can see a city center older than U.S. history, the ruins of Nineveh to the north-east, palace grounds further north, and landmarks that include the Jonah temple and a 6th century monastery. The wall-sized photo may be the only way I will see the sights I would rather see in person. Mosul's previous record as Iraq's top tourist destination may still hold true after the invasion, but given the amount of total tourism in Iraq currently, that isn't saying much. I want to adventure forth, and I feel frustrated. Our security fence begins to resemble prison bars.

I know myself well enough to realize that continuing to view the base as a prison will only further my frustration. To stay sane, I need to find a different focal point. Rather than remaining trapped in my frustration at the lack of exploratory options, I will instead concentrate on our mission. The fence is only a symptom or sign of more complicated issues. Iraq is in political turmoil and needs a reprieve from violence to develop properly. We are here both to give Iraq the security it needs and to give the world a more peaceful Middle East. A daunting task at best. If we are successful, the fence will come down of its own accord. Iraq will prosper, Mosul tourism will revive. I hope to be first in line.

04-24-04 * NEWS FROM THE FRONT

I attend a meeting every Friday at the palace headquarters, on the other end of the city. Here are a few things I learned about the city of Mosul from today's trip.

The soldiers now here replaced the 101st airborne division. The replacements, however, are only a brigade, 1/3 the size of a division. We do not have enough personnel to position soldiers interacting in the community. Iraq may have the same total number of troops as before the rotation, but troops have been allocated to higher threat areas.

Since the 101st left, public opinion has shifted somewhat away from the military. Convoy attacks have increased especially small arms fire and IED explosions. Mortar and rocket attacks against the bases have also increased. Both numbers, however, are still small especially when compared with other major cities in Iraq.

Our community presence in Mosul is more aggressive than interactive. We raid homes, take people into questioning, and drive through the streets at high speed and with little regard for other vehicles. We have undercover operatives in the city and pay people to inform on their friends. At least that is how most of the local population understands our mission.

A Special Forces (SF) unit convoys people from this base to the palace for the Friday meeting. A major and I accompanied them today. These guys take no chances at being the next fatality. Our convoy consisted of two heavily armored HMMWV's with mounted guns. We each had our protective vests and personal weapons loaded and ready for action. The personal weapons that the SF guys carry would impress a group of Montana militiamen. Labeling them SF is just a guess, however, as their uniforms have no names, rank insignia or shoulder patches. If they die, no one knows who they are. Spooky.

The lead vehicle has a special bumper to move vehicles out of the way. They do not stop for anything. If traffic is stopped at an intersection, they go around in the wrong lane, make "illegal" turns, and do whatever it takes to keep moving. A stopped vehicle is a sitting target.

My orders were simple. Stay alert. If someone points a weapon at me, shoot first and ask questions later.

Mosul is a fascinating city, modern and historic, beautiful and dilapidated, economically diverse, but not particularly cosmopolitan. The vast majority of vehicles on the road (95 %+) are at least 15 years old, small, and in poor working order. For a city of 1.7 million I expected more traffic. Many people walk, a few ride bicycles. I saw two donkey carts driven by young men. Broken door vehicles are commonly deserted, which one could be a vehicle bomb waiting for a convoy to stop nearby?

I would rather ride in a taxi in Tijuana than here. The Mosul cabs are typically a Toyota corona or similar era / size car. They are all painted white with orange fenders, no signs needed or used. They often go the wrong way down a street. I even saw a few vehicles head the opposite direction down the shoulder of the highway. Cabs are frequently used or owned by terrorists, but there is no registration or licensing system to track the cabs.

Goatherds and shepherds commonly let their flocks graze along the roadside. A goatherd commented a few days ago that he makes ~ $2500 U.S. per year. Of that he pays about $1200 for feed for his goats, $120 for gas, and the rest on family expenses. Most people in Mosul are very poor by American standards.

The Iraqi police are everywhere with loaded AK-47's. They patrol the streets in vehicles and stand on major intersections directing traffic even though traffic signals are present. The police state atmosphere continues past Saddam's downfall.

Very few buildings are taller than 3 stories. The city sprawls along the Tigris River. Small agricultural plots are visible in various areas of the city. Some of the buildings are crumbling yet lived in. Mosul definitely does not have an enforced building code.

In our 15-mile trip I did not see anything that looked like a gas station or Starbuck's. The only 7-11 in Mosul is on our base and does not resemble any 7-11 I have other seen. I doubt it is a legitimate 7-11 franchise and I bet they don't cash money orders. Merchants sell copycat merchandise everywhere such as "Rolex" watches and DVD's of movies that are nothing more than a CD copy of someone taping a movie in a theatre. But they're cheap!

The palace grounds in Mosul are an incredible complex of buildings, and were once the personal residence for Udai Hussein. The main palace building was hit during the first Gulf War. Udai built another, more opulent building to replace his destroyed mansion while millions of Iraqi citizens suffered because of the invasion and sanctions. The grounds are now home to the northern Iraq command.

The Hussein family lived as royalty in this city. I cannot even begin to describe the architecture, inch-thick marble flooring, hand-painted or intricately carved facades. The main buildings might not be as large as some American mansions, but the grounds are home to dozens of buildings with distinct purposes such as pools, party homes and perhaps torture or death rooms.

04-26-04 * WE ARE NOT ALL HEROES[1]

A U.S. news program played interviews of several soldiers returning home from Iraq. I paused from monitoring message traffic, listening for interesting stories. A young female soldier remarked, "We are all heroes." I strongly disagree.

This is my second voluntary tour since 9/11 but I have yet to perform any acts worthy of the designation "hero." I fear that the new trend of considering all members of military, police or firefighting units as heroes diminishes the honor due real heroes and will decrease the quality of heroes available in the future.

Circumstances do not make heroes; they reveal them. The character of a hero must develop beforehand or events will pass unchallenged. Heroism is obedience to a private impulse, driven by the thought that it can follow no other path.

Heroes see the necessity of their actions while others remain frozen by fear, uncertainty or moral tepidity. Heroes stand in defiance of falsehood and evil, willing to bear the consequences of their resolve rather than succumb to tyranny or oppression. Heroes are frequently impatient, preferring to act quickly and decisively rather than wait for a committee resolution, fact-finding mission or congressional hearing to reveal no more than the hero already knows.

Heroes often walk alone yet they are rarely lonely. Heroes tend to disdain austerity or ostentation, even popularity. They act not for recognition and seldom tell their own tale. Thus, most heroic acts go unrecognized while the public spotlight regales as royalty pompous entertainers who add little worth to society. Duty and virtue mark heroism's nobility. Justice is its hallmark and righteousness its crown.

Societies around the world, and throughout history, raise their children on stories of heroic deeds. We inspire children to greatness with such stories. Heroic stories develop a sense of loyalty, duty and responsibility. One of the most valuable lessons learned from such stories is that society bestows great honor to performers of great deeds. We need to remind each other that honor is earned; the undeserving cannot compel it.

Most soldiers in Iraq will not fire a single bullet in offensive missions or defensive necessity. They are here to support the minority that confronts the enemy in ways that hope to ensure the majority will never need to. The soldiers involved in denigrating their detainees clearly demonstrate that we are not all heroes, yet there are other incidents outside the news. I have seen soldiers disrespect their leaders or balk at simple duties. Some drive wildly through the city streets on patrol, disregarding the safety of the very Iraqis we are here to protect. Others have stolen artifacts that rightfully belong to the people of Iraq. These soldiers may act bravely, at times, but to consider them heroes is a concept I personally find repugnant.

If we now bestow the honor of hero without regard to deeds performed or character revealed, if hero status is achieved with so little struggle, many of our children will fail to develop the discipline necessary to carry them through the painful process true hero character development requires. Already too many of our young people pattern themselves after those who usurp fame while promising at best fleeting pleasure and at worst self-destruction. Past generations helped develop the real heroes we have today. Let us, likewise, prepare real heroes for the future lest none be found when needed most.

More than a quarter of a million soldiers will be involved in operation Iraqi freedom before we all return home. We might all appreciate a hero's welcome but only a few deserve a hero's honor. Deciding in advance that everyone returning home is a hero saves society the time of listening to individual stories and resolving who deserves the distinction. Do we not still value some character traits over others? I hope so. Do we actually believe that a year spent shirking duty is to be as honored as a year spent in unwavering selfless service? Definitely not, or America is no longer the country I think I am here to defend.

I am very grateful that most Americans choose to honor those who serve in this time of increased terrorism. The highest honor society can bestow is that of hero but we do not all deserve this designation. Let us instead take the time to determine the identity of our true heroes and give them the honor they uniquely deserve. If we do, our heroes will benefit and the heroism's virtues will remain strong in our culture.

04-30-04 * OUR LOCAL LABOR POOL

Tuesday I observed hundreds and spoke with several Iraqi people entering the base. We have approximately 1,500 locals who work on the base. Many of them are supervised by or escorted by Iraqis given clearance to do so. Most of the contractors for the various building contracts are Iraqis. A few have even returned here from the U.S. to start companies and take advantage of the current construction boom. One man born here recently returned from LA to start a leather factory in an abandoned building. Another is leasing space in the PX food court to bring some American's franchises such as a pizza outlet and coffee shop. The current coffee shops all use Nescafe, which I dislike about as much as I like Tully's or Starbuck's. Most of the men dressed better than I would expect for manual labor positions. Nobody I saw wore jeans, shorts, t-shirts or anything with tears or holes.

I commented to one man that I observed a higher level of education than I had anticipated. He told me that education in Iraq is free, even at the post secondary levels. The post secondary system is divided into universities and technical schools. There is one high-school grade cut-off level for the universities, a lower one for the technical schools. I did not ask if the goat herders I had seen last week might have had a college education. I assume education is not forced on anyone, but everyone who sincerely strives for education is supported in that endeavor.

Some soldiers treat the Iraqis as an uneducated people. The name calling reminds me of what many slave-owners believed about blacks during the slavery era. One officer lamented that writing contracts with the Iraqis is difficult, as if it is the Iraqi's fault. For example, in the U.S. we might customarily think that a specific end-result includes specific steps. The Iraqi contractor then produces his (always a male) interpretation of the result using different steps. When asked why he didn't do it a certain way, the common reply is because it was not in the contract. While the officer interpreted this trend as a negative idiosyncrasy, I thought it revealed a shrewd or perceptive business quality.

Of all the reasons that might account for Iraq's national poverty levels, an ignorant or lazy population is not one of them. The people I have observed work hard. The going rate for base laborers is $8 per day. This does not sound like a living wage to Americans but it is more than they can make in the local economy.

Iraq, under the control of people such as the ones I have met this week, will be in good hands. The Iraqi people are fully capable of self-government. What we don't want to happen is for terrorists to take over the country before it has a chance to develop and recreate another haven of state sponsored terrorism. The Iraqi people under Saddam were not in a position to be able to tackle the terrorist threat on their own. We would have left them as sitting targets if we pulled out after ousting Saddam. That is why we are still here. We are definitely not at war with Iraq and have no need to do so. We are at war with terrorists and terrorism. I would rather be at home opening my own law practice, but I believe in this mission.

Numerous news reports discuss how the Iraqi people feel about a certain issue, such as the Marines pulling out of Fallujah. One stateside anchor asked a local correspondent, "How do the Iraqi people feel about that?" The first problem with this reporting is that there is no single-thought entity that can be called the Iraqi people. Mosul area Iraqis I have talked with share divergent opinions. Some fear that the withdrawal will result in more violence in this area if the anti-coalition forces here see it as a decline of American will. Others are furious that the U.S. is placing former Ba'ath military officials back in power. A few others believe that the situation in Fallujah does not represent the overall state of affairs and will have little impact here. Very few news reports take the time to represent the spectrum of views held by Iraqis.

A second problem is that reporters rarely discuss the reliability of their sources. In our Intel office, we receive numerous reports from Iraqis. Each report contains a reliability assessment. Acting on unreliable or unverified information that proves false can literally get our soldiers killed. Where does the correspondent get his information? How many Iraqi people does he talk to? Are they actually representative of the Iraqi's as a whole? Does he assess the reliability of his sources or does he run the risk of being manipulated as a mouthpiece for anti-coalition sentiment? Does the reporter have a personal view of the situation his reporting is supporting or is he truly objective? If I would apply our reliability criteria to the news reporting, I would rate most of them unreliable.

A third, and I honestly believe not picayune, problem is the impression given by the question and answer format. For example, the anchor in the above real example asked how "the" Iraqi people feel. This implies one people, one national sentiment. Then the reporter, in one city of this large nation, answered, "Iraqi people feel…" He did not discuss how many Iraqis feel that way. Even if only .01% of the people feel that way, the reporter is making a truthful statement, but because of the question's wording, the answer implies that all or large majority feel that way. Many Americans then believe that all of Iraq feels or thinks a particular way.

Other than frustration at inaccurate or perhaps biased reporting, why does this matter? If we treat the Iraqi's as a congruous whole, any answer to the question of "How to Spot a Terrorist" will focus our military strength in the wrong direction. I have heard it stated that the Iraqi's want stability, thus the instigators are from outside the country. If true, we would focus then on border protection, identification procedures, and have a certain bias to believe reports Iraqis make against alleged foreigners. We would also overlook Iraqis as terrorist suspects. On the other hand, if "the" (all) Iraqis are responsible for terrorism, we could not trust their reports; we should not have them as our security forces, etc. The truth, of course, is that some Iraqis are our allies and some continue to oppose us. The estimate in Fallujah is that the opposition consisted of 80% Iraqi nationals and 20% foreigners. Even if all of the Iraqi opposition came from Fallujah residents (doubtful), the small number of them represents less than 1% of the population. The Iraqi people who oppose our forces do not represent all of Iraq any more than the recent disgusting treatment of Iraqi prisoners represents the way all American soldiers behave toward detainees.

As I write, a news announcer is asking the question, "Do the Iraqis want to kill us?" The answer, worse than the question, may have done more to confuse people than help explain our situation. No, most Iraqi people do not want to kill us. Yes, some Iraqi people want to kill us. The passengers of that SUV were missionaries helping the people of Mosul by working at the new water treatment plant. New to the area, they stopped to look at a roadmap. The reading lamp drew the attention of the passengers in another vehicle. Pulling alongside, they opened fire on the missionaries, killing all four. These murderers, these opportunistic thugs, lived right here in Mosul. We now know their identities and they are on the run. The press, the government, the military, in fact everyone involved, should think about the multifaceted reality they simply call "the Iraqis".

Americans are not the only ones suffering from a precarious groupthink predisposition. Someone of Kurdish descent bemoaned that Americans can't distinguish between the various ethnic groups in Iraq. His implication was that if we could, we would be able to spot the terrorists. His comment, though, reveals a prejudice existent for centuries. A major problem in Iraq, actually, is a deep and ancient mistrust between various groups. Many groups continue to deal with each other as unified wholes rather than realizing their conflict is with select individuals. The U.S. forces will not reach a viable solution if we perpetuate existing bigotry. The enemy cannot be defined along straight ethnic or even religious lines.

How, then, do we spot a terrorist? Terrorists do not wear an identifiable uniform. In fact, they prefer to blend in with their surroundings. Spotting a terrorist is not easy. Terrorists are not always performing terrorist acts. Not everyone who voices opposition to our presence here is a terrorist. Five pieces of empty luggage left in areas of New York recently may be an indicator of terrorists practicing another assault. Which one of the thousands setting a suitcase on the floor in Penn Station is the terrorist? Many terrorists never publicly voice their opinion. A patrol might pass a terrorist and not even know it, if no terrorist activity is taking place.

Our base employs approximately 1,500 locals. Many of them are supervised by or escorted by Iraqis given clearance to do so. Most of the contractors for the various building contracts are Iraqis. Are any of them terrorists or reporting base activities to anti-US groups? How do we know? In the U.S. we might request a police record as part of our inquiry into an applicant's background. In Iraq, however, a police record could indicate the Saddam government invented charges against our applicant, which means we might be able to trust him. Then again, he could just be a criminal.

What if we relied on local informants? Consider this scenario. Under Saddam, people owned a plethora of personal weapons. Most males carried weapons openly on the street. When the U.S. forces assumed control of Iraq, they made a national rule that restricted each household to only one weapon, typically an AK-47. If a search reveals more than one weapon, the extra weapons are confiscated and household residents detained. Knowing all of this, suppose a gang of thieves decides to take action against a wealthy family household. One gang member informs the family that someone is going to rob them on a particular night and harm their women or children. A typical Iraqi family would move the women and children to another family home and have all of the males in the family stay in the targeted home with the weapons from their own homes. Another gang member then reports to the Americans that a group of terrorists is meeting in a particular house. The house is said to be full of men and weapons, but no women or children. U.S. troops raid the house, confiscating all weapons and detaining the men. The house is then unprotected. The thieves move in, emptying the home without meeting resistance. Who do we trust? Why are they telling us their stories? Do American troops ever inadvertently support the anti-coalition agenda by eliminating their enemies? Hopefully not as often as reporters do.

Spotting a terrorist in the U.S. is far more complicated that spotting one on the streets of Iraq. On the street, many of these questions do not matter. When we suit up for a patrol in the city, we only use one simple definition of a terrorist. A terrorist is anyone who points a weapon at us. We shoot first and ask questions later. I hope Americans never need to do this at home.

05-04-04 * FAITH FOCUS—
ONWARD CHRISTIAN SOLDIERS

I joined a group of Christian soldiers discussing aspects of the war from a spiritual perspective. To what extent can the war between America and the terrorists be rightly described as a spiritual battle? Terrorists describe their actions against Americans as justified to punish us for the evils our country perpetrates on the world. Many Americans feel that our cause is the right one, and that God is on our side in this battle. Others take the position that God is not on anyone's side but wants all of us to learn to live together in peace and harmony. One could also argue that God is on the side of those who believe in Him no matter which side of the terrorism battle they fight – a spiritual civil war perhaps.

Are we fighting this war in Iraq as Christians who also happen to be soldiers or as soldiers who also happen to be Christians? I think the answer is obviously the latter. If as American soldiers, then on what grounds do we claim spiritual protections? I once read a bumper sticker with the modern proverb "Don't drive faster than your guardian angel can fly". Have soldiers, who are also Christians, placed our selves in a situation in which God is unwilling to extend His protection? If my pacifist friend is correct about God's opinion of military service we may indeed have done just that.

I firmly believe God reigns and God overrules in the affairs of men. I also believe that the confusion surrounding the effectiveness of prayer and applicability of scriptural promises is resolved by correctly understanding the enemy we fight as Christians. As Americans we are fighting a war against terrorists in Iraq, Afghanistan and other places around the world. But who is the real spiritual enemy faced by Christians today, whether soldiers or any other vocation?

What if a fundamental Islamic extremist repented, apologized, did not convert to Christianity but did everything within his power to live at peace with Christians? No longer a soldier's enemy, would he still be a Christian's enemy? If an enemy at all, and I would argue against that determination, he is the weakest of enemies with no power or intent or opportunity to circumvent my faith. An individual's participation in a different religion does not, in and of itself, make that person an enemy of Christians and we should stop treating them as such.

The true enemy of the Christian is any power or entity that works to destroy our faith in and relationship with God. We have such enemies in our midst today. One enemy of the Christian faith is the Christian leadership furthering the enemy's agenda by convincing people that Satan does not really exist. While I believe that many Christians think of Satan exercising more power than he really possesses, I am fully convinced that Satan will achieve an incredible victory if the church comes to believe that he is powerless or is purely mythical. This decade's old debate parallels the issue of whether sin exists[2] and if sin does not exist then why do we need a savior.

Another enemy of the church is the self-appointed shepherd who fleeces God's flock for his own interests while promising unscriptural, exorbitant blessings from God. They parade success stories in the spotlight while carefully controlling anything that does not support their contentions. These wolves in shepherd's clothing deflect unfulfilled promises onto the givers by asserting the problem must be the sheep's faith. These traitors care little for the damage they do to individual believers since they monitor their ministry's success not in any terms Jesus described in the gospels but by the amount of the contributions they receive.

A third enemy of the Christian faith are those who spiritualize tenets of the faith into meaningless precepts. Some surveys reveal that most Americans consider themselves Christians yet rarely do these surveys first attempt to objectively define what it means to be a Christian. We may have so diluted the definition of Christian that any concept of active faith becomes irrelevant. Could this be what Jesus meant when he asked, "When the Son of Man comes, will he find faith on the earth?" (Luke 18:8).

The most dangerous enemies of the faith are never people. Paul defined the true battle for the faith: "For our struggle is not against flesh and blood, but against the rulers, against the authorities, against the powers of this dark world and against the spiritual forces of evil in the heavenly realms" (Eph. 6:12). A Christian's primary mission in the intergalactic spiritual battle is to reach out and save the lost. Our spiritual weapons should never be directed against people but toward spiritual forces.

If any person ever acts contrary to the Christian faith our job is to pray for them, standing firm in our own faith, reaching out to them in love. Jesus devoted much of His ministry to reaching the one sheep that had left the fold.

Our efforts should encompass that same mission. Every person is precious to God and should be to us as well. May we never join the ranks of those in Jesus' prophecy who, at the end times, "will turn away from the faith and will betray and hate each other" (Matt. 24:10).

05-06-04 * News From the Front

Discussions of our tactics against prisoners continue to dominate the news of the week. We have a detention facility on our base, but I have never seen any such issues surfacing here. I have not heard yet whether the photographs are authentic or manipulated somehow. If the people involved indeed performed actions outside stated policies, they should be held accountable. If their actions were within guidelines, yet reprehensible, the system needs an overhaul. I think the former is far more likely.

I have noticed a disturbing trend in the news. Reporters frequently treat the people of Iraq as if everyone here shared the same behaviors and attitudes. Do "the people of Iraq" want to kill us? How do "the people of Iraq" feel about an issue? Even some soldiers think that way. Unfortunately, the results influence how we perform our mission and how we treat the Iraqi people. About a month ago four young, local Iraqi women who worked at our hospital were gunned down on their way home from work. I discovered the vehicle they were riding in at the time. The people who shot the missionaries also lived in Mosul. Most of the enemy combatants are part of "the people of Iraq". So are the people who risk their lives for us as our security force. Treating the people of Iraq as a homogenous unit demonstrates a grave misunderstanding of both the Iraqi people and the issues involved in helping them create a stable democracy.

News reports periodically mention Iraqi military weapons buried in the sand. Our base is very near such a weapons cache site. I heard a news interview with New York councilman Barron a few days ago in which he said, "we did not find WMD in Iraq; in fact, and we did not even find a firecracker." He is right that we did not find a firecracker, but we are not looking for something that small. We have, however, found so much firepower I am baffled at the continued press that WMD does not exist. We discovered numerous weapons systems capable of delivering chemical or biological agents that are very deadly without the added agents. True, we have not yet found evidence that Saddam possessed the chemicals we know he had in the past, but the delivery systems certainly still exist. I believe a 1,500 lb. bomb could qualify as a WMD, at least according to the FBI definition, even if it does not contain chemicals. Thousands of unfused bombs, rockets and mortars are available in old Iraqi ammo supply points. Most of the attacks against our base are with ordnance stolen from the ammunition depot we are now trying to control.

This week an officer from another unit and I took a drive southwest of the base. I heard rumors of a 5th century monastery and wanted to see it. The entry was blocked by yellow warning tape and a sign posted an order by the base commander not to enter the property. We walked around the structure and looked in a few windows. The stone construction did not appear to contain any wood, used archways rather than doors and small openings for windows. The small personal rooms for the monks contained a stone slab bed and appeared consistent with someone who took a vow of poverty even for that time period.

On our circuitous return we discovered a large field full of Iraqi tanks. It has been rumored that a certain staff sergeant may have been seen climbing into an Iraqi tank. I cannot confirm or deny the rumor (ahem), only mention that certain security personnel would have already talked with this sergeant about his activity. The primary reason presented for not playing with the tanks is that they have not been cleared for chemical residue or explosives. Chemical residue? In a country with supposedly no chemical weapons?

A few people, after reading the Las Vegas essay, have asked how I am doing physically. I went running outdoors for the first time today. I usually work out in the gym. I am well, aside from my mouth tasting like dust all the time. Hopefully the previous health issues will stay in the past. That also means I am not heading home any time soon for physical reasons. I ran inside the fence line for a few miles. At one point two children on the other side of the fence waved, smiled, said hello. I chatted with them, but found their English did not extend beyond saying hi, which is still better than my Arabic. Although separated by a strong wire-mesh fence with strands of barbwire on top and a circle of razor wire in front, they smiled and chatted in Arabic as if the fence did not exist.

When I mentioned the outing to someone, he said that I should not be running along the fence line as the openness and proximity to outside buildings makes me a vulnerable target. In fact, he stated that children could be used to lure a soldier to stop for just that reason. I had considered the vulnerability issues while running (that is my job, after all) but have different beliefs about the composition of the enemy.

What struck me most about the interaction with the Iraqi children is the necessity, for security reasons, of fencing ourselves off from the people we are here to protect. I felt like a prisoner reaching the outer limits of my daily experience, a wall I can see through but am not allowed to cross. I dislike living in this compound structure even if it is necessary for our protection. More than a fence separates us from the local population. While most soldiers I talk with about this issue prefer the fences and other protective measures, I am saddened by what this implies about our relationship with "the people of Iraq".

In his recent Congressional testimony, Defense Secretary Donald Rumsfeld thrice explained, in response to similar questions from three different Congressmen, why the concept of "command influence" prevented him from knowing the full extent of an ongoing court martial investigation. The Congressmen, all Democrats, but that's probably a coincidence, chastised his leadership for not knowing specifics about the abuse. One even suggested, using contrite and apologetic language with only a hint of sincerity that Rumsfeld resign at this implication of incompetent leadership. The questions show either an indefensible politicization of this event or an inexcusable ignorance of military law. Inexcusable, I believe, because these Congressmen sit on the Armed Services Committee.

For those who understandably lack experience with military law and protocol, I want to provide a background through which to better understand the point Sec. Rumsfeld attempted to convey.

The Uniform Code of Military Justice (UCMJ) contains laws for convening a Court Martial and punitive articles outlining violations. The military does not have a full-time court with judges, defense and prosecution devoted to courts-martial. Instead, military officers with the appropriate experience serve as judge and advocates. The judge, attorneys and jury may even belong to related chains of command.

The UCMJ delineates crimes such as murder and robbery. It also lists crimes particular to military service such as absence without leave (AWOL), aiding the enemy, and misbehavior of a sentinel. Many people not familiar with the UCMJ are surprised to discover, for example, that married soldiers can be jailed and dishonorably discharged for committing adultery.

The UCMJ applies to all soldiers on active duty status, anywhere in the world. It does not apply to soldiers in the National Guard, a fact that generated another controversy in the news recently. The UCMJ makes it a crime for any commissioned officer to use "contemptuous words against the President" and other officials. A lieutenant from Massachusetts gave the Democratic reply to a recent Presidential address. This was the first time, I believe, a non-politician has given the reply. He reprimanded the President for his handling of the situation in Iraq. Part of that speech appeared in ads against Pres. Bush sponsored by John Kerry. On the surface this seems like a clear violation of the UCMJ, yet is not.

The lieutenant had been in active duty status in Iraq, but when he returned to his National Guard unit the UCMJ no longer applied. In Guard status, soldiers come under State law. So, even though he is using his military title, and appearing in uniform, the UCMJ does not prohibit the lieutenant from using contemptuous words against the President. The UCMJ also does not apply, for example, to civilian interpreters interrogating prisoners.

My law school "Federal Courts" professor sharply chastised the protection of defendant rights under the UCMJ. He believed that the process gives too much power to the military in the way the court is convened and in certain rules of evidence. Soldiers receive evaluations that factor significantly into the promotion system. They are also obliged to follow orders. What if a commander appoints a junior officer as defense attorney who is barely skilled and is reviewed by the commander? What if the entire court is convened to guarantee a guilty verdict? Our professor called this "command influence". He then quoted the near perfect conviction rate in court-martials as evidence that such influence exists.

A certain amount of command influence does exist. The system significantly relies on the integrity of the officers involved. This may be one reason why it shuns civilian attorneys. To prevent tampering in the case by a higher chain of command, the command is notified of the number and type of court martial proceedings but not the specifics of the case. The military process also can combine the investigation with the trial, meaning that new evidence can be brought it as acquired and new witnesses called by the court with broader tolerance than allowed in civilian courts. The details are forwarded, if at all, when the investigation is complete.

The military also does not appreciate the influence of the press before cases complete. The increasing tendency to try high profile civilian cases in the press before the jury has even heard the evidence does a disservice to our justice system. The press can have an even greater influence on the decision of a civilian case than commanders could ever have over a military trial, but our professor did not seem to have a problem with press coverage.

The main problem with the prisoner abuse scandal is that the investigation is still in process. The first court martial starts in 10 days. To avoid command influence Rumsfeld should not know intricate details about this case, yet the three Congressmen appeared shocked that he only received general notice that such a case existed. They hunted for a cover-up at the highest level while knowing all along how the system works. One commented later than Rumsfeld did a good job, as he should have, of making it look like the President was not directly involved, which he is not.

Someone reported the abuses in January of this year. Within a few days an investigation began. A press conference was held that mentioned the commencement of a case involving abuse of prisoners. No media fanfare, but then again no details such as photographs were released. Six people are currently behind bars and the investigation continues. In late April, before the secret report of the case had even reached the Pentagon, someone leaked it to CBS. Showing the photographs originally to a chain of command that took action means the process works. Showing the secret report / photographs to the press was likely a violation of the UCMJ.

The bottom line is that if the leak had not occurred, the Congressional committee and the American public would probably never have known the details. It took a leak of a secret document to sidestep this process. Instead of expressing outrage that a secret document was released (as Rumsfeld did), the same three cover-up hunting Congressmen praised the offender for making this information public. They waxed indignant that the military could have concluded its business and America would not have known about the abuses. Congress looked far more concerned about its power to review military matters than about the leaking of a secret level document. Who is really covering up illegalities, Congressmen?

Given the constant display of the photographs in the news, and the embarrassment of the President and the military before the entire world, did the release of the document help? Is this really something the entire world needs to know about? I don't think so. There are over 18,000 courts-martial per year that include spousal abuse, spying, drunk driving or being drunk on duty. Sec. Rumsfeld and the Congress do not need to know the details of cases in progress or of most of the concluded ones. Rumsfeld has the right attitude about how the system should work. Several members of Congress do not. If anyone should resign, it should be Congressmen that manipulate a system they do not control for their own political gain.

Despite its imperfections, the court-martial system works. All soldiers involved, no matter how high up the chain of command, will face serious consequences. Any leaders who ordered the abuse will be disciplined more severely than the soldiers that participated. "I was just following orders", as the photographed female soldier claims, is not a complete defense because soldiers are only required to follow lawful orders. Participation in an unlawful order is still a UCMJ offense. What justice is added to this process by the media and Congressional attention? None. In fact, a predominantly honorable institution, if not the entire nation, is being treated as if we need the press and Congress to force us to behave.

A few soldiers behaved dishonorably, if not abhorrently. Yet certain members of Congress and the media are attempting to discredit the President, Secretary Rumsfeld and the entire military. I strongly suggest that they attend to the dishonor of their own institutions before attempting to clean up ours.

The most important local news of the week concerns five American soldiers killed in Mosul. Two of the five worked here at the airfield. This base suffered only one U.S. death from the initial entry into the area over a year ago and our unit's arrival. That death was due to an equipment accident. The recent attacks could indicate either stronger and bolder area dissidents or the dying efforts of a faltering faction. I hope for the latter but fear the former is closer to the truth.

An al-Zarqaiwi press release mentioned that the recent murder of an American was in response to the prison abuse. Other news items recount that the kidnappers wanted to negotiate him for specific Iraqi prisoners and the U.S. would not cooperate. But the al-Zarqawi terrorist group believed responsible for this murder was doing things like this long before the prison scandal broke and even before we invaded Iraq. As to the negotiations, the safety of every American in countries where they operate would be in danger if they thought kidnapping Americans would accomplish their objectives. The most likely reason for the execution is that this is in line with who these people are. Withdrawal from Iraq will not stop them. Negotiating will not stop them. They want to kill Americans. The military, President Bush and Donald Rumsfeld are not responsible for their behavior regardless of what certain newscasters opine. These terrorists are at war with us whether we want to be at war with them or not. These are acts of war and we need to deal with them as such.

Last week I won our local version of the "Who Wants to be a Millionaire" game show. I topped out at the $125,000 level. The prize? No money, unfortunately (or fortunately… for the taxpayers). I won two hours of free Internet usage with a web cam. All 20 computers in the recreation center had web cams in the past, but soldiers stole 17 of them. The recreation center reserves the three remaining web cams as contest prizes, so it is a valuable award.

This past Sunday I played a square on Hollywood Squares. The questions were mainly from 80's television, a decade I think I missed somehow. Fortunately the game show producers handed out the questions they would be asking us along with the answers. We then only had a decision of whether to tell the truth or lie and try to mislead the contestants. I think the squares had more fun than the contestants.

I killed my first camel spider this week. At a body length of only one inch it was a small camel spider, but deserving of death nonetheless. I do not like spiders. Not only are these spiders fast and dangerous, stepping on one sounds squishy with a slight crunchy coating. Perhaps camel spiders could be a delicacy in France if France ever runs out of frog legs.

A couple of weeks ago I decided to dedicate some spare time to learning something in addition to my legal and Bible reading. Many years ago, I started guitar lessons but sold my guitar soon thereafter in a financial crunch. This week I bought a guitar through a local Iraqi shop and started guitar lessons. In only one week, I have progressed up to lesson 1: switching between G & D major chords. This is an as-the-mission-allows goal, but I hope it stays quiet enough around here to continue.

My law office is off to a disappointing start. A female soldier two doors over started a barbershop. She has customers on almost a daily basis. No one so far needs an attorney. I am glad I have a side job as an Intel analyst to pay the bills. When I return home, though, I fully expect the legal business to pick up. At least this is the optimistic story I tell myself.

05-17-04 * BLESSINGS FOR A BUTCHER

A sparrow lighted on a branch nearby, joined in song by others still in flight or nestled amongst the leaves. In this beautiful garden containing roses in bloom, sculptured shrubberies, and a water fountain, I listened to nature's symphony and felt blessed for my respite from the sounds of war. I also paused to admire the architecture of the main house; beautiful stone murals several stories tall, intricately carved columns, a large rear veranda with a spectacular view of the city. I already knew of the two indoor pools, the exquisitely tiled floors, the decorative ceilings and stunning chandeliers. More impressive than the mansion itself are the surroundings grounds. The entire palace complex includes other mansions, one nearby and another down the hill on the bank of a large lake. On the few occasions I am allowed to adventure here, I have discovered a Roman styled terrace with stone steam baths and a huge fire-pit for the rumored feasts, numerous smaller homes, a large garage complex and uncounted other buildings the secrets of which may have died with the previous occupants.

I have been to the Vanderbilt and Hearst castles, J. Paul Getty's residence turned museum and other impressive estates of famous Americans. Our richest citizens do not live in the grandeur lifestyle of Saddam Hussein. The palace grounds in Mosul are, I have heard, less extravagant than his main palace in Baghdad. He actually owned more estates than John Kerry, living a lifestyle parallel to that of royalty in Buckingham and Versailles rather than presidents of democracies. Did Saddam consider himself blessed in these surroundings? Did he or his sons walk in this garden and praise Allah for his bountiful mercies? Did Saddam see these grounds as a reward for his faithful service?

Thinking that monster, that butcher, that most evil of human beings could judge himself blessed disgusts me. The full account of atrocities he and his sons committed against fellow Iraqis is yet to be told. He may have accomplished a few good deeds, but probably for selfish purposes rather than humanitarian. He maintained roads, schools, and the basic necessities in meager conditions required to sustain Iraq and thus his power. The abundance of Iraq's wealth he kept for himself and those loyal to him.

I realize that the rain falls on the just and the unjust, yet the thought of blessings befalling the Butcher of Baghdad for his scant, selfish good behavior violates every concept of justice I hold dear. Those who sow to the wind should reap a whirlwind, not fortune. I first despaired justice could catch Saddam. Even if Saddam was one of the photographed prisoners in Abu Ghraib, the humiliation pales in comparison to how he treated other people. If the Iraqi courts sentence him to death, his humane execution could never seal justice for the thousands of horrible executions he directed. The butcher appeared to have tipped the scales of justice in his favor.

The sparrow's song reminded me of a concept of justice I overlooked. Life's true blessings are not material. More accurate and enduring than the portrait of Dorian Grey, our soul reflects our deeds in ways that cannot escape justice. If someone steals from me, he loses more than I do. I have lost a replaceable possession, but he can no longer look me in the eye. He uses the item in secret, afraid someone will discover the truth. Solomon warned that Folly calls out to the simple, "'Stolen water is sweet; food eaten in secret is delicious!' But little do they know that the dead are there, that her guests are in the depths of the grave" (Prov. 9:7-8). Material possessions may mask our depravity, but justice is never mocked in the recesses of the soul.

In that moment I doubted Saddam ever truly enjoyed the sparrows, roses, fountains or even his power. His spy network, electronic surveillance and intolerance of the slightest defiance to his authority reveal a soul plagued by paranoia. Though surrounded by a dedicated private army, Saddam still feared that what he took by force could be snatched from his grasp in like manner. When justice knocked down his defenses, not even billions of stolen dollars and the power of a president turned dictator could safely hide Saddam. The butcher could only crawl into a spider hole and hide. Some leaders in Iraq may denounce the U.S. presence in Iraq, but I have yet to hear them demanding restoration of Saddam's regime. He is utterly alone.

All the grandeur of Saddam's palaces could not entice me to trade places with him even at the height of his power. No amount of worldly wealth is worth a decrepit soul. Justice has indeed weighed Saddam in the balances, and judged him wanting.

05-18-04 * FAITH FOCUS— WHEN GOOD THINGS HAPPEN TO BAD PEOPLE

The more I contemplate justice as operating in Iraq, specifically with Saddam, the more I am convinced that eternal life and judgment is not designed to balances the scales of Earth's history.

I once traced the words "justice" and "just" through the entire Bible. Reading those passages in chronological order I followed changes in the way Biblical characters viewed the concept of justice. Early books in the Bible describe God intervening on a personal level to dispense justice, ensuring that circumstances rewarded or punished people according to their actions. The story of Job contrasts perceptions of justice held by Job, his various friends and ultimately God Himself. God's perceived personal intervention in human affairs led to a strong belief that good things happened to good people and bad things happened to bad people. Good people died in certain ways and provided an inheritance for their children.

King David portrayed a strong, if not completely black-and-white view of justice. As king he dispensed justice according to this belief even to the point of cursing the family of his Joab. Joab murdered Abner in retaliation for Abner killing Joab's brother. Since Israel allowed retribution, albeit according to rules which Joab did not follow, David and Joab exhibited strong and opposed views of justice regarding Abner. The king sang this lament for Abner: "Should Abner have died as the lawless die? Your hands were not bound, your feet were not fettered. You fell as one falls before wicked men" (2 Sam. 3:33-34).

By time one reaches the Book of Hebrews, the concept of justice portrayed in the Bible changes radically. Hebrews chapter eleven dispels the notion of only good things happening to good people. The author of Hebrews traces historical events where people of faith enjoy success and suffer torture. The level of one's faith cannot therefore be accurately determined by starting with what happens to people and working backwards to faith based on beliefs about justice.

The New Testament does not elaborate on or delineate layers of eternal punishment and reward to compensate or punish for injustices suffered or performed in this world. Christianity radically departs from other major religions by asserting that eternal life is not based on reward and punishment for actions on Earth but is either a continuation of a relationship with a living God or eternal separation from God's presence. Even though I believe this, when I think of Saddam's brutal betrayal and murder of thousands of Iraqis, his displacement of the Marsh Arabs, his genocide against the Kurds, his hundreds of documented uses of Sarin against people whose only crime was their bravery to stand against his dictatorship, I want to curse him and his family worse than David cursed Joab. I want to witness justice in action against him and his family.

One of my favorite professors in law school taught my first year torts class. His final exam wove an elaborate and creative chain of events involving numerous actors into one story followed by one simple question: "What torts and what defenses?" Ensconcing myself in the throne of judgment, I dissected the facts and applied the rules of torts similar in manner to which many people think God will judge the world. During my final exam I missed the impact a few facts played in the litany of events proving, once again, people should be glad I am not God. The history of tort common law compared to the church's message of justice as revealed in available sermons is another fascinating study, but outside the scope of this discussion.

Suppose that all of the people murdered by Saddam appear before the judgment throne at the end of Earth's history. Each one appeals to God for justice. Each one asks that Saddam be punished according to his deeds and that they receive an eternal reward to compensate them for the injustice they suffered on Earth. What result? Would God apply His own type of tort law and award them damages?

I imagine that an Islamic cleric would answer that question differently than I do as a Christian. My belief is that God would distinguish the wheat from the chaff and tell most of them "I never knew you." Their eternal judgment might place them on the same side of the heaven and hell dividing line as Saddam. I have met Christians who believe there must be differences in the way people will experience hell even though the Bible does not provide enough details for such a conclusion. What is certain is that both Saddam and his non-Christian victims are headed for the same eternal destination. I have also met non-Christians and former Christians who state that this lack of eternal justice in the Christian faith is one of the main reasons they choose not to believe.

Although Paul wrote that we shall judge the world and angels (see 1 Cor. 6:2-3), he did not mention what laws will be the standard or what sentencing guidelines may apply. James mentioned in his epistle that we should "speak and act as those who are going to be judged by the law that gives freedom" (James 2:12). After years of study I believe James is not referring to the Ten Commandments, as I was once taught, but do not know for sure what law he meant. I am comforted somewhat in my lack of understanding by the thought that if God wanted us to know now all of the details of how we will judge in the life to come He would have revealed that to us. What He did reveal is part of our job on Earth is learning to apply sound or righteous judgment.

God did, however, instruct us with everything we need to know to prepare for our own judgment. "For God did not send his Son into the world to condemn the world, but to save the world through him" (John 3:17). I know as much of what heaven will be like as I do about hell – not much at all. Still, if heaven is spending eternity with the God I love, then I want to be there. He already finished everything to make that happen. I do not know where or in what capacity Saddam will spend eternity but I know whom I believe in and am persuaded that my eternity will be very different.

We had two more memorial services here this week. Two real people, with families back home who grieve for them, killed in the line of duty. The death of any of our soldiers is an emotional experience for me. No one wants to get a knock on his or her door with this message. "Sir / ma'am, I am with the Army Casualty Assistance Office…" But the knocks come, the tears flow, and life moves on whether we cope or not. Every time this happens I strengthen my resolve to do everything in my power to make sure no one from Casualty Assistance ever needs to call on my home.

I left my apartment (I call it that to make it seem bigger than the 70 sq. ft. space it actually is) a few nights ago and discovered three hills ablaze to our south. At first I feared that the fire endangered the Abu Sayef village to our south, but the nearest flame was several hills to their west. The wind favored the village, moving the fire further west along an unoccupied dry, grass-covered ridge. I climbed to the top of the trailer unit and watched the fire with two other soldiers, enjoying nature's amazing display. I climbed down to find that I had both left my light on and my door open. About a gazillion small flying insects invaded my room. It was flying room only and no bug free location for me to stand. Not that big of a deal except for the malaria and leishmanasis some of the mosquitoes carry.

I watched Rudy Giuliani's testimony to the 9/11 Commission. I thought he delivered straight-forward answers, on point and accurate from what I know of how government & the Intel community work together. I could not believe the headlines I saw the next morning. "9/11 victim families disappointed" that he wasn't raked over the coals. How many families? Very few I imagine, so why does our media focus on their reaction instead of the tens of thousands of New York families who admire Giuliani and are grateful he was the one in charge of New York at the time? I can find no kind words or thoughts at the moment for those whining, ungrateful, selfish crybabies hissing at Giuliani or the reporters who think their opinion deserves even a second of airtime. Fume… Okay, I'm better now.

The prison guard court martial case continues to top news stories here. One astute reader reminded me of the 1971 Stanford Prison Experiments conducted by Professor Dr. Zimbardo. Dr. Zimbardo's research studied how people might treat others if granted certain powers as prison guards. Each side was chosen randomly from a pool of similar people so no real criminals or enemies were involved. Dr. Zimbardo has an informative website which also discusses the court martial cases here in relation to his study.[3] I also researched several news sources for an accurate resource to pass along for those who want truth rather than some of the fiction being released. The *New Yorker* magazine originally broke part of the story, in addition to CBS, and has followed the facts well.[4] I disagree with the author's conclusion, though, that the Abu Ghraib guards could not have done these things on their own. I think Dr. Zimbardo's work reveals that indeed they could have. One of the problems many people have in dealing with this situation is the reality check of what we are capable of doing, even as Americans.

Last Friday I was allowed to accompany a patrol through the city. We went through areas I had not seen before. One section of commercial shops caught my attention. Several city blocks of steel door after steel door, the kind that rolls up like a garage door. The entire block is lined with these doors on all four sides. Merchants roll up their doors, bring their wares out to the sidewalk, and business commences. Most of the shops displayed only one or two items (but multiple units of them). One would have tires, another batteries, and yet another oil. I saw soda stands, a meat market with raw meat hanging in the open, and a coffee shop that seemed to have the bulk of the customers at this time of day. Pottery, sandals, clothing, mats, vegetables, fruit. One open door caught my eye. There was no shop behind it. Instead, the door revealed a passageway wide enough to drive a vehicle into the courtyard of that block. I thought about a report I heard that somewhere in the city is a door that leads under the shops to a terrorist hideout. It is sort of like the gangster movies of the 30's; a certain honk, the door opens, bad guys drive in, door closes, good guys pass it a few moments later unaware. I wish I had my camera, but we carry weapons instead and don't stop to take pictures.

We drove for a while along the river. The riverfront area has restaurants, different shops than the commercial market area, and some beautiful homes. I also saw a sign in English that read "Tourist Island". A small boat transports people to an island in the Tigris, about 30 feet from shore. I saw a Ferris wheel and several other attractions as we sped by. The island seemed slightly larger than the island in the River of America in Disneyland. Although early afternoon, I did not see very many people. I guess this isn't a good tourist season. We also passed the major hotels in Mosul, including one closed due to bomb damage. I think this would be a fascinating place to spend a vacation if we could get the security issues taken care of. So far my requests to go to the Hatra ruins 70 miles south have been denied.

05-24-04 * THE OIL FOR FOOD PROGRAM

A Florida National Guard soldier received one year in jail and a bad conduct discharge for failing to return to his unit in Iraq after returning home on leave. He argued that he refused to support an "oil-driven war". His argument made national headlines, but is neither a defensible position against a charge of desertion nor accurate. Politicians and pundits also accuse the President of conducting a war to benefit big oil oligarchies. Most news programs repeat the criticism as a self-evident fact. Unless someone starts challenging the truth of these assertions, the rhetoric will only intensify throughout the presidential elections.

Who benefits from Iraqi oil production? United States companies did not previously buy oil from Iraq because of the sanctions. Saddam's oil sales benefited himself, his family, and international terrorism, rather than enriching the Iraqi people as should have happened. The Coalition Provisional Authority set up a trust system so that the proceeds of fair market sales of Iraqi oil are used to benefit Iraqis. American oil companies have actually paid more for oil, including Iraqi oil, since the U.S. assumed control.

The oil rich countries in the Middle East benefit from a stable Iraq, but not from Iraqi oil. Iraq is a competitor to, not member of, OPEC. Kuwait, a member of OPEC, no longer needs to spend billions on recreating its refineries and pipelines because Saddam is in one of his moods. OPEC considers the availability and pricing of non-OPEC production into account when setting prices. The win for the Middle East is peace, not oil profits.

The people of Iraq are the primary beneficiary of Iraqi oil production. The profits from Iraqi oil are now rebuilding the country, not promoting the security and sadistic pleasure of Saddam Hussein and family. The people of the free world also benefit. The world's terrorists lost a major source of funding. Like Kuwait, freedom-loving countries everywhere can shift resources from rebuilding after terrorist attacks to preventing future actions. Whether these countries acknowledge it or not, the leadership of the U.S. and Britain produced this benefit for them.

Under pressure from the U.S. and Britain to curb Iraq's state-sponsored terrorism, the United Nations Security Council established the Oil-for-Food

(OFF) Program on April 14, 1995. The resolution limited oil production and forced all funds to be spent on non-military purposes. The resolution also called for evaluations every six months. Iraq exported 3.4 billion barrels of oil valued at about $65 billion under the program between December 1996 and 20 March 2003. Of this amount, the UN allocated 72 percent towards humanitarian needs nationwide. The balance went to: Gulf War reparations through a Compensation Fund (25 percent); UN administrative and operational costs for the program (2.2 percent) and costs for the weapons inspection program (0.8 percent).

Iraq's State Oil Marketing Organization demanded that companies purchasing Iraqi crude oil pay a fifty-cent per barrel surcharge starting on December 1, 2000. The surcharge, paid directly to the Iraqi government rather than into the OFF program, constituted a clear violation of sanctions. The United States responded by forbidding U.S. companies from buying Iraqi oil. The surcharge provided Saddam's Ba'ath party with millions of dollars on a weekly basis.

On November 29, 2001, the Security Council unanimously approved a resolution extending the Oil-for-Food program in Iraq for another six-month period. This resolution allowed Iraq to sell unlimited quantities of oil on the condition that the proceeds buy food, medicine, and other humanitarian goods, and pay war reparations. This resolution also called on members of the Security Council to agree by May 31, 2002, on a list of "dual use" items that would require United Nations approval before Iraq could import them through the program.

President George Bush delivered a State of the Union address on January 29, 2002. In his speech, he identified Iraq, Iran, and North Korea as terrorism's "axis of evil". President Bush also stated, "The United States of America will not permit the world's most dangerous regimes to threaten us with the world's most destructive weapons."

Iraq announced on April 8, 2002 that it would halt OFF exports for 30 days as a gesture of support for the Palestinians' struggle with Israel. Iraq also requested that OPEC would not raise production to make up for lost Iraqi exports. Iraqi OFF exports had averaged about 1.7 million barrels per day to date in 2002. Major Arab OPEC exporters Saudi Arabia, Kuwait, and Qatar expressed unwillingness to join in any embargo.

The Security Council approved an overhaul of the OFF program on May 14, 2002 that created an extensive list of "dual-use" goods (goods that could have a military as well as civilian use). The resolution renewed the U.N. program until November 25, 2002. Iraq officially accepted the UN proposal on May 29.

According to United Nations officials and representatives of the oil industry, on September 18, 2002, Iraq stopped the illegal surcharges on oil it sold through the OFF program. Iraq appeared to cooperate more closely with UN resolutions in the face of increased scrutiny by the United States and Britain. Alternatively, perhaps Saddam found more oil buyers outside the OFF program.

United Nations Security Council Resolution (UNSCR) 1483, dated 21 May 2003, sanctioned the establishment of the Development Fund for Iraq (DFI). Resolution 1483 and the laws and usages of war, authorized the Coalition Provisional Authority (CPA) as the administrator of the Fund. The United Nations Security Council approved the immediate end of 13 years of economic sanctions on Iraq, dating from the time of Iraq's invasion of Kuwait in 1990. UNSCR 1483 effectively granted the United States-led coalition forces control of Iraq until a new Iraqi government is in place. The end of the sanctions also made it easier for Iraqi oil exports to resume without the auspices of the United Nations. Later, on May 27, the U.S. Department of the Treasury lifted most remaining sanctions on Iraq. Secretary of the Treasury John W. Snow stated, "It is no longer a crime for U.S. companies and individuals to do business with Iraq."

Resolution 1483 also authorized the International Advisory and Monitoring Board (IAMB) to ensure that the CPA used DFI funds in a transparent manner for the stated purposes and that export sales from Iraq complied with prevailing international market best practices. The IAMB has the responsibility to approve the independent public accountants selected and appointed by the CPA and to audit the DFI.

About $31 billion worth of humanitarian supplies and equipment were delivered to Iraq under the OFF Program between 20 March 1997 and 21 November 2003, including $1.6 billion worth of oil industry spare parts and equipment. Additional goods and supplies from the program's multi billion dollar humanitarian pipeline are delivered on a priority basis in consultation with the Coalition Provisional Authority, Iraqi representatives and UN agencies.

The UN Controller transferred the OFF remaining balance of $8.1 billion to DFI. In a statement to the Security Council on Nov. 20, 2003, UN Secretary-General Kofi Annan noted that the OFF Program was the only humanitarian program ever to have been funded entirely from resources belonging to the nation it was designed to help. He said that in nearly seven years of operation, the Program had been required to meet "an almost impossible series of challenges", using some $46 billion of Iraqi export earnings on behalf of the Iraqi people. Under the program, nine different United Nations agencies, programs and funds developed and managed humanitarian operations in Iraq, meeting the needs of the civilian population across some 24 economic and social sectors.

April 21, 2004, the Security Council unanimously endorsed an independent investigation into charges of corruption in the UN-administered OFF program. Allegations had arisen in the Iraqi press that foreign administrators of the program were receiving inappropriate proceeds from oil sales before the war. Payments to overlook the illegal surcharges and oil sales outside OFF or was the 2.2 percent administrative fee of several billion dollars just not enough?

In addition to the $ 8.1 billion from OFF, DFI has received $ 9.5 billion in proceeds from oil exports. The $ 9 billion in disbursements from the DFI have been in support of the wheat purchase program, the currency exchange program, the electricity and oil infrastructure programs, equipment for Iraqis security forces, and for Iraqi civil service salaries and ministry budget operations.

Although U.S. companies may now purchase oil from Iraq, that fact does not make them more competitive since they do so at prevailing market rates. The competitiveness of U.S. companies in the oil industry stems from their ability to purchase oil from non-OPEC countries. At 3.4 percent, Iraq ranked sixth in U.S. oil imports for 2003. How many OPEC countries ranked higher? Only Saudi Arabia (second). Our number one country for importing oil? Canada. Go figure, eh? Perhaps the U.S. could replace oil imports from Iraq with increased production from Canada, development of ANWR, or several other non-OPEC countries. Why we do not do so hints more at an environmental conspiracy than oil oligarchy influence.

Why, then, is the oil production in Iraq a major factor in the rebuilding process? Iraq has oil. Iraq will sell oil. The question is who will control how the money is spent. Before the OFF program, the profits built the palaces and armies of Saddam's brutal administration. Even with OFF restrictions, Iraqi oil profits left many of Iraq's citizens in poverty and without basic services. Now, a major state sponsor of terrorism is completely out of business. The sponsored terrorists still in Iraq want their money back. DFI is rebuilding Iraq despite the protests of the terrorists in Iraq and misguided politicians in the U.S. The people and infrastructure of Iraq need the profits from Iraqi oil to rebuild a viable economy. People of Iraq 7, state-sponsored terrorism 0. I am one National Guard soldier proud to be on the winning team.

The one self-evident fact in this discussion should be that those who continue to chastise the effort in Iraq as a pawn for big oil oligarchies have an agenda other than the truth.

There is some good news from Najaf concerning the cease-fire with Muqtada Al-Sadr. The predictions of increased violence until the handover may turn out incorrect. I hope so. Our area still has mortar and IED attacks. No deaths this week. A few more wildfires to our west and one on our base with no significant damage. The electric grid project continues but is still a long way from completion.

Temperatures are in the high 90's with lows in the mid 60's. I like the weather so far but not looking forward to the forecasted 120+ degree days starting in July. Two days ago I went for a run in the twilight cool. About 1.5 miles away from my "apartment" the sun disappeared below the horizon and the bugs appeared. I discovered that, after lights in rooms with doors left open, bugs are most attracted to sweaty bodies. A large cloud of bugs accompanied me for the rest of my run. Fortunately I escaped with only a dozen or so bites.

I accompanied some officers on a business trip to the Mosul palace. While they attended their meeting I wandered around the palace grounds. In a building I call the pool house (since it is next to the large swimming pool on the grounds) I found two mosaics featuring Saddam: in one he is portrayed as generous to an elderly, poor woman, and in the other a child is climbing onto his lap. Someone told me Saddam used the upper floor as an office for meeting with the public. The two-story mosaics reminded visitors of Saddam's larger than life benevolence and warmth.

Monday is Memorial Day. A news broadcast just reported that we now have 802 deaths in Iraq. According to other news items and advertisements one would think that Memorial Day is the unofficial beginning of summer travel, firing up the BBQ, pleasure boating, camping, fishing or other outdoor activities. This Memorial Day weekend take time to honor the fallen.

I may have an opportunity in 10 days to accompany a convoy to the Turkey border. I volunteered to help with security. At first the convoy commander seemed skeptical of my request, but when I told him about my weekly trip with the Special Forces team he placed me on the top of the list. If a seat is available after everyone in that unit is tallied, and my commander agrees, I will be allowed to accompany them.

A week ago I was fortunate to meet a local Iraqi who acts as a translator. I specifically wanted to know his opinion on American presence in Iraq. He is more pro-American than many Americans! He sent me this e-mail:

"What I believe the Iraqi people and people of U.S. are more than brothers and friends. Sir thank you for everything you do for this country and God bless you. Together we will work to the world better place to live. Sir very soon I will send a message to the people of U.S. to tell we are brothers and friends and Iraq is just a second country for our brothers people of U.S. I will let you know before I do it. Then I will see you later and take care sir."

He wants to write letters to people in the U.S., primarily schools, about how important our involvement here is to the people in Iraq. He watches the American news and wonders why they report some of the stories they do. I pledged to support him as I am able. Unfortunately, as are many Iraqis who help us, he is targeted by local anti-coalition forces.

05-31-04 * MEMORIAL DAY

Born in British Columbia, Canada, to American parents, I grew up with traditions on both sides of the border. Unfortunately, many of our society either ignore or have forgotten the rich history that is Memorial Day. Let us always remember.

Canada does not set aside a national Memorial Day, although Canadians do celebrate Veteran's Day on Nov. 11. Canada received its independence from Britain by decree rather than revolution, and the English politely passed on a good opportunity to oust the French by Civil War. Canada had little reason to adopt a Memorial Day until WWI. On July 1, 1916, the Germans killed or wounded almost the entire Royal Newfoundland Regiment at the Battle of Beaumont-Hamel in France. Newfoundland recognized July 1 as a provincial Memorial Day. Unfortunately, Canada already had a holiday that same day (Dominion Day, now Canada Day) and the idea failed to catch on nationally.

Several U.S. cities claim to be the birthplace of Memorial Day, originally known as Decoration Day. The practice of decorating graves traces back not to any particular city but to several women's groups in the south who, before the end of the Civil War, began decorating the sites of their fallen beloved. The Grand Army of the Republic, an organization of former sailors and soldiers, held Decoration Day services at various posts after the war ended. The Grand Army first widely observed Decoration Day on May 30, 1868, when its national commander, General John Logan, directed all posts to arrange such fitting services and testimonials of respect as circumstances may permit.

During the 1868 celebration of Decoration Day, General James Garfield made a speech at Arlington National Cemetery, after which 5,000 participants helped decorate graves of the more than 20,000 Union and Confederate soldiers buried there. New York became the first state to set aside Memorial Day as a State holiday in 1873. By 1890, all of the Northern states recognized it. The South refused to acknowledge the day, instead honoring their dead on separate days until after World War I, when the holiday changed from honoring those who died in the Civil War to honoring Americans who died fighting in any war.

In 1966, President Lyndon Johnson declared Waterloo, New York, the birthplace of Memorial Day. The decree probably had more to do with the influence of NY Governor Nelson Rockefeller and newly elected Senator Robert Kennedy than the influence of Waterloo on the creation of Memorial Day. In 1971, Congress declared Memorial Day a Federal holiday, celebrated the last Monday in May rather than May 30, perhaps because the Federal employee's union prefers consistent three-day weekends.

To remind Americans of the true meaning of Memorial Day, Congress passed the National Moment of Remembrance resolution in December 2000. The resolution asks all Americans, at 3 p.m. local time, "to voluntarily and informally observe in their own way a moment of remembrance and respect, pausing from whatever they are doing for a moment of silence or listening to Taps."

Today, Arlington National Cemetery remains the national focus of Memorial Day. On the preceding Thursday, soldiers from the Third Infantry Regiment decorate each of the cemetery's now over 260,000 graves with a flag. They also stand guard until Memorial Day to make sure all of the flags remain standing. The President customarily gives a speech honoring the contributions of the dead and then lays a wreath at the Tomb of the Unknown Soldier.

My father's family fled the Netherlands during WWII, settling in New Jersey. I know little else about them. On my mother's side, I knew one uncle was a veteran. Several of his friends died in combat but I never asked him about them. My maternal grandfather passed away before I had an opportunity to get to know him personally. To my knowledge, no fallen soldiers grace my family history. Though blessed to be part of a family and community that taught the significance of Memorial Day, its observance remained more historic than personal. Names on memorial walls meant little, although I felt grateful. That started to change a few years ago.

For most of my life, I did not feel comfortable talking to people. From early elementary school years, I felt little apprehension speaking to or performing in front of groups of people without regard to the composition of the audience. On the other hand, the opportunity to dialogue with individual people scared me. Discussing interpersonal subjects proved especially difficult. I did not feel comfortable initiating conversations on a multitude of subjects that involved the expression of feelings. The stronger the feelings involved, the less I wanted to talk about it. I especially avoided the topic of the death of a loved one, perhaps the strongest emotional experience common to human beings. For example, if someone mentioned that a loved one was deceased, I usually muttered, "I'm sorry", and then changed the subject.

My apprehensions to discuss death or the passing of loved ones started to change during a beautiful sunset on a public pier in Seattle several years ago. As I watched the sunset with a friend, an elderly man approached the rail. I said hello and smiled. He returned the greeting but said nothing further. My friend also said hello, then engaged him in conversation. He remarked that he and his wife loved to walk there before she passed away. I anticipated that she would respond with "I'm sorry" and discuss something else, a course of action I think I would have pursued. Instead, she remarked, "You must have really loved her." Tears came to his eyes as he reminisced about his wife. Although sad, he also seemed happy for the opportunity to tell someone about his wife and keep her memory alive. Before leaving, he thanked her for listening to him. I began to realize that allowing people to talk about their deceased loved ones honors the departed, allows the living to relive fond memories and blesses the hearer as well.

The following Memorial Day I placed flowers on my grandfather's grave before heading to other events. My grandmother stopped by that evening and thanked me for remembering him. We talked about my grandfather for almost 30 minutes, longer in one day than the combination of previous years. My grandfather became more real to me that day than he had been since my childhood. I discovered my grandmother spoke willingly; almost eager for me to know more about the incredible man she loved. I could have received the treasure of better knowing him, my family history and myself years before if I had only asked. My grandmother passed away shortly thereafter.

In the years since I endeavored to learn how to connect to people. I still feel far more comfortable speaking to groups rather than getting to know people through individual conversations. Yet, I am blessed to have quality relationships with many people patient with my stumbling efforts. Some of those people are veterans; others lost loved ones in service to America. The recompense of hearing their stories far surpasses the challenges I faced in learning to reach out to people. I wish I could honor them all in person today. I wish I could stop by the graves of my grandparents and decorate them with flowers. I wish I could stand on a pier in Seattle and engage a stranger in conversation. Instead, I am halfway around the world from those I love and want to honor the most.

The current Iraq conflict has already added over 800 names to the list of one million soldiers killed in the line of duty since the Revolutionary War. These are soldiers I have met, soldiers who served on this base, even soldiers from Washington State. Although they died here, we cannot decorate their graves today. We sent their bodies to the care of their families or a military cemetery in the U.S. We entrust their families and friends to present the honors due them this day.

The soldiers on our base have been protected in many potentially disastrous situations. For example, one soldier received several pieces of shrapnel through the wall of his trailer only inches above where he lay sleeping. If he had sat-up or jumped out of bed at the sound of the blast, as most of us did, he would have been hit. Two trailers received direct hits while the occupants had stepped out for a few minutes. The miracle stories impress me as similar to those told by George Washington about the hand of providence guiding the troops during the Revolution. Students of the founding days of our country realize that something miraculous took place, whether they attribute it to God or not. Faith is a shield in these times as well. I don't like to get political while on duty because that is not the place of soldiers, but when Ralph Nader had the audacity a few days ago to chastise the President for being a man of faith, I wanted to reach out and thonk him on the nose. Faith is all some of us have to keep us hopeful. That faith, however, was shattered for some this week.

We received the most mortars and IED (improvised explosive devices) attacks in the Mosul area for any week since our arrival. Some of the close-call stories continued. The most disturbing local news concerned an attack involving our base chaplain, Father Tim Vakoc, severely injured while on convoy to conduct mass at another base. He does not carry a weapon. In fact, he prays for the Iraqi people and ministers to them in addition to caring for American soldiers. Some nameless, cowardly Iraqi attempted to kill him and everyone in his vehicle. Father Tim was the only one injured. The news of the attack shook many soldiers here people. It does not matter to me that the terrorist did not realize he attacked a chaplain. The fact is the terrorists do not care. They might even get extra points for chaplains in their skewed way of thinking. While the media and Congress are increasingly hindering us from taking appropriate action to resolve hostilities against us, nothing is said about the blatant disregard for human life displayed by the Islamic terrorists.

My trip to Turkey this weekend is cancelled. My day off that made the trip possible was given to someone else so the convoy will go without me. I am not happy about the cancellation either but that's life in the Army.

The new president of Iraq is from Mosul, so we hear numerous stories about him. So far I have only heard good reports, even from someone who previously said he did not trust anyone on the governing council. The president's popularity seems to stem from several factors. He wears the typical Arab clothing, but the symbol of his tribe rather than the Muslim prescription. His tribe is respected and located all over the country. He is pro-Iraq, but not necessarily pro-America. I think he is a good choice for Iraq even if D.C. prefers someone else. Of course, this makes him a top target by the groups that what an Islamic caliphate and feel bound by God to destroy any alternative.

Some readers scolded me after reading about spending time near the fence, but how can anyone resist saying hello to children like these? I heard that one of the kids was trying to sell something they call alcohol through the fence at $20 per bottle today. Fortunately, or hopefully, most soldiers are not that desperate. I heard a story of one soldier dying (months before we arrived) from drinking a concoction sold in like manner. That story could be an urban or military legend but no one around here is taking any chances.

"You buy, only $20. Good stuff! You buy!" the child-hawker kept repeating as I jogged past. The contents of the bottle look like camel urine. Probably tastes about the same. Childhood here is not all innocence, flowers and smiles.

The provisional government recently signed into law intellectual property and copyright protections. The new laws are not yet reflected in the local movie pirating trade. We already have *Shrek 2* and *Troy* on DVD. The quality does not live up to American standards but at $2 per movie I have not heard anyone complaining too loudly. We can also buy the same "Rolex" watches sold in Mexico and Nike brand clothing at sweat-shop prices.

The Iraqi author of the quote I included last time confided to me that he would like to meet American women. No, I did not immediately show him pictures of my daughters. He is not the only Iraqi to voice this sentiment. Perhaps some entrepreneurial reader could start an on-line service with that specific result in mind. The Internet will become a booming business here.

I watched the opening ceremony for the WWII Memorial with grateful sadness. The courage of those soldiers and the cooperation of an entire nation facing the horrific evil of their time deserves a memorial of this majesty. It's about time. It reminds me of a poem by Herb Wells, WWII veteran from St. John's Newfoundland:

> As nature's healing through the years
>> Reclothes the stricken battlefields;
> So mercy gives us joy for tears,
>> And grief to proud remembrance yields,
> And mindful hearts are glad to keep
>> A tryst of love with them that sleep.

06-05-04 * FAITH FOCUS—
WHEN BAD THINGS HAPPEN TO GOOD PEOPLE

Normally I sleep well between shifts but not today. Father Tim's injuries disturb me more than the thought of mortar attacks, camel spiders, scorpion stings, or stray bullets. He prayed for God's protection over every convoy. He prayed for soldiers by name. He did everything Christian soldiers do when they desire God's safety and protection. Yet he was the only one injured. This makes no sense to me spiritually and this aspect of the tragedy bothered a few other soldiers well.

As a teenager I attended witnessing classes that trained the energetic and perhaps naïve attendees to bring people to an understanding of their need for a Savior with a concept called "the sinner's prayer". One evening, after several people came forward for prayer, I overheard someone telling another youth counselor that she asked for God to come into her heart many times but did not feel saved. He responded that was because she had not said "the sinner's prayer". He then read a few pages of a booklet and led her in the prayer at the conclusion. She left feeling saved but returned several weeks later with the same need.

I stopped attending that church shortly after the experience. I am more convinced today that there are no magic words to salvation. What audacity, what pompous arrogance must God attribute to those who think they can manipulate the Creator of the universe with repetitive incantations. I am repulsed by the idea that particular prayers can automatically place the initiate in a saving relationship regardless of the condition of the heart or soul. Now I am questioning even whether prayer itself really accomplishes anything other than calming the soul of the praying Christian.

I have been told in the past that the magic combination is faith plus righteousness, implying that if our prayers are not answered it must be because we lack faith or we are not righteous. Did not Solomon write, they tell me, "The Lord is far from the wicked but he hears the prayer of the righteous" (Prov. 15:29). The Apostle James reminded us "The prayer of a righteous man is powerful and effective" (James 5:16). And Peter encouraged early saints by quoting

Psalm 34, "For the eyes of the Lord are on the righteous and His ears are attentive to their prayer" (1 Pet. 3:12).

We often repeat these verses before praying in a church service as if reminding ourselves our prayers will be heard because we are righteous people. But the Bible offers no guarantees, not even for righteous people with immeasurable faith. Instead, the Bible includes numerous stories where the prayers of God's people, righteous people, are not answered in the manner requested. Now, here in Iraq, we have another hero of the faith, another righteous, God-fearing man whose prayers appear to go unheeded. Part of me wants to throw up my hands in despair stop praying altogether.

Father Tim prayed for protection but he was not protected. That haunts me.

Father Tim prayed. I do not know what it feels like to have an epiphany but I do know the feeling of finally seeing a solution right in front of me the entire time. Father Tim prayed. He visited wounded soldiers. He performed baptisms and last rites, delivered sermons and officiated at funerals. He has seen the worst side of war and the best side of life. Father Tim knows better than I do that there are no magic phrases or formulas. Yet he prayed. Prayed fervently. Prayed every time, every convoy, every church service, and every bedside. Why?

Prayer might not guarantee the positive realization of every request yet prayer is not without power. Prayer brings hope. Prayer increases faith. Prayer reminds us of the most important values in life. Prayer is an opportunity for listening to God and tuning in to God's design and God's priorities.

Surrounded by the world, I sometimes lose sight of the spiritual drama unfolding to universal history. We pray for physical safety in this physical battle in Iraq but the more important battles and greater dangers are those waged in the spiritual realm. Father Tim prayed for spiritual safety as well. It is in the spiritual realm perhaps that his prayer for safety was answered. It is also possible that God is preparing Father Tim for an even more important mission either here on Earth or in Heaven.

Rather than lose heart it is time for action. Father Tim's transfer to Landstuhl Regional Medical Centre in Germany leaves opportunities for service. Perhaps some of the believers here became too confident in the prayers of one chaplain. Yes, Father Tim prayed. What about the other Christians in the convoy? How many prayed for Father Tim? I do not want to imply that Father Tim was injured because some of us failed to pray for him, yet I do believe that the power of prayer increases with a plethora of believers united in prayer.

If there is a lesson to learn from Father Tim's story that lesson is to increase both prayer and the number of people praying. Praying for our lives in the physical realm and also our souls in the spiritual dimension. Beginning today. Beginning with praying for Father Tim's physical healing and my spiritual strength. I have spent too much of my life in despair already.

06-07-04 * HEART OF A CHAMPION

Soldiers rarely make the news without either a singular act of bravery or criminal behavior. Most soldiers do their job without complaint. Some, as the protagonist of this true tale, strive for excellence. Their stories deserve to be shared, but circulating stories of soldiers in action increased in difficulty with privacy laws and operational security concerns. With a plethora of lower ranked officers on base I can safely call him "LT" without violating operational security.

LT decided to run the six-mile course around the airfield. Not a stupendous feat if judged by that criteria alone, but looking deeper one will see the heart of a champion. LT had not run more than two miles in at least that many years. He finished his previous fitness test's two-mile run barely within qualification time, vomiting a few steps past the finish line. Running continued to make him nauseous; a detrimental characteristic in today's Army to say the least. We share this bizarre characteristic, although perhaps for different medical reasons, which led to his asking me to help him with his running program.

"Why are you doing this, LT?" I asked as he stretched.

"Leaders need to occasionally require their soldiers to push beyond limits, try harder than they may have ever tried in their life. When I am placed in such a position, I want my troops to remember that what I ask of them I first demand of myself."

"Lead from the front; I admire that. But why running? Why not something that isn't going to make you sick?"

"Running, or at least the feeling I have after running, is something I fear. I don't know what will happen to me if I run for more than two miles and for years I have been afraid of finding out. Today I hope to change that."

He set a 9-minute per mile goal. He did not want to have the watch on his person, reasoning that not maintaining his arbitrarily chosen time could demoralize him along the way. For that reason, and perhaps for personal security reasons as well, he asked me to run alongside. Flashing an anxious smile at me as I clicked the stopwatch, we headed south.

His running shoes appeared worn. I doubted a new pair of the most expensive Nike's would significantly improve his time, as if they really do for anyone. Shortly into his foray, LT reached a section of road recently watered to reduce dust. A layer of slick mud coated the soles of his shoes. He plodded on. LT passed his usual turn-around point and noticed that he did not feel the apprehension he normally associated with reaching fifty percent of his goal. He wondered if the physical necessity required the two-mile limit he previously set for himself or if he had simply created a psychological defense.

Around the two mile mark LT did not feel winded, but he did feel a need to stop. Even though he started out shortly after sunrise, the temperatures already reached 80 degrees. Not knowing how he would react to the run, LT earlier consumed 1.5 liters of water to ensure hydration throughout his ordeal. Now, pressure from his bladder guided him to a lone chemical toilet on the edge of the truck convoy assembly area. The smell triggered a wrenching nausea. He started heaving before exiting the unit. A few steps later, the heaving turned to a full-fledged vomit. LT felt better and resumed running.

LT reached the assembly area exit shortly before the halfway point. He ran alongside the convoy as it slowly exited the compound. A memory of a childhood friend flooded his mind. In a similar position, his friend had slipped, falling in front of the rear axle tires that took his life. Unfortunately, the terrain prevented LT from moving over. He concentrated on his footing, glad that the water truck had not turned this segment of the road to mud even though he coughed in the dust and diesel fumes. The memory faded as the convoy turned to exit the airfield and LT continued north. Feeling slightly woozy from the diesel fumes LT slowed to a walk. The feeling passed after a minute and he resumed running, determined to reach his goal.

Training to recognize potentially dangerous situations carries a curse. Solomon truly observed that with increased wisdom comes increased sorrow. While the uninitiated merrily, if not capriciously, continue in their routines, a select group seemed destined to carry the burden of precaution on their behalf. A broken curb could hide an explosive device; a man standing for a long period of time near a restricted area might prove a spy. Trained reconnaissance observers seldom notice how their mental calculations diminish their capacity to enjoy a vacation, a date, or time to themselves. Once one habitually practices full alertness, relaxation becomes all but impossible. At a point on the circuit where he could have congratulated himself on running farther than he had in years, his mind remained occupied with watching the fence-line, open fields and people lining the road. LT also noticed the small loose rocks on the road as a vehicle drove past at 30 mph. Years earlier, LT witnessed a tire spin a rock into a jogger at bruising velocity. He suddenly felt better about paying parks and recreation taxes for groomed trails nestled in quiet forests back home.

Rounding a bend, the familiarity of his surroundings helped him comprehend how far he had come. LT's confidence rose as he realized his proximity to the finish line. His steps seemed lighter although his pace was noticeably slower than when he started. I spotted him cutting across the final corner, once again heading south. I examined the stopwatch. Close.

"Come on, LT!" I yelled. "You're almost there!" I do not know whether cheering actually helped him, it just felt right. I thought of jeering him, Drill Sergeant style, but let the temptation pass unsatisfied. Participating in several running events, I realized years ago that runners finishing first may receive the ribbons, but the loudest cheers are often reserved for participants who overcome tremendous personal odds, even if finishing near the end of the pack. I noticed the same phenomenon at my college graduation. The crowd erupted into applause not for the summa cum laude students, but for those who persisted long after their family and friends abandoned hope of ever seeing them in a cap and gown. Human nature delights in triumphant stories, yet our entertainment industry continues to parade for our attention the bizarre or the disgusting. Here is a story, I decided unanimously, more worthy of 15 seconds of fame than any guest on Jerry Springer.

I clicked the stopwatch as LT crossed the starting line. We slowed to a circling walk. I waited while his breathing stabilized.

"How... long?" he panted.

"Fifty six minutes." Two minutes slower than his goal.

LT stopped walking, bent over, and placed his hands on his knees. He sighed. I tried to encourage him.

"You did it, LT! Six miles!"

He nodded, looking at the ground a few feet in front of him.

"You're crazy, you know that?"

LT nodded again, this time with a smile.

No Army regulations forced him to confront himself by running six miles that day. He did not do it for publicity or only after receiving assurances of success. People who wait for guarantees seldom accomplish anything worthwhile. The Army already made him a leader. To LT, though, his six-mile run that day strengthened his right to say, "Come on boys, follow me!" I, for one, would be proud to do so anywhere we need to go.

Mosul, unfortunately, made the lead story on CNN earlier this week when a few terrorists tried to blow up a top Iraqi official with a car bomb. They cut between the official's vehicle and his front security car, blocking the VIP near a staged parked car filled with explosives. They were a few feet off. The VIP received only minor damage, but the terrorists killed themselves and nine innocent bystanders. We do not know if the terrorists were recent recruits paid to do this act or more sophisticated cell members who misjudged their location slightly. If new recruits, then we know the recruiting efforts are working and the people behind them are still alive. The families receive more money than their dead family member could earn in a lifetime of labor, and the recruit gets a fast track ticket to the Promised Land. It is a temptation to some even if they do not fully support or understand the politics involved. This incident does not mean that a growing number of people in Mosul are becoming anti-American as some news stories imply. The situation is more complicated.

I enjoyed lunch with my Iraqi friend I wrote about two weeks ago. According to him, those who help the coalition forces may have a hard time finding employment after we leave. He wants to become self-supportive in the computer field, but training here is limited right now. He hopes to become one of the first MCSE certified Iraqis in the area so he can teach English and computer technology at the university. He wants to use his classes to also educate people about the democratic process and the United States involvement in freeing their country. One major obstacle is how to get MCSE certified in Iraq for very little money. He is hoping that he can receive books, study on his own, and then take the certification test somehow.

Ronald Reagan's death dominates many conversations here. I decided to move to the U.S. when Americans voted Reagan into office for the second time in the same year Canadians voted Trudeau in for the fifth time. I wanted to move to the country of Ronald Reagan. I thought the Americans a more intelligent people for choosing such a leader. I told numerous people in 2000, only half-jokingly, that if Al Gore became President I would change my mind about

Americans and move back to Canada. I admire Ronald Reagan for many reasons. I especially love his sense of humor, something I need to work on myself.

Iraq now has three television stations. The TV industry is in its infancy but growing fast. The main channel watched here actually comes from Qatar. A company there produces a channel specifically for Iraq with local news, etc. I watched a clip recently (in Arabic so I could not follow the dialogue) portraying new Iraqi film producers and how they produce their films. I also watched a music video featuring Khadim Alsaher. Khadim was popular with the people during the Saddam regime, which made him an enemy of the State. He fled to Canada where he became even more popular and wealthy. Now he is returning frequently to Iraq to help rebuild his country. Although I have only seen one video by him, he produces numerous videos with songs supporting the people of Iraq and those trying to help them. I watched Iraqi music videos for over half-an-hour, something I can not stand to do at home with what MTV and BET market these days. Most of the videos are filmed outdoors as production studios do not yet exist in Iraq. Most of the movies and music videos shown are from Egypt and Lebanon. I toured Iraq by watching the videos, asking the Iraqi people there (I was the only American in the restaurant at the time) about the locations represented. No Madonna, Britney Spears or Janet Jackson lewdness, just well dressed Iraqis in beautiful natural surroundings singing lyrics I couldn't understand. Personally, I hope we do not export too much of America over here. Some parts of our culture would not be an improvement.

I may be able to visit the Iraq / Turkey border this weekend. I will know for sure tomorrow, but so far, it looks positive. A few asked me if this is a safe thing to do. It is as safe as we can make it and that is all I ask.

A firefighter here shot a seven-foot viper. In addition to camel spiders and scorpions, we now have deadly snakes. I am thinking of opening a petting zoo. Terrorists get free, unlimited admission.

A complete comparison between the U.S. and Iraq constitutions would require a law review article. A brief description of the Iraqi constitution may, especially to those familiar with constitutional law, provide an overview of what we can expect from Iraq at its formation. The following quotes are taken from the Interim Iraqi Constitution.

Their preamble states:

> "The people of Iraq, striving to reclaim their freedom, which was usurped by the previous tyrannical regime, rejecting violence and coercion in all their forms, and particularly when used as instruments of governance, have determined that they shall hereafter remain a free people governed under the rule of law."

The U.S. preamble does not contain any references to the governing system it replaced. Instead, our preamble looks forward in time to state what the people of the new union want to create rather than what they want to avoid. The people of Iraq are engraving in their formation documents a reminder of the tyranny and violence of Saddam. Psychologists insist that stating what we want is more powerful than reciting what we want to avoid, but this preamble does both. The people of Iraq are a determined assembly. I wonder, though, if their determination will allow them to remaining free while rejecting violence and coercion in all forms.

"The system of government in Iraq shall be republican, federal, democratic, and pluralistic," with powers shared between "the federal government and the regional governments, governorates, municipalities, and local administrations." The relationship between these powers remains to be developed. Many Iraqis remain skeptical of a strong federal government, as did a majority of colonials. I do not see an Iraqi version of Alexander Hamilton arguing for federalism. In the U.S., some view an increase in democracy as necessarily decreasing our republican form of government. Iraq strives to become at once republican and democratic, federal and pluralistic. Future comparative politics classes will undoubtedly include a focus on this potentially unique government.

"Islam is the official religion of the State and is to be considered a source of legislation... This Law respects the Islamic identity of the majority of the Iraqi people and guarantees the full religious rights of all individuals to freedom of religious belief and practice." Our experience with Islam, at a fundamental level, leads me to doubt that Islam as an official religion and source of legislation could lead to full religious freedom. The U.S. now favors a lack of religion in its officials to the extent that any official expression of religion brings out more attorneys than a celebrity murder trial. The law itself arguably usurped religion's former role in our society. Iraq intends to combine both.

The Kurdish communities in northern Iraq present a problem of proportions exceeding slavery and the civil war in the U.S. The Kurds want their own country, but Iraqi neighbors vehemently reject the idea. The Kurdish area, once a separate country after the Ottoman Empire, contains large oil reserves currently providing income to Iraq. The area also supplies a significant amount of electricity to Iraq. Although there is more historical evidence to give the Kurds their own country than the Palestinians, the U.S. is not pressuring Iraq to create a Kurdistan. Rather, the TAL offers consolation to the Kurds by making "[t]he Arabic language and the Kurdish language the two official languages of Iraq." I hope that this will not mean Iraqis need to learn both languages like Canada thrust the French language on less than appreciative western Canadians. Neither ethnicity will warm to that idea.

"Each Iraqi shall have the right to carry more than one citizenship." The U.S. rarely allows this. In Iraq, though, it should work. This does not force other countries, such as the U.S., to recognize the dual citizenship nature of Iraqis.

"All Iraqis are equal in their rights without regard to gender, sect, opinion, belief, nationality, religion, or origin, and they are equal before the law. Discrimination against an Iraqi citizen on the basis of his gender, nationality, religion, or origin is prohibited. Everyone has the right to life, liberty, and the security of his person. No one may be deprived of his life or liberty, except in accordance with legal procedures. All are equal before the courts." I guess discrimination against non-citizens is allowed. The courts may straighten that out in the future. Other protected freedoms include:

- The right of free expression;
- The right of free, peaceable assembly,
- The right to join associations freely,
- The right to form and join unions and political parties freely;
- The right of free movement in all parts of Iraq and the right to travel abroad and return freely;
- The right to demonstrate and strike peaceably;
- The right to freedom of thought, conscience, and religious belief and practice.

These freedoms are not stated as recognition of God given rights even though their religion might support such a claim. Rather, they appear granted by the state. The extent to which the state can later revoke these rights remains undetermined.

Iraq also grants every individual the right to "security, education, health care, and social security." In addition, within resource limits needs, the government "shall strive to provide prosperity and employment opportunities to the people." Conservatives in the United States might deem this a failing proposition. Although it sounds unrealistically utopian, the people of Iraq have one advantage to cold war communism; a multi-billion dollar, continuously replenishing trust fund. A trustworthy management of the oil reserves is an essential key to Iraq's success.

Each citizen has a duty to protect public property. Duty might not imply the same legal obligation the word conveys in the U.S. If it does, the elected government will likely determine the extent of that duty and appropriate punishments.

"Each Iraqi citizen shall have the full and unfettered right to own real property in all parts of Iraq without restriction." This clause might prove problematic in small villages owned entirely by the local sheik, but through most of Iraq this clause is only restricted by financial limitations.

The Iraqi council, following its anti-violence resolve rather than the U.S. second amendment, does not permit Iraqis "to possess, bear, buy, or sell arms except on licensure issued in accordance with the law." Under Saddam, Iraq resembled the Wild West days in the U.S. The Coalition Provisional Authority allowed each household to keep one AK-47. Anything in addition was subject to instant forfeiture.

Two interim constitutional articles echo the preamble's rejection of anything Saddam. The law does not allow a member of the military to serve in the federal government "unless the individual has resigned his commission or rank, or retired from duty at least eighteen months prior to serving." Reiterating the balance of power debate, "The design of the federal system in Iraq shall be established in such a way as to prevent the concentration of power in the federal government that allowed the continuation of decades of tyranny and oppression under the previous regime."

At that time of the American Revolution, the formation of the colonies into a republic was a radical and unproven idea. The new government of Iraq is also a new and equally radical idea, unparalleled in the Islamic world. May they succeed as well, if not better, than we did.

I finally received permission to accompany a convoy to the Turkey border, as long as it did not interfere with my scheduled duties. I worked the previous night and slept only two hours before attending the first convoy briefing at 0800. The convoy of six vehicles left shortly after noon. Wearing our required and uncomfortable equipment, seated in a cramped HMMWV rear seat with no air conditioning and a broken window that will not open, sweltering in temperatures exceeding the external 110 degrees, and holding a loaded weapon in my hands, the trip hardly resembled a Sunday drive through the country. The armor enhanced vehicle provided only necessary visibility. Still, I enjoyed looking at countryside.

The Iraqi police station checkpoints at key locations on main roadways. I counted three between our base and the border. The terrorists know these locations and use alternate dirt roads so smuggled weapons or people find a way into the city undetected. Outside the city limits only the highways are paved ("pavement" generously defined). There is no highway patrol, no enforced speed limit or any warning signs such as posted speed limits or "curve ahead" warnings. Lane boundaries are not marked with lines, which also mean an absence of no-passing zones. Descending a mountain pass on a single width of pavement wide enough for four lanes, the downhill traffic occupied every inch of the cliff walled road even though a curve ahead severely limited visibility. That same stretch of road included three burned vehicles off to the side. A solo fuel tanker had collided with the mountainside and burst into flames. At the other scene, a fuel truck hit a passenger car head-on, killing everyone involved. Our troops drive this deadly road daily but so far without any serious accidents.

While approaching our base on the return trip I heard several mortar rounds exploding near the runway. A piece of shrapnel from one mortar that landed near our headquarters ripped through one of our unit's bravest men. He lost so much blood that if he arrived at the hospital (one block away) only a few minutes later he would not have survived. I sat with him shortly before the medical staff prepared him for his flight to Germany. Still unconsciousness, his entire body appeared swollen. I prayed with him, stroked his arm, and talked for a few minutes. I do not know if he heard me, as I could not decipher any signs of recognition in his eyes or face. His eyes remained closed, the only body movement detectable occurred as he breathed through a tube. He will regain consciousness slowly, awaken to new surroundings and adjust to his new life. I am sad for the grief and the changes this incident imposes on him and his family, yet very glad the prognosis predicts a solid recovery.

We take malaria prevention pills weekly. The pharmacist would only give the bottle to us after we signed a statement verifying we understand that we cannot donate blood for three years. My friend needed a replacement of almost his entire blood supply. That blood all came from the U.S. via the Red Cross and other donation programs. Many ask me what they can do to help soldiers, usually meaning what they can send us. Donating blood does not appear on care package suggestion forms yet it is a high priority need.

This week included the assassination of three top Iraqi council leaders, although not necessarily by the same organization or for the same reasons. One of the ministers also happened to be a high-ranking Ba'ath party member with a thirty-year record of Saddam affiliation even before Saddam's rise to the presidency. That minister had many enemies who may support the current government but do not want him (or any other ranking Ba'ath member) part of their new democracy. Since justice did not seem to force that minister to atone for his past actions, it may be that otherwise American coalition supporters coordinated that assassination. An Iraqi revealed this as common knowledge among the locals, but I do not see the new Iraqi government acknowledging that possibility which leads me to think that self-appointed justice may plague Iraq until Iraqis can trust the system to dispense appropriate justice. His death looked more like a targeted attack rather than attacks engineered to do as much damage as possible.

Our soldiers confiscated a large cache of weapons and munitions this week, including 2,900 7.62mm rounds, 50 20mm rockets, 25 14.5mm rockets, 67 rocket propelled grenade rounds, 19 RPG boosters, one RPG launcher, four AK47 rifles with six full magazines, one anti-tank mine and six live hand grenades. The suspects are in custody and no soldiers were injured during the search.

06-25-04 * News From the Front

Last Friday our office received a report that a vehicle from our base was involved in an IED explosion. The vehicle was a HWMMV that, fortunately, sported the unattractive armor add-on kit. The gunner received shrapnel wounds to his face. All four tires were blown. Shrapnel also penetrated the frame and severed the transmission cooler's fluid lines. Despite the vehicle damage, the vehicle continued from the attack zone to get the wounded solider to the nearest U.S. aid station. The report did not mention that I was in that vehicle.

A voice in my head often takes notes as I observe items that might interest people back home. A minute before the IED explosion that voice jotted down the phrase "This is the first trip to the palace that has been hit..." Hit? I became more alert. I could not see anything! Due to the people and equipment in the vehicle, from my rear passenger side seat I could only see diagonally over the steering wheel and directly out the window in my door. I looked right just as the IED exploded. Light, sound, shrapnel flying, the gunner dropping, blood. A solid hit centered on the passenger side doors. No time for shock. The occupant of the driver side rear seat and I attended to the gunner. The driver attempted to control the vehicle yet reach help as fast as we could. The front passenger called in the report.

I do not know why some prayers for safety are answered but not others. Chaplain Vakoc did not pray any less than I do or have fewer people praying for him. Yet I came through an IED explosion mostly unharmed, just a cut on my shin and a sore back from slamming into the center equipment. The armored door had three penetrations in the outer layer but nothing made it through. Only the gunner, with the upper half of his body extended above the vehicle, received serious injuries. The medics report that he will recover, although he will not look the same.

As we shared our observations later I admitted that I had not seen any indication of the danger. Realizing that, I wondered how my mind knew. The premonition had not helped us. Although I experienced a heightened awareness it made no significant difference. I did not know what to do differently. In hindsight, if I trusted what I heard I could have shouted at the gunner to get down. It all happened so fast I am not sure whether he would have had time to react and it might have made him more vulnerable if he turned right and down to face me because he would have been looking directly into the blast. A skeptic or atheist would not consider the voice I heard proof that God exists, yet I feel assured that there are forces at work here beyond sensory comprehension.

Although that experience shook us up and felt traumatic in some sense, many of our soldiers here have suffered far worse. Our police, firefighters and emergency medical personnel at home experience similar tragedy. I think that I have a better feel for now of the risks they take to protect us. The dangers or trauma they face are often initiated by the very people they swore to protect.

The Iraqi police (IZP) have specific checkpoints around the city. They waive us through or around any checkpoint we approach. One odd aspect of our IED explosion is that it took place at one of the checkpoints where, every week prior, we encountered IZP in place. This is not the first time an IED attack occurred where IZP were noticeably absent. Our local liaison to the IZP confronted the police with this information and received the names of the police on duty at that location and time. The police's internal investigation concluded that the officers were absent from the scene because of a shift change. Some believe that the IZP tolerate the terrorists if not collude with them, a tradition that probably began early in the Saddam administration. That may help explain a few events but I also know that the IZP are targeted perhaps more often than the U.S. military. We work with the police and depend on them as much as they depend on us.

The Iranians held and are now releasing eight British soldiers who wandered into restricted Iranian territory. Iran is sending several messages with this event (my personal Intel analysis). Muslim states, including the new Iraqi council, do not want a reputation as puppets of Western countries. Iran wants the world to know that they are still in charge of their borders. Iran is also demonstrating that they are different from the terrorists who have kidnapped and executed people recently. The video shows the Brits treated humanely, not needing to beg for their lives. That video could be used by some anti-coalition (or anti-Bush) groups to compare the evil Iran (as Bush called them) treating prisoners well compared to the U.S. treatment if prisoners in Iraq.

An observant friend pointed out that *Special Report with Brit Hume* on FOX recently aired a piece about Task Force Olympia in Mosul Brigadier General Carter Ham and staff. I did not see the interviews. As the report undoubtedly pointed out, the General work out of the palace grounds to our north. They get all the press, which is fine by me. That is the base I go to on Fridays, a 25-minute drive north of us. Actually, today will be my last trip to the palace. Our office is changing to 12-hour shifts rather than 8-hour. We will work six days / 72 hours per week instead of 7 days / 56 hours per week (with one day off per month). I originally volunteered to attend the Friday meetings at the palace because our thin staffing did not easily accommodate a day shift person attending (and because I just wanted to). That made Thursday-Friday a very long shift for me. With the consolidated staffing, the day shift can now afford to release one. I doubt I will miss that weekly trip even if it was my one chance to leave base each week.

As of the time of this writing Mosul is experiencing numerous explosions. Details are sketchy at this point. Perhaps your news will cover some of it. Reports state events are happening in other areas as well. Today's trip to the palace was cancelled because of security risks. So far the thrust of the attack seems directed at the police.

06-25-04 * Iraq— Turkey Border

Passing the palace grounds I felt like Samwise Gangee at the edge of the meadow in *The Fellowship of the Ring*. "One more step and I am the farthest away from camp since I arrived in Iraq," I whispered to an imaginary Frodo Baggins. The prospect of adventure kept me awake even though I had only three hours of sleep after working all night. Buildings disappeared when we passed the city limits. If Mosul has any suburbs they are not to the north. A dam northwest of the city restrains a large reservoir that required half an hour to leave behind. Along the way, we passed several villages of perhaps a few hundred people each. Barefoot children ran to the side of the highway from every village, waving at us or gesturing for us to give them something. One small girl even blew us kisses. I have no idea if troops in central or southern Iraq receive the same attention, but the people of Northern Iraq seem to love Americans.

Villages do not invite traffic with promises of commercial enterprises. No McDonald's, entertainment venues, or small curiosity shops. We did pass a few of what I would call truck stops; a restaurant, fuel pumps from above ground tanks, and an outdoor area for do-it-yourself repairs. Huts speckle the roadway near every village, offering drinks, gasoline from tin containers, melons, ice or cigarettes. Each hut exhibited only a few items of its specialty. One vendor might have five gas cans available. Another vendor displayed a few trays of produce, a third, six blocks of ice. None of them sold tourist items, just necessities. I cannot imagine a life of sitting by the roadside in this heat just waiting for someone to buy from my melon trays. The road vendors remind me of children in the U.S. earning summer cash with a lemonade stand, but here adults occupy the merchant chair as if this modest inventory represents their livelihood. Most vendors display their items in the sun, even the ice blocks, using the small shelter for personal shade.

We only stopped once on the trip north, circling into a large dirt lot. "Rest stop", the convoy commander explained. I did not notice any typical rest stop facilities. However, I did spot several soldiers standing next their vehicles relieving themselves. The two liters of water already consumed to combat the heat compelled me to join them. A group of children appeared out of nowhere, jumping excitedly, waving, and some gesturing for us to give them something. At least that is how we interpreted their hand signals. Given our level of exposure, the laughter and gestures could have meant almost anything.

The smiles on these children's faces could melt even the most indifferent soldier's heart. A few weeks ago, a young boy approached me, gesturing and asking in Arabic for something I carried. I gave it to him only to have the boy's father give it back to me. I tried to tell him that I had more than enough to spare. Although we could not communicate with language, his gestures told me that he did not want his son growing up to beg. I remembered that incident as I watched the children now surrounding me. Are we really helping them if we give so much to them? I know we mean well, but sometimes I wonder whether we create dependency rather than promote self-sufficiency. Another voice scolded me for taking this moment so seriously. With what they lived through under Saddam, did it really matter if we helped them celebrate a few Americans in their midst? I joined the others in handing out some hard candy we brought for such an occasion.

The American presence at the Harbor Gate border crossing occupied one building on the grounds of the Iraqi customs offices. The only other U.S. facilities in this compound are the portable mess trailer and a shower tent that reminds me of the one in *M.A.S.H.* They have no PX to buy personal items from, very limited food choices, two cash-only phones that reach the U.S. at $1.50 per minute, and three computers for off-duty use. They also have real grass, more moderate temperatures, no dust storms, no mortar attacks and no problems with the local predominantly Kurdish population. None of the soldiers I spoke with would trade places with me even if the Army would let them. The reputation of our base in Mosul had preceded me.

The soldiers I accompanied drive to Harbor Gate, stay overnight in a room of bunks on the bottom floor of the glass and marble four-story building, and return to the airfield the next morning accompanying a convoy. The restroom facilities in that building are on the top floor as the entire water system is gravity fed. That means every trip to the bathroom requires ascending four flights of stairs after donning a complete uniform, still better though than the outdoor trek required in Mosul. My first time visiting the restroom I approached three doors, each depicting a vacancy. I opened the left door, and then froze in the doorway. The restroom consisted of a hole in the floor, a tank on the wall that drained water over the ceramic plate surrounding the hole, and a hose connected to a low faucet. A sign read, "No paper products of any kind are allowed down the drain." Hence the hose? I wondered if the phrase "Turkish bath" refers to this room. The other two stalls contained a toilet, but also a wastebasket as the "No paper products" ruled applied to them as well.

A soldier pointed out the veranda enveloping three sides of fourth floor. I noticed a switch-backed trail on a hill to the south leading to a small crop of buildings. He mentioned that some of their unit used that as a PT run. I asked directions to the trail and learned that I could only go if others went with me. Commander's orders. I raced down the stairs to the convoy group.

"Hey guys, anyone want to go with me up the hill run in the morning?" Blank stares. One soldier turned to his neighbor and said, "I think he's serious!" Another looked at me with a mock scowl. "We don't do that kind of thing. We're Air Force." They returned to their electronic recreation. I asked some of the soldiers stationed there if they would accompany me. No luck. Maybe I am the only one in the military who deems it fun to run up a steep hill shortly after sunrise in 80-degree temperatures. I will need to wait until my next trip to find out if I enjoy the experience as much as I imagine I will.

The main reason I wanted to accompany this convoy was that I heard the soldiers at this station could visit the local town of Zahko, located about two miles away. Taxicabs constantly circled through the customs buildings, conveying people between this business center and the town or beyond. I discovered that a Commander's decree prohibited soldiers from riding in the taxis. In fact, any trip to town required accompaniment by a security team and at least one translator. Unfortunately, all personnel normally available had escorted several soldiers to the city of Dahuk, a half-hour drive to the southeast. If we had arrived in time, I could have accompanied them. Alas, I once again remained confined, little better off than a prisoner under house arrest.

07-02-04 * NEWS FROM THE FRONT

The transfer of sovereignty occurred a few days early. No notice of large scale celebrations around the country or even smaller ones here in Mosul. The government here imposed a three-day curfew, and then downgraded it to a "holiday" in which they strongly advised everyone to stay home. No locals on base. A little eerie, actually, as one of the indicators of an impending attack is an unexplained absence of local population. The thrust of attacks still focus on the Iraqi police and Iraqi National Guard. Elsewhere, three Marines died when an IED detonated against their vehicle.

I have been easily frustrated lately with the increased restrictions. I feel like a caged animal, helpless, unable to take proactive action against attacks we know are coming, or to help the community as I would like. Someone asked me yesterday how I enjoyed my job here. I told him that I was not enjoying it. He paused, and then said, "You are probably the luckiest person on this base." Then he touched my arm in a few places. I gave him a questioning look but did not speak. "Not a scratch," he explained, and I understood. Even though I rarely mention the IED explosion everyone seems to know I am one of the lucky ones. My frustration gave way to gratitude and a renewed willingness to do what I can when I have the opportunity.

Last week I mentioned that a coordinated attack had occurred only a few hours earlier and promised more this week. This attack is important for more than the resulting casualties and damage. Six cities, hundreds of miles apart, experienced explosions happening within minutes of each other. This is a well-coordinated effort. I assume the Homeland Security Department is analyzing the details so we will know them to prevent such attacks on U.S. soil. The attacks targeted the Iraqi police and Iraqi National Guard. These attacks refute the suggestion that all it would take for the violence to end is for the U.S. to pull out. Zarqawi cells took credit for the attacks down south but did not specifically mention Mosul. We should not live our lives in fear of these people, but we should understand their operations and take appropriate action.

After working all night, I had less than three hours of sleep when a loud blast rocked my room. Doors and windows blew open, shelves and contents fell off walls, people hit the ground or scrambled into bunkers. Radio reports all confirmed a close detonation. The blast actually occurred over two miles away, the most powerful explosion on record since American arrival.

According to the Nineveh Provincial Governor's Office, the attacks killed 72 Iraqi citizens, including a number of police officers and private security force members. The number of wounded was reported to be more than 250.

I spoke with one soldier who works on the grave registration team. She told me that the closest victims were hard to identify as the bodies were all in pieces. She also told me of a family gathered around a table for breakfast. A car, thrown by the blast, crashed through the roof and landed on the children sitting at the table while the mother watched in horror a few feet away, preparing the meal.

The attacks began at 9:05 a.m. when car bombs exploded outside the Iraqi Police Academy and the Al Wakas Police Station in western Mosul. Another explosion occurred near the Al Jamhori Hospital but later was confirm as being directed against a police station in the vicinity. At 10:15 a.m. another car bomb exploded near the Sheik Fatih Police Station in western Mosul. Iraqi National Guard soldiers moved to secure the Sheikh Fatih Police Station in response to reports that terrorists had taken it over, but terrorists fired at the Iraqi soldiers from across the street at the Mohammed Al Nooryi Mosque.

Coalition forces moved to the Sheikh Fatih Police Station to support the Iraqi soldiers and received fire from the mosque as well. Iraqi Security and Coalition forces returned fire on the terrorists in the mosque. In less than two hours, Iraqi National Guard soldiers secured the mosque and Coalition soldiers from 1st Battalion, 23rd Infantry Regiment took back the Sheikh Fatih Police Station.

One Task Force Olympia Soldier died. Three Task Force Olympia Soldiers were injured, and five Iraqi Police officers were wounded in this series of attacks. At 10:10 a.m., a private security company came under small arms fire in west Mosul. One security guard was killed and another was injured. The injured guard is at the Army Hospital in Mosul.

At 10:15 a.m., an explosion of unknown type occurred in the vicinity of the Sheik Fatih Iraqi Police Station. At 11:20 a.m., June 24, in response to reports of terrorists taking over the Sheikh Fatih police station in southwestern Mosul, Iraqi Security Forces moved to secure the site and were fired upon by Anti-Iraqi forces that were shooting from the Mohammed Al Nooryi Mosque across the street from the police station. Coalition forces moved to the site to support the Iraqi Security Forces and were fired upon from the mosque as well. Iraqi Security and Coalition forces returned fire on the terrorists in the mosque. At 1 p.m., Coalition forces reported that Iraqi Security Forces and Soldiers from 1st Battalion, 23rd Infantry Regiment have taken back the Sheikh Fatih police station from the Anti-Iraqi terrorists. Iraqi National Guard soldiers have secured the Mohammed Mosque as well.

Reports indicate another series of attacks on the 4th of July. We will be on high alert, rather than celebrating the holiday as we would like. I hope that everyone in the U.S. celebrates for us and with us in spirit. We are here in part to guarantee that free countries around the world can celebrate independence and liberty.

I was asked a few days ago to give the sermon for this Sunday's noon service. Many years have passed since I last appeared behind a pulpit. I am more nervous about my sermon that I have been about traveling to the palace or accompanying a convoy.

07-02-04 * WE GOT A MIGHTY CONVOY

While most of the Turkey-Iraq border follows a rugged mountain range, the river valley affords rare road access. This border crossing, slightly larger than the commercial vehicle crossing in Blaine, Washington, processes over 2,000 trucks per day. Our troops oversee the creation of two convoys per day. One convoy averages 100 – 120 trucks containing goods purchased by the military for troops stationed around Iraq. Examples include bottled water, PX inventory, living containers but not military equipment or soldier personal items such as mail. The other convoy, typically 700 – 800 trucks, consists of fuel trucks loaded with fuel, purchased by the U.S. for distribution to the Iraqi people. If only I could listen to some CW McCall music!

I noticed a border crossing guard on the Iraqi side measuring the gas tank of a truck crossing back into Turkey. Thinking this an odd scene, I asked someone why the Iraqi government would care about the size of a truck's fuel supply. I found out that Iraq practically gives fuel away to its citizens. Gasoline in this area of Iraq sells for 53 dinar per liter ($ 0.137 U.S. per gallon). Water sells for 600-dinar per liter. The exchange rate is currently 1463 dinar per U.S. dollar. Turkey sells gasoline for $4.85 (U.S.) per gallon. The Turkish drivers cross the border on fumes then fill their tanks at prices designed to benefit the Iraqi people. Iraq restricts the size of the gas tanks based on vehicle size. If fuel tanks are larger than allowed, the drivers must pay a fine.

This fuel price discrepancy creates other interesting dynamics as well. The fuel imported into Iraq is not refined in Turkey but shipped from elsewhere. The trucks are sealed after they are filled at the ports with the quantity carefully measured and logged for each truck. In early days of the program, some drivers would break the seal, sell gas out of their truck in Turkey, refill the truck in Iraq and pocket the difference. One duty of the troops stationed at the border crossing is to compare the quantity in the tank with the paperwork for the truck. The drivers are fined if there is a difference. Many drivers who sell part of their payload in Turkey top off their tanks with water to avoid detection of a volume difference. If caught, drivers are financially responsible for the entire load.

The fuel trucks are coordinated into a daily convoy of 700 – 800 trucks. A separate security team escorts the fuel convoys to a staging area just north of Mosul. Convoy movement teams divide the large convoy into smaller convoys by destination. A similar process occurs at the Iraqi-Kuwait border for southern Iraq destinations. KBR, a division of Halliburton, holds the contract for delivering this fuel. Last December, the contract came under strict scrutiny by some members of Congress investigating whether Halliburton overcharged the government. Halliburton claimed that they billed for expenses incurred plus 2 percent but promised to return any amounts billed in error.

The fuel convoys rarely lose vehicles. I have a theory on why this is the case. Iraq's refineries have not yet reached pre-war production levels. Terrorism primarily accounts for the decrease as American troops did everything they could to avoid damaging refineries or supply lines. The United States purchases this fuel at closer to world prices and sells it at Iraqi prices as a humanitarian aid mission. Daily life around Iraq would almost collapse without this aid. Since fuel is so inexpensive, a fuel truck driver makes more money for delivering the load that he could selling it on the black market in Iraq but less than if he sold it on the black market in Turkey. Terrorists in Iraq have inexpensive access to fuel so they do not need to steal it. The fuel helps Iraq rather than U.S. soldiers so they are not hurting us if they blow up a fuel truck. We get our fuel through different channels.

One of the soldiers in charge of assembling the fuel convoys told me that he receives numerous complaints from the drivers, predominantly Kurdish and Turkish, that the Iraqi police frequently hassle them for money. Truck drivers must maintain a log signed at the checkpoints to prove that the drivers did not bypass required stops. The police often demand money from the drivers before they will sign the driver's log. Drivers who refused to pay had their windshields smashed or received personal threats. Drivers reported demands of up to $5 U.S., a significant amount considering their wages.

Commodity truck cargoes, on the other hand, tempt both terrorists and truck drivers. The cargo would sell for more than a driver makes for transporting it. Our commodity convoys, which support the military rather than the local economy, do not follow the checkpoint log rules. That may change after the transfer of authority. The return trip escorting the convoy required at least five hours. We attempted to maintain accountability of all of the trucks in the miles long convoy in case drivers had an agenda other than delivering the goods to our base. It reminded me of cowboys on a cattle drive, rounding up the strays and guarding against poachers.

When the commodity convoys started, the Army accepted 30% truck loss as an acceptable risk. Weeding out faulty trucks and opportune drivers combined with enhanced escort tactics now limits the typical loss at 6 – 10 % of the convoy. Anti-coalition forces can affect base supply levels and enhance their own by stealing trucks. Most of the trucks were older model MAN or Scania single frame (rather than tractor-trailer types). The few new trucks were all Volvo models. Not a single Peterbuilt or Kenworth. Two of the newest trucks towed trailers with insignia from the Netherlands. Some vehicles had no markings other than the convoy placard in the front window.

Six trucks did not finish the convoy with us. One old flatbed loaded with pallets of bottled drinking water could not make it up the pass. A similarly painted truck pulled over to help. The drivers attached a tow bar between the vehicles. The second truck only lasted a few feet under the additional load and then it could no longer move. We left them behind. Troops recently discovered a warehouse in the area full of our water. PX items and bottled water are the most common loads lost in transit and are the most lucrative. Near the top of the hill a truck with an enclosed, locked trailer stalled. The convoy commander rummaged through the load declaration sheets to cull the one for that vehicle. I did not notice the contents. An Iraqi mechanic heading in the opposite direction pulled over and offered his assistance. He promised to help the driver get the vehicle back to the staging area for the next day's convoy.

We later noticed a truck moving barely five miles per hour. Two other trucks with matching markings followed closely behind it. All three trucks clearly held bottled water cargo. We tailed them until they turned into the lot of a restaurant with an outdoor repair facility. A pin holding the bed of the ailing vehicle had broken off resulting in a list to starboard. We tried to convince the drivers of the functioning vehicles that they needed to continue with us, but they would not leave the other driver to his own fate. I wondered at the probability that at least five of our six stranded vehicles contained bottled water. A conspiracy of thieves?

07-05-04 * FAITH FOCUS—RESTORATION

Sometimes I can't remember what I had for lunch the day before, although on a military base in Northern Iraq who would want to. But one day, nineteen years ago, I will never forget. The day a staff member of the department of religion at Loma Linda University recommended I pursue a different career.

At the end of the school year I ranked second in my class academically even though I worked full-time to take care of my wife and three young children. The department awarded me a scholarship for the following year. I felt elated as my meager farm wages would now all benefit my family rather than pay books and tuition. That summer I also attended our church's world conference as a student delegate. A church in Whittier accepted me for a one-year internship. I loved my wife, adored my children and pursued my dream of becoming a minister with all the energy I possessed. Like the Glen Campbell song, I felt "On Top of the World".

I do not know what life is like for a young wife, away from her family, three children under five years of age, with her husband at school or work most of his waking hours. Although years before she supported, in fact insisted, I follow my ministry dream one day she decided she did not want that life for herself. She left. My world left with her.

That fall I tried to continue my studies. The scholarship helped but I still needed to work to feed and clothe my children. People surrounded me with love and support but none of it healed the deep, heart-shattering ache I felt inside. My motivation for school changed as I searched for answers on how to cope with a quick divorce I did not see coming and all the corresponding hurt and anger.

A few weeks into the fall quarter a department head asked me to come into his office. He explained the reality of the ministry to me, how more people wanted to become ministers for the church than the church had positions available. The church needed bilingual pastors. If I was a native Spanish speaker perhaps the church could hire me but… a pause that seemed an eternity. He recommended that I pursue a different major that year and perhaps we could revisit the issue after more time passed. The church preferred married pastors for several reasons, including parishioners misinterpreting the beginnings of a romantic relationship for a single pastor as varied moral faults.

Discovering the goodbye note my wife left sent me reeling. This announcement knocked me down for the count. Signing away tens of thousands of dollars in scholarship money I left school instead of changing majors. I moved back to Lynden, Washington to be near my family. I felt as if I failed God's plan for my life. I failed to take care of essential needs in my wife's life or overlooked something. Every day I went to work reminded me that I was called to do other work. Every time I spent time with my children I thought about my failures as a husband that culminated in their mother's abandonment of our family. I lived in a cloud of my own creation as if I carried a spiritual dry-ice machine that pumped a chilling, dense fog twenty-four hours per day, for ten years.

Life is not like a limbo dance where the goal is to see how low one can go. Steeped in a constant attitude of viewing myself as a failure, however, reaching new lows was the only thing I did successfully. One day, tired of the cycle where I thought I couldn't go any lower only to prove myself wrong, I took myself for a walk. I looked at cars whizzing past and wished I owned one. I admired houses along the highway and wished I lived in one. I paused to look at a stream, temporarily mesmerized by the water flowing over rocks in the hard clay bed. One rock about two inches long reminded me of a shield. I picked it up. I thought about Paul's description of the shield of faith and resolved to strengthen my faith. I carried that rock with me everywhere as a reminder to myself that faith in God is my only necessary shield against adversity. I still have that rock today, even here in Iraq.

Around the same time as I found the shield rock I read a verse that seemed to speak directly to me. "But I have prayed for you, Simon, that your faith may not fail. And when you have turned back, strengthen your brothers" (Luke 22:32). June 1994 I turned back to faith. I sensed that even in failure God protected me; Jesus prayed for me, faith sustained me. On a foundation of faith I could rebuild my life and in the process strengthen others. In 1994 I resolved to do exactly that.

Life changed for the better and is still progressing. Of course it could honestly be said the only way to go was up. When I hear people say that phrase I sometimes caution them. I have proved too many times the human capacity for finding lower ground. At the age of thirty-three I joined the Army National Guard. I was the second oldest member of my boot-camp class, older than even one of my drill instructors. After returning home from basic training I enrolled in evening classes at a Whatcom Community College. One year later, fortified with an AA degree in not much of anything, I transferred to a four-year university, went on to law school and now proudly serve in Iraq. More importantly I strengthened family relationships, healed some deep emotional wounds, and blazed a trail for my children rather than continuing to just sit around and wish.

One dream remained unfulfilled since leaving ministerial studies nineteen years ago, the dream that someday I would be asked to preach again. Preaching is both an incredible honor and a grave responsibility. I accepted years ago that I would not become a full-time pastor yet I hoped that somehow, someday, I would participate in the church's greatest calling. Yesterday, July 4th 2004, ten years after I turned back to faith, I preached in a gospel service in Mosul, Iraq.

Today my hands trembled as I reflected on the nineteen-year journey since leaving Loma Linda University. I felt, perhaps, something akin to what Simeon felt when he held the baby Jesus in his arms in the temple. (See Luke 2: 25-35). People who always get what they want, when they want it, never experience the feelings that spring up like an artesian well at the fulfillment of a decade long dream. Unlike Simeon, though, I am not ready to go. There is too much work to do.

I am watching the Saddam trial proceedings with interest. In the past few weeks, I have worked with some of the attorneys here to understand the criminal court process in Iraq. It is very different from the U.S. system. No juries, no circumstantial evidence, no attorney arguments.

My Iraqi friend who was injured in the huge explosion of two weeks ago is out of the hospital and almost fully recovered. Someone donated MSCE training materials for him. If he is as smart as I think he is, he may be the first Iraqi to achieve certification in this country. The gunner that was hit in the IED explosion is also doing well. This is heartwarming news in the midst of the national headline tragedies.

We hosted another memorial service this week; an MP on duty at the police station that was the target of the huge explosion two weeks ago. He did not have his helmet on at the time of the attack. The explosion removed about 30% of his brain and skull. I found out that, instead of protecting himself or running for cover after the first blast, this MP fired into the approaching main vehicle as it sped toward the police station. His action killed the driver and caused the vehicle to hit a pole, detonating the bomb perhaps 50 meters from the intended compound. If it were not for his heroism, many more people would have died. He and I share the same birthday. He leaves a wonderful wife, two daughters and three step-daughters, a combined family like I have. I did not know him well but our lives are similar in a few ways and it really hit me. He is a true American hero.

Some quick bullet points on changes and ongoing operations. Our firefighters on base are training Iraqis to build a fire department for Mosul. The Iraqi civil defense corps is now the Iraqi National Guard operating under similar laws as the National Guard in the U.S. Iraqi police and ING now patrol the cities more than multi-national forces. The university here is getting security equipment and a better trained security force. Several new medical clinics are under construction around Iraq. The Iraqi Air Force now actually has two aircraft. A hospital in the southeast now has power and clean water restored after several years of inadequate service. A sewing factory that employed 995 Iraqi women will open soon after a half-million dollar renovation. The mosque on our base and several other bases are now open for services to Muslims that work on the bases.

A few days ago the airfield hosted a ground-breaking ceremony for construction that will upgrade the airfield to civilian standards. The ceremony featured the demolition of one of the military bunkers on the base. When the 101st Airborne first arrived here, they engineered the airbase with dual considerations of military and ultimate civilian purposes. The airport may open to civilian aircraft before we leave. If so, maybe some of you can stop by and say hi. There is a new billboard near the as yet inoperable terminal. The billboard depicts a welcome to Mosul in several languages. I think it is interesting that the two planes pictured on the billboard are from an Iraqi airline and a plane from Air France.

The Iraqi National Guard, Iraqi Police and U.S. soldiers conducted a large search operation in the neighborhood of Al Somer and detained two members of a known terrorist group wanted for planning and conducting anti-Iraqi activities. During a search of the residence, IED making-materials, seven AK-47s, two Russian-made machine guns, a container of artillery powder and assorted electronics equipment were seized.

Last Monday soldiers discovered a weapons cache containing 54 100mm and four 90mm High Explosive Anti-Tank rounds, 200 37mm anti aircraft rounds, 50 propelled grenades, three AK-47s, two machine guns and a night vision device. An explosive ordnance disposal team destroyed the cache on site and the detainees remain in custody. The previous Saturday soldiers located and destroyed two weapon caches after they received information regarding their location southeast of Rabiya. One cache contained 85 100mm, 37 60mm and 11 90mm high explosive mortar rounds, as well as two anti-tank rounds, two RPGs and 12 grenades with fuses. The other cache contained 32 60mm and two 82mm mortar tubes. An explosive ordnance disposal team responded to the site and destroyed the caches. Lots of weapons are still in circulation. The most recent attacks on our bases in Mosul involve rockets larger than any we have seen yet (107mm). No one was injured in the attacks which is a miracle considering the firepower.

We have a new theatre on base that shows movies (from a DVD player projected to a large screen); no charge for the admission, the popcorn or the sodas. The movies are shown in the evening, after my shift starts, so I have not seen any movies yet. Rather than fuss about my frustration, since it baffles me that we can even build a theatre to watch movies in a hot combat zone, our night shift decided to do something about it. We now use my laptop and a Proxima projector to play our own movies on a screen of white butcher paper taped together.

I was asked to video our Harley riders on base riding a Harley that one of the civilians bought in Kuwait. We took a few stills and video samples to send to our higher command, which is forwarding them to a news station in Tacoma to correlate with footage from a motorcycle ride back home. During one of the video clips I commented that the bike owner should tell the General, "I have one and you don't… nya-nya." Everyone laughed. One of the guys sent the samples without editing the audio. Now the comment does not seem as funny.

Since we moved to 12-hour shifts I do not get out much-not that there is any place to go if I did have the time. We watched the movie *Groundhog Day* recently during an early morning lull. Bill Murray's activities changed even if the day did not. Here we cross off calendar dates but nothing changes. Work, eat, sleep, react to loud noises and things that go bump in the dark. Day after day.

In other news, one Iraqi National Guardsman was killed and nine wounded after their convoy was attacked with small arms fire as they traveled near Mosul University. Soldiers returned fire killing one of the anti-Iraqi terrorists before they fled.

Dr. Usama Kashmoula, the Governor of Nineveh Province in northern Iraq, died from wounds received in an attack on his convoy while he was traveling on his way to Baghdad. Governor Kashmoula was enroute to Baghdad for a meeting with the President of Iraq. The attack occurred between Baji and Tikrit. The attackers threw a hand-grenade into his vehicle then opened fire. The governor died in a hospital in Baji.

I went to church on Sunday hoping for an attitude adjustment, glad that I was not scheduled for a role in the service. When I looked at the program, however, I noticed my name next to the congregational prayer. For that particular prayer, in the gospel service, everyone stands and holds hands in a closed ring around the altar. Typically the size of the audience means the ring extends around the entire inner perimeter of the church. The minister offering the congregational prayer stands inside the ring and prays for all of the prayer requests, which can take as much as 5 – 7 minutes. The prayer is preceded by a time of testimony where people share ups and downs for the week. Most of the testimonies include prayer requests. One newly arrived unit experienced its first casualty the previous day, a gunner lost in an IED explosion that sounded remarkably like my experience. The driver was severely injured. Two other people shared tragedies and asked for prayer for everyone involved.

I felt spiritually unequipped to lead 80+ people in an exercise they hoped would bring them comfort and spiritual help. I could have asked someone else to fill in, but I decided to check my attitude at the door and do my job as I do every night I enter the office. I first prayed a silent prayer for God to help me pray for His people. He did. People wept, hearts received hope, and strength and peace seemed to fill the room. People thanked me afterward, but it wasn't me. Wanting to avoid sounding unappreciative of their gratitude I asked them to thank God instead.

Bill Davis, a country singer, graced our dining facility with a concert. I worked that night but snuck away for 10 minutes to listen to him. No one else in the office even heard of him before. And my co-workers say I am out of touch with contemporary culture! He was the California Country Association's entertainer of the year in 2000 and has won several other country music awards. He took a break to give two Fender acoustic guitars to the chaplains. I went to the stage and said hello. After learning I could not stay for his performance, he offered to stop by the office later. And he did! He even gave me a set of Pearse strings for my guitar. I have a prized photo with Bill Davis, the Everyman Band and me with a huge smile. Monique Martinez, a comedian from Indianapolis, appeared with Bill but I could not see her show. She stopped by the office with Bill and offered to send a couple of CDs since I had to work through her show. Bill following through on his promise to stop by the office reinforced once again how people can make a difference in someone else's bleak situation.

Four Marines were killed in a vehicle accident a few days ago while providing security for an oil pipeline. This is a part of the price of gasoline not reflect at the pumps. Saboteurs attacked pipeline operations over 130 times in the past seven months causing billions of dollars in lost revenue and damage. Did terrorists attack the pipeline during Saddam's regime? If not, why not? Would Saddam kill them or their families whereas we don't have the resources to even track them down? The proceeds of the oil sales still go to the Iraqi development fund. The main difference is the administration of the fund. I believe that the anti-US rhetoric does not provide an adequate explanation. I find it more probable that Saddam either paid money to certain organizations so they would not attack Iraq or he directly supported and directed terrorist organizations.

Kidnappings in Iraq continue to make the news. The Philippine government is pulling out at least part of its 51-member humanitarian mission to save the life of one kidnapped citizen. The terrorist bullies are forcing a humanitarian mission to pull out! I think this news would be enough to dispel the theories of those who believe that peace would come to Iraq if the American troops pulled out. The terrorists want everyone out, which leaves them unrestrained or unaccounted control over a significant income stream.

As an interesting side-note, a news article about the President of Mexico mentioned over 15,000 kidnappings occurred in that country in the past 10 years. Mexico suffers so many kidnappings they rarely make U.S. headlines unless they involve a newsworthy individual. The kidnappings in Iraq involve people that would not necessarily make the news if they occurred in Mexico, yet every one here makes international headlines. But then Mexican kidnappers don't videotape and televise beheadings of people they kidnap.

07-20-04 * DEALING WITH STRONG
EMOTIONS SUCH AS DEPRESSION

D epression, like terrorists, cannot be reasoned with. Commanding myself
to feel happy or logically arguing with myself that I should feel other than
how I really feel does not work for me. Depression is not the same as feeling sad,
in fact, it is not a single feeling at all; it is a way of interpreting the world around
me. Depression interprets events in ways that further the depression. Arguing
with the depression's interpretations does not help either.

I also studied depression clinically in university. Depression is a depressed
mood or markedly diminished interest or pleasure most of the day, nearly every
day over a two-week period; accompanied by at least four other indicators that
include: significant weight loss or gain; decrease or increase in appetite; insom-
nia or hypersomnia; feelings of worthlessness, excessive or inappropriate guilt
(which may be delusional); diminished ability to think or concentrate; and re-
current thoughts of death (not just fear of dying) or suicide.

The worst episode for me happened in the fall of 2001. I manifested almost
every DSM-IV indicator for clinical depression over several months. Not a good
way to start my second year in law school. Fortunately I found a doctor who
believed, correctly, that I did not need drugs or confinement and developed a
behavior modification program that worked.

We discussed every aspect of my life; every substance I added to my body
and how I spent every minute of my day. I discovered that the onset of the
symptoms coincided with a fat-burning supplement I started taking as recommended by a health club instructor. Today Hydroxycut is manufactured without
Ephedra, but in 2001 the general public did not know about many of the more
serious side effects. Before using the supplement I read the warning label that
recommended people with a history of depression or other emotional problems
should not use it. I ignored the warning since it did not apply to me, or so I reasoned. Several weeks into an emotional tailspin I still did not associate the severe
depression with Ephedra but with the stress of my second year in law school and
financial difficulties.

Discussing the *Reader's Digest* version of my life, Dr. B pointed out the numerous battles with depression I had attributed to other problems. He taught me some coping techniques that I still use and need today. There are activities, people and even foods that help me cope better. Nutrition, exercise and rest all play a significant role. I tend to work more and stay busy during non-work hours with projects that keep my mind and body busy.

There are times when my mood changes from happy to withdrawn in less than a second, but reversing the process takes hours, days or longer if I am feeling particularly hopeless. The sooner I start working on the issues the sooner I return to full function but having someone tell me to get working on my issues usually just fuels the anger side of the problems.

For me the worst part of depression is the emotional hurt I sometimes cause in others when I am strongly agitated. Depression can be especially cruel in that it affects not only the depressed person, but acts through them to affect everyone around them as well. Someone who is depressed can be very difficult and draining to deal with. A depressed person's relationships can become strained to the point where others actively avoid having anything to do with them. This further contributes to a worsening self-image and makes the person feel even more isolated, intensifying the depression.

Depression is an exceedingly heinous illness, preventing those it afflicts from finding treatment, and plunging them into ever-deeper isolation. No other disease, physical or mental, reinforces and feeds itself as depression does.

The week plus long session here in Iraq lasted as long as it did in part because I did not want to recover. I felt I had no control over the issues that triggered my anger and resentment and I thought, in the twisted type of thinking one does in depression, that I had no hope of feeling better until others resolved the issues. I totally gave control of my emotional state to people I did not even know, who were hundreds of miles away and who could not care less about how I felt. I still followed my daily routine of work, eat, exercise, sleep but I did not enjoy anything, even talking with Philese on the phone. To her credit she remained supportive and encouraged me to continue writing and other fulfilling activities.

Commitments are important to me. In the past I have walked away from a promise I made such as spending an evening on the town with Philese and then breaking the date because I did not feel like it anymore. Honoring commitments helps me overcome so I resolve to honor every single one whether I feel like it or not. Feeling totally unable to fulfill a commitment to help at a church service made me realize that I needed to take control of my emotional state.

I find that if I constantly work on my attitude, nutrition, exercise, sleep, etc., the volume and depth of depressive episodes decrease significantly. Military life in Iraq did not allow me the flexibility I wanted. That resentment triggered others and depression took control. Today I feel back in control, determined to find ways to maintain a daily regiment that will help keep me on course. Even with continued mortar, rocket and IED attacks, fighting depression may be the most important battle I face here.

Learning to deal with strong, negative emotions does not mean that I do not have them anymore, but experiencing such feelings does not scare me anymore. I learned that feeling angry, for example, does not make me a bad person and does not mean that I will do anything harmful. I am more in control of the behaviors I exhibit when flooded with emotion. I can even enjoy emotions or at least live in the moment with them without feeling like running from them or hiding them.

One serendipitous result of all this work is that I relate to people better. I am able to connect with others on an emotional level where in the past I could only relate to people intellectually or in physical activity such as sports. I find that life is richer when lived with emotional connections.

07-22-04 * FAITH FOCUS—SHOULD CHRISTIANS EXPERIENCE DEPRESSION?

In the late '70's I attended a concert in Vancouver, B.C. featuring The Archers. Looking forward to the music, I felt impatient when Joni Eareckson[5] wheeled herself onstage to share her story. Like me, some of the crowd did not recognize her name, did not know Joni was part of the program and listened impatiently. Joni soon had us all giving her our utmost attention. I have been grateful ever since for her life and message. She shared with us the pain of dealing with Christians who told her she obviously lacked faith because God did not heal her. Listening to her life unfold, I felt inspired by her battle with her spinal injury. She epitomized a life of faith that night as she encouraged thousands of, predominantly, teenagers to strengthen our relationship with God even in the midst of pain or surrounded by Christians who do not understand.

Years later I forgot her message when I needed it most. Some Christians today shun members of their church who go through depression as if it is a lethally contagious spiritual disease. Denouncing depression as a moral or spiritual blight, they judge, opine, lecture, condemn, or ridicule, doing everything other than become part of the solution. It is a sad commentary on the church when a Christian needs to leave their community of believers to find the support they need to spiritually survive.

Another tendency I notice in some church circles is to support someone through depression the first time and then consider their work complete. When Jesus heals He heals completely, they say, so any recurrence of depression must be because of sin, or backsliding or a lack of faith in God's ability to heal. Someone caught in depression is viewed like someone who breaks their leg doing the same stupid thing they did the first three times they broke their leg. After a few episodes, like the boy who cried wolf, the number of people rushing to help diminishes greatly.

In the past I blamed Christians, in part, for the depths of my depressive episodes. Now I realize that most Christians do want to help, they just do not know how and I typically do not make it easy for them. I am now convinced that even if depression distances me from people I love it does not separate me from the love of God. (See Rom. 8: 35-39). Depression happens. The good news is that, with God, I can control depression rather than be controlled by it.

I made immense improvements in controlling depression when I stopped blaming other people for my level of despair. This can be a tough lesson to learn. I still need to remind myself, although not as often, that God loves me, that He already supplied everything I need, that other people are not the problem and that there is hope. There is always hope.

Not only did I need to stop blaming other people I also needed to stop blaming myself. I did not understand depression. I gave it too much power, viewed it as something to fear because of what I might do when under its spell. I made the problem bigger than reality. God is bigger than the problem of depression and God is willing to help anyone who is willing to listen to His wisdom.

In God's wisdom healing is not necessarily the absence of a problem. Healing also includes living an abundant life in Christ regardless of our problems or circumstances. God's church demonstrates to the universe that there is no problem too big for God, no aspect of humanity that God cannot reach. Do you despair of living the Christian life because you are from a tough, inner-city neighborhood? God's family includes many people from such neighborhoods learning how to live and walk a life of faith. Do you deem yourself unqualified to become a Christian because God could never use someone who did the things you did? There are Christians growing in their walk with God inside the toughest prisons, coming to know Him after performing deeds of darkness too horrible to describe. Does your continuing conflict with anger, depression, discontentment, ungratefulness, worldly pleasure or other emotional states cause you to believe that perhaps God is not listening to you, perhaps God or circumstance or fate singled you out for a life of miserable struggle? There is not a single struggle in our human experience where the results improve by addressing the challenge alone rather than with God.

Christians play an interesting psychological game. When confronted with unwanted events in their lives, they pose a hypothetical question to themselves as if originating with an opposing attorney in a heavenly court; "Will you continue to believe in God even if God does not deliver you from this time of trouble?"

Rather than question whether Christians should experience depression, or any other malady, we should question where God exempted Christians as a corporate body from any type or category of human suffering.

Another three memorial services on base this week, all the results of IED attacks against convoys. One a young gunner only two weeks out of Special Forces school, the two others each part of our convoy driving teams. We also sent a few soldiers home with serious injuries sustained in mortar attacks. Earlier this week I commented to a group of soldiers that I hope the politicians in DC realize on a daily basis that the military is not just a pawn in an international chess game but real people with real lives on the line. As we sit here helpless to significantly retaliate or take proactive action since the transfer of authority, I sometimes wonder to what extent politicians go to bed at night with the effects of their decisions on their conscience.

I asked our commander if I could play a stronger role in community affairs. He asked me for a suggestion. I offered to run for Governor. He reminded me that the last one was assassinated. I told him that's how I knew the position was vacant. He still said no, but suggested I could run for governor of Washington later.

Mosul continues to make news; although I do not know the extent it reaches hometown media. Iraqi police found a headless corpse dressed in an orange jumpsuit in the Tigris River. I noticed one news source reported that this occurred in Mosul, but in fact happened near the town of Baiji, about 150 km south of Mosul.

Iraqi Prime Minister Iyad Allawi vowed to destroy insurgents behind a wave of deadly attacks in Iraq. Mr. Allawi unveiled plans for a mukhabarat, a new intelligence unit, which he said would "annihilate those terrorist groups". A little over a year ago, the word "mukhabarat" would have sent shivers down the spines of Iraqis, but many say they supported a new domestic spy agency if it helps end rampant violence. Others are afraid that the power of the new government will resemble Saddam's regime too closely for their comfort. I think it will take a very strong government to take on the terrorists, which may generate questionable headlines in the States.

Allawi personally executed six detainees at a Baghdad police station shortly before the Coalition handed over power to the new Iraqi administration. This could be characterized as an Iraqi leader who shoots those that oppose his leadership. Sound like Saddam? I would not be surprised if Allawi is equated to Saddam in the press, and the United States is accused of giving the Iraqi people nothing better than they had before. A Zarqawi group offered a reward of $282,000 on Sunday for killing Prime Minister Allawi.

A member of the Turkman National Front was assassinated in a drive-by shooting in Mosul. Gunmen opened fire on his car, killing him instantly and wounding two passengers, including his 7-year-old son. A Turkish truck driver was killed and another kidnapped in an attack targeting a fuel convoy in town. Hard to tell if the violence in Mosul is in fact escalating, but definitely getting more diverse compared to the previously exclusive American focus.

A security team discovered a roadside bomb on the west side of Mosul that consisted of five 155mm artillery rounds near the side of the road. To put this in perspective, that IED would make a very big boom. The explosive ordnance disposal team reduced the device. This week we uncovered several IEDs before they could hurt anyone. Comforting on one hand, yet the deaths this week by similar IEDs diminishes the good news for me. American lives for Iraqi security. I know that the bigger picture includes American security and American interests, but that is difficult to see sometimes at the explosive street level.

I chatted with an Iraqi interpreter about his explosion experience. He was injured in a recent blast that killed over 40 people. He personally witnessed the American soldier who sacrificed his life to shoot the vehicle driver before hundreds more were killed. He told me that this is his seventh involvement in an attack. In Iraq they have a saying that a cat has seven lives and perhaps the next might be the last. Still, he will not quit helping us. He remembers all too well Saddam killing his father and confiscating their family's wealth. I told him that because of his help for Americans, he gets two extra lives because our cats are said to experience nine. I am inspired by his determination.

A few days ago, I woke up to the sounds of someone screaming in pain. I dressed and went outside, knowing not too many people remained in the area during the day. I met someone who also heard the screams but we could not find anyone else. Weird. We react to noise differently here than in the quiet neighborhoods of Bellevue. A sharp crack and we duck; a boom and we hit the dirt or instantly stop our vehicles. I wonder how long it will take us to adjust to home life after we return, or for our families to adjust to our new behavior patterns. But that is months away, unfortunately.

Finally, in the category of things not to do in the military, this story just in. The Sergeant Major of the base was in a staff meeting this morning with all the sergeant majors and first sergeants of the various units on base. One of the attendees presented him with a weapon that someone found in a portable toilet. The Sergeant Major promised to "talk" to the soldier assigned to that weapon. Heads nodded knowingly as evil grins chiseled into the stoic military faces. He traced the serial number to a member of his own unit! He knew that he could not just brush it aside since all the unit sergeant majors could either accuse him of favoritism or cite his example when failing to discipline their own troops. Even worse, the soldier is a staff sergeant, an NCO leader who should know better. Wow. I sure would not want to be in his boots! Now if I could only find my weapon so I could get to the office.

07-30-04 * ROOM SWEET HOME

In true military fashion, our activation orders did not include a location more specific than "Report to Kuwait for duty in Iraq." "Where in Iraq?" I asked of anyone I thought might have an answer. The replies sounded like a rehearsed script, "It does not matter. You will find out when you hit Kuwait." It mattered to me! I hoped to focus my preparation time specifically on climate and other conditions on my duty station but had to settle for the generic Army deployment prep procedures designed to prepare one for any kind of duty.

I decided to first acquaint myself with the military sleep system issued at Fort Lewis. I assembled the cot, then unrolled the three piece sleeping bag on top if it. The multi-section sleeping bag replaced the cold-weather mummy bag formerly in my duffel bag. In addition to the sleeping bag portion, the trio also consists of a cotton inner liner and an external wrap. The washable liner is used solo in hot weather and, when used inside the bag, allows easier cleaning. The outer liner adds an extra layer of protection for extreme cold climates. A tri-part sleeping bag on a narrow, short cot; not exactly a replacement for the down duvet covered Stearns & Foster Kedleston bed set in our bedroom.

Trying out the cot in the bedroom did not seem military enough. Lacking a floorless canvas tent, I decided to move the cot into the garage. Based on past military exercise experience, I cleared a section large enough for the cot with a two foot clearance on all sides. Now I only needed a tent flap instead of a door, a generator outside noisy enough to keep all but the truly exhausted awake, and soldiers to wake me up every two hours to ask "Sorry, wrong cot, but do you know where Private Jackson is sleeping?"

When I arrived in Kuwait, the desk sergeant directed me to a large tent reserved for soldiers waiting for flights to Mosul. The tent contained two columns of cots on a plywood floor. Luckier soldiers occupied cots within range of the air-conditioner. I chose one near the doorway, regretting my choice as soon as I tried to sleep. Every fifteen to twenty minutes someone clumsily tried to maneuver through the overlapping flaps in the dark. Fortunately, I only needed to wait two days for a seat to open on a flight north.

Someone told me the 101st Airborne originally set up the airfield base with an entire division (over 15,000 troops). Those true heroes of the war created stability in Mosul so a force less than ten percent of their size can now maintain the mission. They slept in tents, in truck beds, under canvas suspended from vehicles or trees, in buildings, Iraqi bunkers and anywhere else they could find room to spread out their Army issued triple layer sleep system. I expected nothing better.

Communications between Kuwait and Mosul failed to inform my unit of my departure and projected arrival. The plane landed shortly after midnight, long after most base operations ceased for the night. A kind soldier helped me find our supply sergeant who, after several military expletives and apologies, gave me a key and gestured in the dark to a door about twenty feet from his. The vehicle driver helped me carry my duffel bags and containers to the door then bade me a good night. Key in hand, I starred for a minute at the door and window of my new home.

My quarters resembled a panel-lined shipping container divided into two 7' x 10' sections. One central overhead light provided illumination for the entire unit. On the far wall, I spotted an air conditioner and another window. Each section contained a freestanding wardrobe eighteen inches wide, a three-foot high 4-drawer plastic snap-assembled unit that would need a huge boost in quality to qualify as a K-Mart Blue Light special, and a bed! Only an aluminum frame supporting a segment of plywood and a 4-inch think polyester covered hard foam, but I doubted a high roller on the Vegas Strip ever viewed his complimentary accommodations more gratefully. This time I chose the bed farthest from the door.

I overheard two soldiers talking about an experience one of them had the night before. One male soldier seemed to be excusing his behavior with the phrase "A year is a long time." Perhaps, but compared to what? A few soldiers, fortunately none in our unit, must believe that no one will ever find out if they cheat on their spouse in Iraq. Is a year a long time to go without intimacy compared to the years of lying to one's life partner? How about comparing the few moments of what they consider bliss with being able to honestly tell someone back home that he or she is the only one?

The faith some people place in their "She will never know" mentality astounds me. Why is their primary criterion whether their spouse will ever find out? What about their own personal integrity or moral fortitude? What about placing faith in the verse, "you will be sinning against the Lord; and you may be sure that your sin will find you out" (Num. 32:23).

Granted, not everyone who gets married makes God a party to their vows. Not everyone who becomes married even vows to remain sexually monogamous. Such people may feel no reservation in developing short-term relationships here. Their spouses are probably doing the same thing at home if that is how they created their marriage. Of course, the military takes a dim view of adultery, a crime still punishable by disciplinary action under the UCMJ. I wonder why the Army believes unfaithfulness is bad for moral and discipline in the military while so much of our society seems to dismiss the significance of a life-long, monogamous relationship.

Solomon remarked "He who brings trouble on his family will inherit only wind" (Prov. 11:29). A few episodes with a fellow soldier and what does that soldier inherit when he gets home? Sands of time flowing through his fingers, time spent in pain, regret, wondering how wonderful life might have been for a few careless indiscretions.

If I had to choose where to place my faith, I would rather believe that God rewards the righteous than believe that a sin as deceptive as adultery will not bear fruit to destroy a relationship.

One of these weeks, I would love to report that we had no fatalities. This is not one of those weeks. One soldier died in an IED explosion while on a convoy earlier this week. We also had the worst attack against our base since our arrival, resulting in one Iraqi soldier fatality and more than a dozen US and Iraqi soldiers injured. Several U.S. news channels reported four fatalities including a mother and child. I discovered that the early official news release from our headquarters to the north related that the vehicle contained a female driver and child. Our final report sent to the headquarters listed a solo male driver. While I did not discover the exact source of the confusion, I did learn enough to conclude that the military, not the press, caused the confusion in the reports. Here is a fuller and more accurate account.

On the 26th, an unknown assailant drove a vehicle rigged with explosives (VBIED—vehicle born improvised explosive device) toward our south gate. A quick thinking Iraqi guard spotted the vehicle approaching too fast for normal business operations and went out to challenge the vehicle. His actions forced the driver to detonate the vehicle 50 meters south of the most dangerous, and probably intended, location. Although he will probably not receive a purple heart, bronze star or other American medal, his actions are among the bravest, selfless and heroic I witnessed in Iraq. I don't even know his name. If the vehicle had reached the gate many more people would have died. That soldier lost his life in the explosion. Several American soldiers were close enough to the explosion that they would have died were it not for intervening barriers that absorbed the bulk of the blast. As tragic as this event is, a series of intervening circumstances prevented a more serious casualty count.

Our office took several pictures of the event. One of the photos was picked up by CNN through the public affairs office but CNN did not credit the photographer, the 116th's own CPT. David Kalamen. The explosion took place in the middle of the car, cutting the car in half, propelling each half in opposite directions. An analysis of the blast fragments revealed the thrust of the explosion went through the front and rear of the vehicle rather than the sides. That also saved some lives as there were people standing on either side; some inside a circle of barriers and several near the truck on the middle left.

Another point on the truck: that entrance is closed at night and the truck is parked there to deter gate-crashing. When the gate opens for business some-one backs the truck into an on-guard position. That morning, for a reason still unknown, the driver could not get the truck started. The stalled truck caused a back up of vehicles to the gate that the suicide driver had to drive around, a suspicious activity that caught the eye of the Iraqi guard. Later that day the truck started normally.

The front half of the propelling vehicle knocked over two heavy, connected cement barriers. The rear section careened into a parked car and set it on fire. Other car parts flew in all directions, injuring bystanders, knocking out windows or doors, landing on rooftops. Iraqis congregated in a nearby plywood shelter, awaiting escorts to take them to their work locations on base. An American soldier in charge of area security decided earlier to move them farther north, a decision that also saved many lives as the shelter was completely leveled by the force of the explosion and flying debris.

We are fortunate for two reasons that an inexperienced person assembled the explosives. The first is the direction of the blast. The vehicle engine and trunk compartments absorbed more of the explosion than if the bomber aimed the device to explode out of the doors. The second reason is that less than 20 percent of the explosive discharged. The bulk of the firepower scattered on the ground without being set off. The explosives experts postulated several theories; old ord-nance, incorrect detonation cord, poor design. Either way, I am very grateful for the resulting decrease in casualties.

The VBIED we experienced contained a comparable strength to the huge explosion that killed 44 people a few kilometers north of us a month ago. The informed reader may realize a similarity in the day of the month as well. I per-sonally do not believe that the factors combining to result in only one multi-national force fatality are unrelated coincidences. If even one of them had not transpired as experienced, the death toll could easily have exceeded last month's mass casualty disaster. Many Iraqi and American soldiers and civilians thanked their God for protecting them.

At the time of the explosion, I had been off shift about two hours and asleep perhaps 30 minutes. Although my sleeping area is on the opposite end of the base, the crack of the explosion woke me up. Later that afternoon, we had a mortar attack very close to our living area. Another wake up call. Working in the operations office, I deal indirectly with the incidents; receiving intelligence, directing responses, writing reports for the commander and higher headquarters. I would rather work as part of the response teams, or the community interaction teams, but I work on the sidelines like a part of a baseball team's back office rather than a player. That's life in the military.

In other Mosul incidents this week, gunmen attacked a retired Iraqi general, Salim Majeed Blesh, 58, as he headed to a mosque to pray, killing him and a bodyguard. Blesh worked for the former U.S. occupation government. The assault against people willing to assume leadership positions in the new Iraqi government continues.

Our VBIED incident will not remain in the news for more than a day or two basically because our media equates the seriousness of an event with a body count of fatalities and injuries. Since only one person died, the media will quickly drop our attack from their coverage. Body count, however, is only one measure of comparing attacks.

Number of terrorists on the scene: One terrorist in one vehicle. According to the typical terrorist cell structure we cou ld assume the involvement of more people in the surveillance and assembly stages of the attack. Even so, this VBIED incident ranks rather low in the number of terrorists involved when compared to other types of attacks in Iraq.

Ten 155-mm artillery rounds linked together: The potential explosive power of this incident is one of the largest we've seen in northern Iraq. The high explosive variant of a 155 mm round has a 100% kill radius of 50 meters and carries the equivalent of approximately 8 kg of TNT. I do not know whether we can accurately calculate the potential impact of this attack if all of the rounds detonated. I do know that this VBIED could easily kill more than 300 people if placed in a crowded, civilian area. But we wouldn't count this as a weapon of mass destruction because such things don't exist in Iraq.

Casualties avoided: I imagine a news service in Heaven publishing an article under the headline "Divine Intervention Thwarts Iraq Disaster, Hundreds Could Have Died". The subheading states "Number 4,275,148 in our continuing series on Angels in Action". The first photograph, taken with a spiritually discerning lens, reveals a grinning angel leaning over the engine compartment of a Deuce-and-a-half truck while a frustrated soldier attempts to start it. The second photo depicts a close-up of that smiling seraph with a caption "I am humbled that God asked me to perform this mission." Angels, of course, do not admit to being proud, remembering what happened to the last cherub who did.

The article later quotes a critic of the operation from the Hell Isn't So Hot public relations firm, "If God really wanted to prevent a full catastrophe, why not have the artillery rounds completely detonate in the desert with only the driver and a stray hare in the vicinity? Are rabbits now worth more than people to God?" Even God deals with critics.

If we compare this event using a scale of casualties avoided rather than casualties realized the recent VBIED attack on our base might be on the top of the charts and that is worth celebrating rather than ignoring. Did God really intervene? People who believe in God think so. Non-believers just shrug at the chain of coincidental events. It starts when a soldier attempts to move a truck that is blocking night entrance to the gate. The truck starts every morning, starts later that same day, but just at the particular moment when it is still possible to diminish the impending attack the truck will not start. The soldier is frustrated. Vehicles waiting outside the gate to pass turn in or pass through are stop. A line begins to form and more people become frustrated. One American soldier in charge of gate area security decides to move all of the Iraqis waiting to get on base to work north to another waiting area. He is also frustrated as over one hundred Iraqis complain to him about his decision. Still, he is in charge and they move as other soldiers follow orders to move the crowd away from the gate.

Frustrated motorists wait in line. One does not. Focused and determined, he drives around the entanglement. An Iraqi guard becomes irritated with his fellow countryman and walks out of his post to tell the driver to get back in line. The south gate of our base is a morass of frustrated Americans and Iraqis who are all, coincidentally, repositioned from where they would have been if the truck had started and moved to its daytime operation position.

The morning is not going according to plan for the terrorist either. Unfortunately he is too far along on his path of destruction to turn around. Perhaps he thought he could roll down his window and explain, "Excuse me, fellow countryman; I do not intend to harm Iraqis. I just want to kill Americans. Could you possibly step aside and allow me to drive next to where the Americans are standing?" But he does not stop to ask, perhaps because terrorists do not really care who they kill. Perhaps they, or their families, get paid the same either way. Perhaps in their system of eternal reward killing Americans and killing Iraqis who work with Americans earns them the same Islamic honors. Perhaps, but he does not stop. Instead he detonates the fuse.

At that point another set of coincidences, unrelated to the truck's mechanical difficulties, reduce the possible number of casualties. Only two of the ten artillery rounds detonate. The rounds are also not positioned properly for maximum effect. The driver dies and takes one brave Iraqi soldier into eternity.

If the rounds exploded in the desert, depending on the exact location and subsequent inquiry, we might not have known the plan. The military would have raised the threat level but might not have changed the way we handled gate operations as we did following the blast as realized. The terrorists would certainly try again as it was the driver who failed, not their plan. I doubt soldiers would discuss a desert blast as divine intervention the way we talk about the truck not starting.

Does God interfere in the affairs of mankind? This incident does not prove the issue conclusively. Nebuchadnezzar testified in Daniel chapter 4 that God ruled and overruled in the affairs of men. The Book of Revelation indicates God isn't finished with us yet. Two thousand years after the Bible finished cataloging God's interactions with the human race many people wonder; does He or doesn't He?

I am not gratified that a fellow soldier died, yet I am grateful that this attack spared so many lives. I actually thank God that the truck did not start and the fuses did not work. I wonder whether the driver felt thankful in the moment. Perhaps I can learn a lesson here about my attitude when events do not proceed as I planned. From a spiritual perspective frustration might be a blessing in disguise.

08-05-04 * THE REAL FREEDOM FIGHTERS

The death toll for U.S. combat operations in the War on Terrorism topped the 1,000 mark this week. That number includes fallen heroes in Afghanistan, Iraq, Kuwait, Djibouti, Cuba and the Philippines. One thousand soldiers who leave behind families who love them and communities that miss them. One thousand memorial services, 1,000 knocks on a door followed by "Hi, are you..."

According to the *Army Times*, these casualties were: 81 percent active duty; 53 percent ranked E-4 (specialist) and below; 71 percent white; 73 percent Army; 68 percent by hostile acts, 48 percent age 24 and below, and over 97 percent male. Eighteen of the 1,000 claimed Washington as their state of residency.

It is not for me to say whether their sacrifice is worth the prevention of another terrorist attack on American soil as if we can glibly sacrifice this group of real human beings for a larger group of imaginary citizens. I leave that determination to the loved ones left behind.

When I hear ungrateful disdain for our military sacrifice from people who could easily have become part of that larger group, I wish I could segregate them from the supportive majority and tell them, "I am not in Iraq for you!" However, we fight for the freedom and security of all Americans and even for the security of countries that did not support our president's decision.

The coalition military delivered a knockout punch to global terrorism, which fell harder than Mike Tyson at his comeback match, but terrorists are not out for the count. They constitute a clear and present danger to the United States and they are madder than a wasp colony finding their hive destroyed.

On August 1, at 8:15 a.m., a car bomb exploded outside of a police station in southeastern Mosul during the morning shift change at the station, killing two Iraqi police officers and wounding 10. The explosion also killed three Iraqi citizens and injured more than 40. The speeding vehicle crashed into the concrete barriers in front of the station and exploded.

The guard at the entry control point shot and killed the driver of the vehicle as he approached the barriers, saving many lives compared to a detonation within the barricades. The guard was one of the Iraqi police officers killed in the explosion.

That evening, a car bomb went off outside a church, incinerating a passing motorist and wounding four others. The toll would have been higher if all of the mortar shells stuffed inside the car had detonated. Based on verbal reports that reached our office, the arrangement and components of the explosive device appear to be the work of the same group that delivered the faulty car bomb to our entrance gate last week. Because of the differences between the explosive device detonated in Mosul and Baghdad, we do not officially know to what extent the Mosul terrorist cell is connected with the Zarqawi cells that claim credit for the masterminded concurrent explosions in the capital.

On August 4, a series of coordinated attacks in Mosul targeted Iraqi police, Iraqi National Guard and multinational forces. At least 14 Iraqi citizens died and 31 were wounded. The number of terrorists killed is not released.

Iraqi police and Iraqi National Guard soldiers responded. Multinational forces served in a supporting role, providing additional support where and when the Iraqi leaders involved in the attacks requested it. No multinational forces or Iraqi security forces were killed in the attacks. Attackers also attempted to disrupt the power and health care system in the city by attacking the Mosul Power Plant and the Al Jahmouri hospital in west central Mosul with small arms fire and rocket propelled grenades.

The new Ninevah province governor, Duraid Kashmoula, stated, "What has happened today, destruction by burglars and criminals, proves that they are not real Iraqis." He also remarked that, "The Iraqi police, the National Guard and the Facilities Protective Service personnel faced them and killed or arrested many of them." This statement should be enough to counter Michael Moore and pals who continue to comment that the terrorists in Iraq are the freedom fighters.

For a one-week vacation Philese packs enough clothes to keep two porters busier than a private in basic training. For eighteen months in Iraq the Army allows four work uniforms and two PT (gym) uniforms. I needed to fit a 30" x 70" bed, 18" wide closet, 4-drawer plastic dresser and eighteen months of clothing, equipment and personal items into a 7' x 10' area. A cell at Alcatraz is 6' x 9'. One extra foot in each direction and a fenced compound that I am not allowed to leave, but I retain the key to my door and don't have to use a toilet in my own living area.

I needed to raise the frame several inches to accommodate the new Army Tuff Bin footlocker under my bunk. When I sit on the edge of the bed, I can dangle and swing my legs as I did as a bored youth finding ways to entertain myself in grown-up church services. The hard plastic box is crammed with mandatory field equipment untouched since my arrival. A wooden weapon crate, required for checking an M-16 into commercial airline baggage, hides behind the footlocker. The other occupant of the makeshift storage area is a drab-green duffel bag, as equally full and untouched as the Tuff Bin.

One remarkable feature of my room is its close proximity to nothing essential. The bathroom is a four-minute walk south over an ankle-twisting combination of dirt and gravel. The dining facility is five minutes north, and my favorite Internet café is a six minute westerly jaunt. Although one could argue that Bill Gates probably walks a similar distance to get from one end of his 66,000 ft.^{2} home to the other, he can do so in air-conditioned privacy sporting silk pajamas and slippers; whereas our treks require a full uniform, dog-tags, combat boots, a 30lb protective vest, a Kevlar helmet and an M-16 with at least one full ammunition magazine strapped somewhere on our weapon or person.

I cannot imagine anyone buying four identical suits and wearing them every day for a year, but that is the extent of my clothes selection when I get ready for work. Deciding what to wear takes less than a New York minute. One desert camouflage uniform, one brown t-shirt, two black socks, tan boots. The only wardrobe choice left to my own discretion is what underwear to don on any given day. I do not care as long is it is reasonably clean and odor free. When not on duty we may sport a clean Army PT uniform; black shorts, grey t-shirt, white socks, running shoes and reflective belt. Army uniform regulations govern our appearance any time we step out of our room, although even the toughest sergeant major makes allowances for emergency runs to the bathroom. Just don't leave your weapon there.

At home, I find two bathrooms often inadequate for our family of four. One wife and one teenaged daughter can occupy two bathrooms for hours.

Knock, knock.

"Who's there?"

"I really need to use the bathroom, sweetie, love of my life!"

"Use the other one!"

"Victoria's using it!"

"Walk to the Chevron station, I need to get ready."

"You've been in there for an hour!"

I only said the latter phrase once, not because it wasn't true other times, but because I am a quick learner when it comes to repeating a calamitous faux pas. My family unknowingly helped me prepare for life in Iraq even before my activation, a blessing I did not fully appreciate at the time.

Here, a bathroom unit seats seven, stands two and accommodates three at the sink. Our living area, maximum occupancy 320, includes three units designated for males and two for females. I have not witnessed even ten females residing in our area. One hundred men to share one bathroom unit that is cleaned once every afternoon, but the females almost have an entire unit to themselves. Come to think of it, since the females I know need vast and continuous bathroom facilities, perhaps continuing the same ratio arrangement works best. Being Army guys, we really don't mind. Pigs don't know pigs stink. Life on our base is better than the Iraq bases where living space is half the distance between cots in a GP Medium tent and personal hygiene means access to a portable toilet and five-gallon water jug.

The Sergeant Major of all American forces in Iraq stopped by our base to say hello. His office requested certain units to send two representatives to have dinner with him. Our unit included me as a representative, which forced me to shower, wear a clean uniform, and mind my manners in the dining facility. He shared two ideas I want to submit for your rumination. First, he believes soldiers in Iraq face as much combat in one year as soldiers in Vietnam encountered in two years. Second, he opined that today's military is perhaps the best military in U.S. history. I mentioned that I do not see in some of our troops the level of discipline and sacrifice evidenced in stories of soldiers in World War II. Although he did not dispute that observation, he added other factors prevalent at that time such as physical abuse of boot camp privates, racial tensions and gender discrimination. I still do not view our generation of soldiers in the same light as Tom Brokaw's description of the greatest generation. I focused on individual values while the sergeant major concentrated on the overall military system. We may both be right.

The living conditions in Mosul, Iraq proved infinitesimally better than the cot filled tents of Kuwait. The quality of the shower facilities, however, decreased as dramatically. In Kuwait, the shower units would require a wide load sign if transported on a flatbed truck. Permanently installed like a mobile home, they contain a dozen individual shower stalls in a horseshoe pattern around bench seats and a separate drying or changing area. The entrance includes a 90-degree blind corner so even with the door ajar; patrons enjoy complete privacy from passersby. The changing area, just inside the door, prevents dirt buildup on the shower area floor. External tanks and pumps quietly regulate water temperature and pressure better than many American city systems. None of this held true once I arrived in Iraq.

Some smaller bases in Iraq utilize the shower tents as portrayed in the M.A.S.H. TV series; a drab-green tent with a wooden floor and green plastic sheets dividing the shower area into six sections. Males and females use the same tent, just at different times, at least according to the rules. The shower tent operates only a few hours each day. The hot water supply consists of water heated in a hefty pot and dumped into an aboveground large canvas bag. Another bag holds the cold water. Gravity delivers the water to chest-high showerheads. The showers close when either bag empties. Soldiers stand on pallets covered in soap slime, hair, dead skin and bugs that crawl up from the tent floor and stick to the grotesque patina. Whenever a complaint about our showers enters my mind, I instead express gratitude that I do not work on a base with shower tents.

To grasp the intricacies of shower arrangements on our base, imagine a corridor twenty feet with a door on one end and a window and air conditioner at the other. On one side of the corridor install seven shower stalls with interior dimensions of 30" square, shower heads with a 70-inch vertical clearance, a shower curtain with half the holes ripped from the hooks, and one hook for clothes screwed to the outer frame of each stall. Across the corridor from the showers, place two sinks, a water pump, two water heaters and space at the end of the corridor for air circulation. The narrowness of the corridor means that someone stepping out of the shower would butt up against someone using a sink. No benches, no separate changing area, floors constantly wet and dirty, and less room to maneuver than in Apollo space capsules. The water pressure drops to almost nothing in two minutes, then the pump kicks in and rebuilds the pressure. The water temperature changes with the pressure, oscillating between cool and scalding. There is one shower facility for every one hundred males and one per ten females.

When we first arrived in Mosul, one of the shower units designated for females did not have the appropriate sign on the door. One of our male soldiers did not receive the warning to stay away from that building. If a female enters a male shower point, men would greet her with open arms, escort her to an available shower and invite her to return any time. A male in a female shower room receives a very different treatment. Due to the scarcity of females in our living area, he used the female-designated but unlabeled shower several times before encountering any of the intended occupants. He marveled at his good fortune, always walking into a clean and empty unit. While scrubbing his dirty self one day, he heard the door open and two female voices enter the unit. He stayed in the shower until they departed, frozen in the fear of discovery. He no longer uses that shower unit.

I tend to use shower stalls in the back of the room because I can set clothing items on the top of the water heaters and because I do not need to concern myself with exiting the shower into the backside of someone using a sink to shave or brush his teeth. Finding the rear showers occupied one day, I used one just inside the door. As I toweled off, aû naturál, shower curtain aside, the wind slammed the door open. In my high school days, I was one of the kids too shy to have a shower after gym class. Now gregarious and flamboyant, I continued drying myself, feigning obliviousness to the open door, a feat I do not intend to try at home.

The only irritating part of showering on our base is the occasional wind driven dust cloud that covers my damp body on the return walk to my room. Clean for less than three minutes. I noticed the other day that the seldom-used female shower is significantly closer and on the other side of the dirt road where I encounter my dusty hygiene nemesis. I wonder. As long as I don't sing, maybe they won't notice.

An American civilian security guard stopped by our office to report an attack on their convoy. He brought two of his co-workers to our hospital but left a third behind, burning in another vehicle after dying in the impact. I watched the horror expressed in his tears. They are not soldiers and do not drive military vehicles. They provide security for the Iraqi government, perhaps an even more dangerous job now than military convoys since they lack the military firepower and armor to protect them. The decision to mobilize 125,000 troops rather than the 400,000 first discussed included a decision to switch duties such as these convoys to private contracts. I don't hear many news commentaries about the amount of civilians in Iraq and the dangers they face. Our work in Iraq would not succeed without them.

I stepped out of the office the other night for a breath of fresh air and view of the stars. A few minutes later gunfire erupted to the northwest. I wanted to head to the area and support our perimeter security. Instead, I returned to our map-lined windowless operations center to assume my battle coordinator role. Military success requires that all soldiers, from tower guards to base commanders, maintain their positions. This call to duty supersedes desire, convenience, weather, support, fatigue or fear. I often prefer to become directly involved, especially when the radio reports contain inaccurate speculations or events inflated by senses pounded into frenzy by indiscernible noises. Inaccurate reports significantly increase the chances I make an erroneous decision that could jeopardize someone's life.

The Rules of Engagement (ROE) and the Laws of Armed Conflict (LOAC) govern our actions and reactions during enemy encounters. Misunderstanding or ignoring these rules can mean the difference between a hero's medal or murder charges. Application of the ROE and LOAC changed after the transfer of authority. Ordinarily the Judge Advocate General (JAG) office develops ROE/LAOC training. Headquarters in Baghdad sent a training class that addressed issues germane to their location but inapplicable to our operations. Our base commander asked me to write a new training class. I considered the heavy responsibility of applying the ROE/LOAC to our activities. If a soldier followed the training, yet a military court found him guilty of a violation, I would feel some responsibility for that soldier's actions. Yet I also wanted to allow our soldiers as much latitude as possible to handle dangerous situations. The final training program received full approval and dissemination. Writing an ROE training program does not make news or earn medals. If I had not participated in Operation Iraqi Freedom someone else would have written it, perhaps better than I did. Still, I feel proud of the product produced. My singular contribution to the effort in Mosul.

Shortly after arriving in Iraq I started an LL.M. (Master of Laws) degree in Estate Planning and Taxation. Most soldiers specialize in computer games, e-mail or watching movies in their off-shift time. A few industrious soldiers study foreign languages or take military correspondence courses. I wanted to maintain some level of proficiency with my legal skills. I completed the first semester with 4 A's, a better grade point average than law school. The second semester is the tougher challenge as it consists entirely of the thesis developed from the work done in the first semester. I plan to finish the degree before we return stateside.

Someone e-mailed me with an observation that I must really miss my family. I do. My wife's birthday is today. She is my strongest cheerleader, my best friend, my primary motivation for returning home safely, an angel who graces my life. Many people think she deserves a sainthood nomination for putting up with me. I agree. I talked to a chaplain about the possibilities of canonizing St. Philese. He said our chances would be a lot stronger if we were at least Catholic.

News reports continue to follow the conflict in Al Najaf against Al-Sadr and his militia. I do not welcome reports of his death. Al-Sadr is not an opportune terrorist, launching mortars, rockets or IEDs and then hiding like a coward. He fights for his country and religious beliefs. Unfortunately for him, and for Iraq, Al-Sadr chose an anti-US path rather than a pro-Iraq position. He could use his militia and influence to rid Iraq if its actual enemies, yet his beliefs clouded his mind as to the true nature of the conflict here. As one Iraqi watch seller said, "Iraqis are standing in a pit, and Mr. Sadr's followers think America is a big devil. But if the devil is telling me, "Give me your hand and I'll get you out," why shouldn't I take it? Yes, it's the devil, but I'm dying in this pit."

The Iraqi soccer team beat Portugal 4-2 in round one Olympic play. Neighborhoods around the airfield celebrated with flares and AK-47's fired into the air. I am very happy for the Iraqi team and the nation. Iraq needs some non-military heroes. I just wish the soccer fans could express their joy with methods that don't accidentally kill people on the way down.

Update on local contract work: The Rapid Regional Response Program (R3P) completed almost $2 million out of $14 million in approved projects in Mosul's Nineveh Province. Projects that received money through the R3P were selected by the former Coalition Provisional Authority in partnership with local Nineveh leaders last fall. Between December 2003 and June 2004, when the CPA ceased to exist and the Iraqi interim government took control of the DFI account, 50 local contractors were awarded contracts, creating more than 10,000 temporary jobs. Mosul received about $850,000 for developmental projects within the city. The projects include graffiti removal, various road construction and repair projects, orphanage renovation and the construction of road and traffic signs throughout the city.

Educational projects made up $290,000 of the total funding. Multinational forces helped rebuild and repair schools and colleges throughout the Nineveh region. I hoped to accompany a school renovation team this week but could not get approval for the time away from my regular responsibilities. I felt frustrated, if not angry, at the decision process, but such is life in the military. My first duty is to my assigned position, as I reminded soldiers in the ROE training class.

A new public library and library for the University of Agriculture College were also constructed. I saw the impressive UAC library on my trip to Turkey. The construction of a soccer stadium and Shuhada Park, completed at a total cost of $190,000, concentrated on providing the Nineveh youth a fun and safe recreation area. The remaining $12 million in projects, to be completed within the next five months, include road construction and repair projects, bus transportation upgrades, purchase of waste removal trucks, and completion of the Mosul Environmental Testing Station.

08-20-04 * COMBAT DENTIST

Bored, tired of sitting at a computer station, I unwrapped a Starburst and chewed slowly, dissolving it in my mouth to savor the flavor as long as possible. As strawberry and banana flavors my taste buds my tongue also detected a solid chunk of foreign matter. I discovered a piece of a tooth sticking to the gooey Starburst. A quick surface scan of my teeth revealed a large hole in the backside of the upper right bicuspid. I pressed the hole with my finger and the rest of the tooth snapped off at the gum line in two pieces. More in shock than pain, I stared for several minutes at the three small shrapnel of bone in my hand. I wondered if I could get triple indemnity from the tooth fairy even though all of the pieces came from the same tooth. The practical side of my brain told me more serious problems required my attention as the level of pain sharply increased.

The dental office occupies two small rooms of a single story structure scheduled for demolition. The window placard read "For Rent". As these practitioners do not need to advertise to attract customers, no signs out front hinted at the diabolical dentistry performed within. I pulled open the rickety screen door and took two steps to the front counter. I laid the tooth particles in front of the soldier behind the desk. He looked at them and asked, "Did you break a tooth?"

"Wow, this guy really knows his stuff." I sarcastically commented to myself.

"Yeth," I replied out loud, opening my mouth and pointing to the gap between an eye-tooth and a molar.

"Have a seat." He pointed to a stool in front of a laptop. Our dentists do not have x-ray film or a developing room. Instead, they rely on an x-ray camera connected to a laptop for digital imagery. My original impression of a state-of-the-art facility in a combat zone quickly faded when I received an instruction to hold the imaging plate behind my tooth with my index finger while the lab tech pointed the camera at it. After a few tries we successfully reproduced an x-ray of the tooth on the monitor.

"Yes, it's definitely broken," he announced with the surety of an apostolic revelation after examining the digital image. Then he turned to the other occupant of the room. "What do you think, doctor?"

The dentist glared at the screen for several seconds. "We'll need to do a root canal." I hate root canals!

He directed me to sit in a patio lounge chair, the plastic tri-part type popularized by Fred Meyer that can have one end raised for the head and the other lowered for leg comfort. The light resembled one late-night book worms would clip to their reading material. No rinse sink, no visual reality options, no music, no nitrous oxide, not even the gurgle of a fish tank. The artistic décor consisted of a poster of Fiji and another of dolphins wearing sunglasses. I tried to relax, but the surroundings failed to generate a peaceful confidence of satisfactory results.

Soldiers and units frequently borrow or appropriate supplies to continue their mission. The dentist office was no exception. The dentist prepared my gums for a shot and lifted a needle that once belonged to the veterinary unit.

"This should only hurt a little bit," soothed the dentist. His comment was followed by a pain so intense I would have preferred hitting my gums with a hammer. Two minutes later he commenced drilling, using a bit procured from a construction jackhammer team. He then asked his assistant for a file. The dentist's helper, a recent graduate of the Dental Assistance School for Troglodytes, handed over a file large enough to facilitate a prison break.

"No," the dentist explained, "I mean those small files there. Hand me the white one."

As the assistant complied, he asked, "What are those little numbers on the side?"

"The numbers refer to the diameter of the file. This one is too large; do we have a smaller one?"

The assistant fumbled with a few files but could not locate one smaller than the 20 in the dentist's hand and my mouth.

"Well, we will have to make do. I am sure this will only hurt a little bit," he told me in the same pacifying voice I no longer trusted.

The drilling continued for several minutes, and then the dentist put down the drill and his safety glasses. He announced to no one in particular, "I think there should be two roots in there!" He walked over to the laptop screen and studied the x-ray of my tooth.

"Get me out of here!" I yelled to myself, knowing resistance would be futile.

The dentist returned to conduct an exploratory drill. Finally, he found the root and proceeded to finish the job.

"You can tell when a root is active," he sadistically narrated, addressing his eager assistant, "when it squirts blood like this." I did not feel as overjoyed. Maybe he drilled too far and did not want to admit it?

"Do you want me to make up some filling material?" the assistant asked.

"No, we don't fill root canals the first time. We pack in some medicine to kill any infection and then seal it. We will fill it when he returns for the follow-up."

After packing the hole with whatever a combat dentist uses (I did not dare watch) he issued my final instructions.

"Here is a prescription for antibiotics. Take them three times per day until finished. Oh… I better give you a prescription for pain-killers. Are you allergic to codeine?"

I shook my head, unable to say anything coherent.

"Good, you'll need them. Come back in a month and we will finish the filling. When you return back to the states you can get a crown or bridge or whatever you want to finish the job."

I smiled, nodded, and left as quickly as I could. I wonder if the "For Rent" sign in the window means they might not even be here a month from now.

08-23-04 * NEWS FROM THE FRONT

Our base received a couple of mortar attacks this week. A few wounded, but no casualties for which I am very glad. Other bases and convoys in Mosul are not as fortunate.

On the 18th, a rocket hit a market in the centre of Mosul killing five Iraqis and wounding 20 others. No one claimed responsibility for the bombing.

Our most dangerous threat continues to be IED attacks coupled with RPG (a shoulder fired rocket propelled grenade) or small arms fire (such as AK-47s). Private security companies, rather than American soldiers, escort convoys that carry supplies for the Iraqi military, or for non-military operations. A private convoy encountered an IED and RPG fire earlier this week. One driver died instantly. The IED immediately rendered his vehicle inoperable. The second vehicle pulled alongside to allow the remaining passengers, all wounded, to escape the overwhelming AK-47 fire. They called in their position and sped to our hospital. Another died here and a third needed emergency evacuation south.

The second security team arrived at the incident scene in time to witness the attackers removing the deceased driver but could not get through the heavy traffic to stop them. The terrorists did not likely take the body to give it a proper burial.

I do not know how many American civilian security personnel are in Iraq. Many of them are former military and those I met are well trained. I do know that the terrorists do not distinguish between soldiers and civilians. They do not operate according to the Laws of Armed Conflict, as we must regardless of their actions.

The terrorists behind the IED attacks are not simply mad at the American presence. They continue to kill Iraqi police, Iraqi National Guard, and Iraqi politicians. They disrupt oil production, electricity and other essential services. They promote chaos and wield power through intimidation. Now is not the time for any country to pull out of Iraq. Kidnappings may cease if they do, but the terrorists will win back control of Iraq and recreate the state sponsored financing they enjoyed under Saddam.

The good news is that the people of Iraq persevere. The national conference on the new government continued in Baghdad despite the threat warnings and Iraqis continue to apply for positions with the police and guard units. Contrary to some stateside news reports, Iraq is not responding to terrorism with open retaliation characteristic of the Wild West. The government strongly believes in a rule of law and pursues the terrorists with all legal means available. This does not mean that the interim government views terrorism as a criminal problem solved only by arrest and prosecution. While not wanting to become a military state, Iraq does not restrict military involvement in domestic law enforcement the way we do in the U.S.

The Iraqi leaders involved in creating the new government want to create a system that includes preventative safeguards against another Saddam-type regime even though that level of absolute power right now might solve the terrorist problem faster. I think this is a very important lesson not adequately discussed in the major news.

Some critics still harangue that this level of terrorism never existed under Saddam. A few even suggest that Iraqis experienced a better life under Saddam than they now currently enjoy. How do they then explain the adamant resolve of Iraq's leaders to ensure that future presidents of Iraq do not have Saddam's power? If life had been so much better under that system, and the council could recreate it if they wanted to, why the reluctance against granting such powers to the new government?

Assuming the representatives to the national conference this week reliably indicate national will and sentiment, I find myself feeling a renewed hope for this country and pride for our involvement. The battle for Iraq could be one of the most important battles for freedom and security in the world today.

The Hawaii-Iraq Partnership for Revitalizing Agricultural Higher Education and Development held a workshop this week on horticulture, food services, plant protection, and agriculture economics. Participants included faculty from colleges and universities across northern Iraq. The University of Hawaii, funded by a $3 million grant from the U.S. Agency for International Development, will be working with University of Mosul College of Agriculture and Forestry and the University of Dohuk College of Agriculture to improve higher education and teacher training as well as stimulating economic growth and agricultural sustainability in northern Iraq. This area produces most of the agricultural products for Iraq so the program is a potentially huge benefit to the entire Iraqi economy.

I finally ventured into our new theater to watch *Lady Killers* with Tom

Hanks, more from boredom on a night off than because I wanted to see that particular movie. The theatre resembles a multi-purpose lecture hall with a wide video screen and audio-visual projector. At the beginning of the movie, shown in regular format, an employee changed the aspect ratio on the projector to fit the movie to the wide screen. This made the movie 30% wider without a corresponding height adjustment. *Lady Killers*, features several people already wide enough without the ridiculously rotund enhancement. A reader asked me recently if all base movie theatres in Iraq are free. Our theatre does not charge admission, but I discovered that others in Iraq do. AAFES operates ones that charge while movies shown in our hall come under the morale and recreation contract to Kellogg, Brown & Root (KBR, a Halliburton subsidiary). Most of the soldiers I talk to would rather pay admission to an AAFES theatre than watch KBR sponsored movies at no charge. Recalculating aspect ratios is only one of the reasons.

08-26-04 * Is Iraq Free?

A recent advertisement supporting George Bush for President features the flags of Iraq and Afghanistan as the narrator says, "And this Olympics... There will be two more free nations... And two fewer terrorist regimes."

Pres. Bush delivered a speech in Beaverton, Oregon on August 13th during which he mentioned the Iraqi soccer team. "The image of the Iraqi soccer team playing in this Olympics, its fantastic, isn't it? It wouldn't have been free if the United States had not acted."

Grant Wahl interviewed the Iraqi soccer team for *Sports Illustrated* and asked their reaction to these two quotes. His article, published Aug. 19, portrays the Iraqi team as sharply critical of Bush's attitude. They do not view Iraq as a free country.

None of the soccer players support the Saddam regime either. Last year the International Olympic Committee (IOC) ethics commission confirmed allegations of abuse against athletes by Udai Hussein. Athletes reported violent and humiliating punishment including rape. The IOC responded by suspending Iraq's Olympic status, reinstating them in February. With little time remaining before the Olympic deadline, only five Iraqis qualified for individual events; track, boxing, swimming, tae kwon do and weightlifting. The soccer team qualified with several unforeseen wins culminating in a match against Saudi Arabia. In the history of the Olympics, Iraq won only one medal, a bronze for weightlifting at the 1960 Games in Rome.

Although Iraq's 2004 Olympic roster does not include anyone directly harmed by Udai, the soccer team members know many players who were tortured for crimes as innocent as missing a shot. Every player expressed gratitude that Udai is no longer Iraq's Olympic Committee Chairman. Gratitude for the absence of the Hussein family does not, for them, automatically equate to support for Pres. Bush.

The *Sports Illustrated* article quoted Scott Stanzel, a spokesperson for Bush's campaign, as reiterating that Iraq is free as a result of the actions of the coalition. I think that if Scott would come here and attempt to spread that message he might be forced to rephrase his declaration. In fact, I think President Bush should fire Scott and hire me. I would perhaps set a record, though, for shortest tenure of a campaign spokesperson, as I cannot envision myself saying anything I do not believe just because the President said so.

The major cities in Iraq experience deadly violence on almost a daily basis, a continuous nightmare since the Feb. 2003 invasion. True, people are free to criticize the government, a privilege literally shackled in the era of Saddam's secret police. Freedom of speech may be the only freedom common to the United States and Iraq.

Iraqis, even many supporting the Americans, do not trust their government. The current assembly was not voted in by the national convention as promised but selected as a slate by an interim council already viewed as a U.S. puppet. The selection process focused on ethnic, regional, gender and religious diversity but many groups do not feel represented. For example, Kurds on our base believe that the Kurds in the assembly were chosen by the council because of their support for a particular political agenda, rather than their representation of the Kurdish population.

Iraqis lack many basic services. Most of the infrastructure in Iraq has not been properly serviced since Gulf 1, a situation some Iraqis blame on sanctions initiated by the Americans. U.S. reconstruction authorities poured more than $200 million into the Baiji power station, one of several such projects in Iraq. Electrical supply still hovers around 50% of demand. A unit on our base installed a donated air conditioner in a village school last week, but the school does not have enough power to run it. Students who live in major cities frequently experience outages that halt homework and other evening activities. The students might not complain but their parents certainly do.

Are Iraqis free? Free to do what? The continued violence hinders the national soccer team from practicing as they wish. Many cities lack proper sanitation, banks sometimes close lacking enough cash to complete daily transactions, stores close when the anti-Iraqi forces broadcast specific threats. What does freedom really mean if Iraqis live in constant fear, mistrust their government, lack essential services, watch their oil proceeds disappear in a quagmire of contract chaos and have no solid hope for effective change? Would it surprise Pres. Bush to discover than many Iraqis view their current situation as little different, if not worse, than under Saddam? We did not give freedom to Iraq. We helped them exchange one nightmare for another. Freedom is something they will earn for themselves with our support, if they still want it.

Sometimes Americans talk about freedom as if our brand of political freedom is the only true freedom available in the universe. Other Americans, usually multi-level marketing recruiters, promote a freedom lived by those whose income does not solely depend on their individual efforts. Parole officers remind their new wards to embrace their freedom and refrain from activities that would result in re-incarceration. Madison Avenue agencies spend millions of client dollars convincing us to purchase products that will endow us with the freedom of additional free time. The American Civil Liberties Union (ACLU) and the National Organization for Women (NOW) believe in reproductive freedom. Our Constitution guarantees freedom of the press, assembly, exercise of religion and address of grievances. Americans are swimming, or perhaps drowning, in freedom.

Our federal politicians court favor with political action committees rather than the voters. The two national parties decide whom to favor with candidacy. Elections resemble a choice between the lesser of two evils since political pay-offs at taxpayer expense continue no matter who is in office. The government bureaucracy and unconstitutional appropriation of power reserved to the people increases annually. I feel increasingly disdainful during election cycles as politicians triumph freedom, remind me of my duties to vote in our free society, yet fail to uphold their own constitutionally mandated responsibilities. Where are the politicians who will reduce the government's authority and return real freedom back to the people?

Someone high in a multi-level marketing program once told me that I was not free if I worked for someone else. Having made a free choice to work for a church at that time, I quoted "if the Son sets you free, you will be free indeed" (John 8:36).

He replied, "You are not free if you are trading time for dollars."

"I am already free," I insisted. He claimed to be a Christian yet deemed his material wealth earned for him by the efforts of other people a freedom superior to grace freely bestowed by God available for the asking. He totally missed my point and probably thought I missed his.

I would not want to be confined in a prison cell yet most of the apostles spent time in jail and lived free. They gladly traded their personal freedom for the privilege of suffering for the cause of Christ. Human physical, social, political or academic constraints cannot inhibit the freedom God gives to His children. People God sets free possess a liberty judges, parole boards or the conclusion of sentences cannot grant.

Most people I know back home are busy. Incredibly busy. Some too busy to raise their own kids. Others too busy to even say hello. They promise to do lunch, give time to charity efforts, or finish a private project when they have the time. Surrounded by a plethora of time saving gadgets they still have only 24 hours in a day. Their live style of convenience ends up owning them as they work to maintain payments, insurance and a house big enough to store everything they have no time to use. Madison avenue may promise free time but it never delivers. People would possess more freedom if they remember that merchandisers sell merchandise and advertising agencies sell advertising.

I learned early in life that if I would plant a seed in fertile ground it would start growing. We used this principle to grow vegetables in a garden and grains in a field. I learned that the seed changes almost immediately. No matter which way one plants most seeds the sprouts grow up and find the essential air and sunshine. If disturbed too early the plants will not grow properly. Life for plants begins the moment seeds combine with the necessary soil environment. When does human life begin?

Some political organizations such as the ACLU and NOW ignore the question of when human life begins to focus on the mother's reproductive freedom. I would rather live in a society where abortions are legal yet never happen than a society in which abortions occur despite their prohibition. The law is not the issue. Abortions do not happen because they are allowed, they happen because women exercise their reproductive freedom to end an unwanted pregnancy, to end a human life growing inside of them.

I am not convinced that caring Christians should focus our efforts on making abortion illegal. If a woman does not want a child can we trust her to properly nurture that life growing inside of them? Should we force her to abstain from alcohol, tobacco and drugs? Should we force her to consume nutritional supplements, play classical music, read to her baby and lovingly involve the child's father in her pregnancy? Yes, human life begins at conception, but human life is more than a biological process. What good have we achieved if we force someone to deliver her baby and she brings a child into the world who has no chance to survive? Reproduction is not a freedom. It is a responsibility.

We typically use the word freedom to mean a state in which somebody is able to act and live as he or she chooses, without being subject to any undue, restraints and restrictions. As He did with so many human concepts, Jesus redefined freedom. He came to set us free from the power of sin and death, from having no choice other than to serve our sinful nature, from the concerns and worries of human existence, from the love of money. We should cherish and promote God's freedom above all others.

08-27-04 * News From The Front

Our unit celebrated our halfway milestone with a synthetic luau. We entered the "in-country" phase of our tour six months ago. A half-way party is more speculation than assured reality as the military could extend our orders past the promised maximum one year in-country as it has for several units in Mosul already.

Our officers purchased a palm tree, hula skirts, parrots and even a female hula dancer all made of inflatable plastic. The luau feast contained non-alcoholic beer and wine, smoked salmon, stale pepperoni, chips, salsa and a few expired dips from the back of the refrigerator. My laptop, connected to computer speakers, played a remix of luau party favorites including *Blue Hawaii*, *Wipe Out*, and several Beach Boy imitations.

A couple of the guys donned coconut shell bikini tops over their PT uniforms. We laughed at silly antics, told stupid jokes and listened as unit storytellers regaled us with memorable incidents all while rotating at least one person to constantly monitor the radios and phones.

Later than night, the Iraqi soccer team defeated Morocco to earn a spot in the Olympic semi-finals. The locals celebrated with increased AK-47 fire and flares, this time including several mortar rounds that landed on the airfield. No injuries or significant damage ensued. Fortunately the terrorists do not have accurate delivery systems for their mortars and rockets.

More people would describe me as impassive rather than emotional, logical compared to intuitive. There are times, however, when logic fails to adequately explain life's twists of fate or sort through my morass of coagulated feelings. Logically I can explain why I would feel a greater sense of loss at the passing of someone close to me. Logically I understand that soldiers die in combat zones, as did four marines in Baghdad today. Logically I know that more Americans die on the highways of our own country than die on the roadways in Iraq. Logically I cannot explain why the passing of a lieutenant I do not know leaves me feeling despondent.

Twenty-five, happily married, and father to a two year old daughter, we knew the lieutenant as a cheerful man who loved his family and country. He supported our work in Iraq and accompanied his unit's convoys even though his position did not require him to do so. He led from the front, never asking his platoon to do anything he would not do himself. The IED killed him on his wife's birthday. One bright flash later and he heads home early in a body bag, wrapped like a present with his wife's name on the delivery tag.

The lieutenant is the second fallen soldier from his unit since they received extension orders keeping them in Iraq past their one-year deadline. Tomorrow I will focus on my duties and carry on with the mission. Today I feel we should just leave Iraq to fend for itself.

A Turkish citizen, who also owns a home in Ft. Lauderdale, opened a food court with four separate stations that serve pizza, Mexican cuisine, fried chicken and hamburgers. He hired young men from Turkey, brought them to Iraq and taught them to create American favorites. To me, the food does not seem worth the price, especially considering we have food available four times per day at no charge. Nevertheless, he sold $6,800 worth of pizzas his first day. Our shift asked me to pick one up for the office. While I waited for the pizza the owner asked if I would be willing to converse with a Turkish worker who wants to learn English. The owner mentioned that he heard me speaking to the staff and thought my articulation would facilitate the learning process. I am sure he had his reasons for not selecting the guys from Alabama and Mississippi ahead of me in line. The Turkish young man asked me questions that one might ask while traveling. When he asked me my age, I answered his question but told him that he should avoid asking American females their age.

That evening I left the office after an hour, figuring I spent enough time there on my night off. The Turks were having a volleyball game on a sand and gravel court with a net strung between two poles wedged inside garbage cans. One side of the court abutted demolition scrap metal. One side only fielded five players so I asked them if I could join. They welcomed me graciously. The first game seemed to be "pick on the American" by the other team. Almost every serve came my way no matter my rotation position. I held my ground and earned acceptance in the group. Only one of them spoke a smattering of English yet we communicated through gestures and smiles. I enjoyed the time with them. The experience reinforced to me that the differences between people do not need to be walls or barriers to friendship or cooperation.

A patrol recently discovered a cache containing more mortars and rockets that we historically receive in a month of attacks. I hoped the confiscation would lead to at least a temporary decrease in indirect fire. Today, however, an anonymous mortar team lobbed a double volley at the base. No injuries, very little damage, just lots of paperwork.

The Iraqi soccer team lost their semi-final game so they play in the Bronze match on the 27th. I read an article on the soccer team's reaction to statements made by President Bush about the freedom we gave Iraq. I do not often disagree publicly with the president but I think he should find another way to express the Iraqi Freedom campaign.

After a few weeks most soldiers learn to distinguish sounds of mortars, rockets, impacts or explosions from garbage dumpster lids banging shut and the wind knocking equipment over. Shortly before midnight, we heard a thwump, then a second, third, tenth, fourteenth. So much for the cache discovery diminishing their delivery. Even though the mortars landed near a living area, no injuries resulted. On the same day as the lieutenant's memorial service many others are spared the same fate.

The day after largest volley of mortar rounds we finally a quiet day on base. The violence in our area, while lamentable, pales in comparison to Najaf and Baghdad. Both Ayatollah Sistani and cleric al-Sadr are calling for people to march to the shrine in Najaf; Sistani calling for a peaceful rescue of the city and al-Sadr fomenting a violent expulsion of coalition forces. Howard Cossell might call it "The showdown of the Shiite clerics in Najaf". Fox News originally reported that American forces launched a mortar attack against one mosque acting as a gathering point for Sistani followers. We do not possess any of those mortars in Iraq. News blurbs now blame unknown insurgents. The battle fought in the press may be as important as the one fought in the streets. I still pray for a peaceful resolution to this extremely important event.

I find explaining intuition a difficult exercise. I do not know how it works. Between thought and feeling lies a realm of human experience that answers to neither. Intuition reveals the truth behind façades, explains events impenetrable by deductive analysis, and can produce a certainty in unforeseeable future occurrences. I walked to the office Monday evening feeling certain that we were in for a busy night.

The night before I had believed the opposite. One of our officers asked the seven people present to predict how many and what type of mortar or rocket rounds we would receive that night, together with when and where they would impact the airfield. I told him emphatically that we would not receive any rounds during our shift. I felt certain even though we had received indirect fire consistently for several nights in a row. Some scoffed, others chuckled, and I maintained my position. When the sun rose, and our shift ended, the event board remained blank.

Monday evening I hoped that same officer would not repeat his quiz. I did not know when, where, what type, I only knew attacks were coming. I walked into the office and spotted five boxes with my name on them. They contained one hundred individually bagged donations for Iraqi school children. I did not even have a school trip lined up yet. I stowed the boxes in a corner and started reading reports. Even though I could find no specific indications of terrorist activity that night from any sources, my conviction did not waiver.

In less than twelve hours, we had five separate incidents involving rockets, two types of mortars, IEDs, RPGs and small arms fire. One US and one Iraqi National Guard (ING) soldier killed, one US and six ING soldiers hospitalized, numerous civilians injured, and a few vehicles destroyed. The entire night remains a blur, thoughts and emotions still swirling from one event when the next one started. By the end of our shift, my brain's analytical value rivaled the Jell-O desserts in our dining room.

What purpose does intuition serve if tragedies cannot be averted or prepared for? People did not sleep easier Sunday night because I strongly believed we would not receive any attacks. Even if I had the power to change any of the airfield operations Monday night, I would not. Based on what? One guy, walking across a gravel parking lot, after eating a military dinner for his breakfast because that's when he wakes up every day, has a strong feeling, a premonition, a precognitive pseudo-revelation with no angels, no parting of the heavens and no helpful details. We are already at the highest alert status and do not need a frenzied prophet shouting generic indications of impending doom.

I returned to my room that morning with my first battlefield souvenir; a 4" x 1.5" section of the brass base plate of a 107mm rocket. Not pretty, hard to polish and containing several sharp ridges from the explosion, I kept it because I do not yet have a brass paperweight for the attorney office I expect to occupy next summer.

Some mornings I run around the airfield rather than exercise in the gym, an activity frowned on but not restricted. While exiting my room in my PT clothes, I heard another explosion to the north of the airfield. The captain that lives next to me stepped out of his room, listening to radio reports of the incident. I am glad not to warrant issuance of a radio to connect me with the office 24 hours every day.

"Did you hear that boom?" he asked.

"Yes," I responded. "It sounded like an IED north of the airfield." We both listened to the radio for a few minutes. We could also hear several volleys of gunfire from the same direction. All reports indicated a situation to the north with no impact directly on the airfield.

"Are you still going running?" I wondered if he meant to imply that I should cancel my itinerary given the current intensity. I paused, hoping for some intuitive declaration. Nothing.

"Stupid, useless intuition" I thought to myself.

"Yes," I replied audibly to the captain.

"Well, stay safe," he urged and held the radio closer to his ear.

The run did not reduce my stress levels as much as it usually does. For the first time I did not feel fully at ease running around the perimeter. I also did not sleep well following my shower. I woke up frequently to even innocent noises. Two hours ahead of schedule, I stopped trying to force myself to sleep and decided to put my restlessness to more productive pursuits.

I located the office of someone rumored to have connections to school trips. A co-worker thought he might return later in the evening. No luck. I dropped off two uniforms at a laundry facility and then walked to one of the local shops for their version of a fruit smoothie. Four soldiers sat around a table, two of them holding a tiny kitten each. One of the soldiers moved his pinky while the kitten tried to paw at it. The second kitten completely rested in the other soldier's hands. I watched them for several minutes. My wife is convinced I wanted to hold a kitten myself, but I felt content to remain to the side. Seeing the kittens helped me get out of my personal fog of war and back to life. I wish I had my camera with me to help me remember seeing four macho soldiers tenderly playing with kittens. I headed to the chow hall for my dinner-breakfast and the start of another shift.

As I headed to the windowless room where I spend most of my waking hours, no intuitive impressions of potential shift events crossed my mind. Instead, I laughed at the thought of trying to answer someone asking me, "So, how was your day yesterday?" I decided I would simply reply, "Busy. How about yours?"

09-10-04 * News From the Front

While finishing the e-mail for last week I learned that a drive-by shooting killed four women who work on our base. In the past few weeks, many Iraqis who work on our base received threats in person or by letter. These women, 19–21, had not reported receiving threats. They were simply gunned down on their way home. I did not know them personally but know several people who worked with them. The women worked cheerfully in the hospital laundry.

The incident caused other workers to evaluate their support for our base. The number of local workers dwindles daily. The tribal or family retribution system protects some; others now live on base, protected as long as the military remains here. The terrorists frequently favor Muslims with greater tolerance. The four assassinated women were all Christians, perhaps the singular characteristic that brought about their selection as examples for others who support the United States.

The memorial service held in our chapel brought tears to many, both to those who knew them well and those of us who missed the opportunity.

Mosul's police department does not appear to be doing everything it can to bring such thugs to justice. Rumors of high-level corruption abound, implicating police leadership in looking the other way in exchange for money or promises of safety for themselves and their families. At the same time our government continues to pour millions of U.S. taxpayer money into strengthening the police department. Although I have no evidence to support this opinion, I would not be surprised if the police chief left quietly in the night and audits revealed significant shortages.

Benign official reports about the clash in Tal 'Afar on September 4th disturb me for reasons that I shall soon explain. First, a synopsis of the reports from the military press and from a local TV station.

As described by U.S. military official reports:

Military operations to bring stability and security to the city of Tal 'Afar began this morning when Soldiers from the 3rd Brigade, 2nd Infantry Division Stryker Brigade Combat Team (SBCT) entered the city in search of Anti-Iraqi

Forces (AIF). Soldiers detained one and killed two AIF. At approximately 8 a.m., Stryker Brigade Soldiers initiated operations to capture or kill members of a known terrorist cell operating in the Tal 'Afar area, approximately 50 kilometers west of Mosul.

Around 9 a.m., an OH-58D Kiowa helicopter made a controlled landing near Tal 'Afar. The two crew-members received non-life threatening injuries during the landing. They have both been evacuated to our military hospital. At approximately 9:20 a.m., a Stryker vehicle securing the site of the downed helicopter received rocket propelled grenade fire, disabling the vehicle. There were no injuries to any of the Stryker crew-members. Recovery operations began for both the Stryker and the Kiowa. While securing the site of the vehicles, Multinational Forces (MNF) continued to receive enemy fire. MNF returned fire, killing two terrorists. At approximately 10:40 a.m., in response to continued enemy fire, close air support was called in, dropping a bomb in an area near the city. No casualties have been reported.

The city of Tal 'Afar has been a suspected haven for terrorists crossing into Iraq from Syria. Multinational and Iraqi Security Forces have targeted the city to rid it of the AIF conducting terrorist activities throughout the northern region and to bring peace and stability to the innocent civilians who live in the city.

According to an Al-Jazeera broadcast:

[Reporter] al-Jazeera has learned that clashes are under way between gunmen and the US forces in the city of Tal 'Afar. There have been reports that dead and wounded people were taken to the city's hospital. I have with me from Tal 'Afar hospital Dr. Khalil Rashid. Dr Rashid, can you tell us the number of the wounded who arrived at the hospital?

[Rashid] The number of the wounded is about 50 and the number of martyrs is about 12. The clashes and the air bombings continue. Five minutes ago, the Iraqi Army opened fire on citizens in front of the hospital. A citizen was martyred five minutes ago.

[Reporter] What are the causes of their wounds? Were they hit by gunshots?

[Rashid] Most of the wounds were caused by warplanes. Houses were damaged over the heads of their inhabitants. Most of the wounded we have received were hit by shrapnel of missiles fired by warplanes.

[Reporter] Are any of the wounded civilians?

[Rashid] Yes, all of them are civilians—children and women. We have transferred five women suffering from fractions and others who are seriously wounded to Mosul. We have in the operating room citizens who are seriously injured. They are all civilians.

[Reporter] Did you learn from the wounded who managed to speak about the reason for this raid and these clashes?

[Rashid] The pretext is that there is armed resistance in the town. The city has been surrounded since this morning. There are huge vehicles and planes. The district has been besieged since this morning as if it has become a closed military zone.

[Reporter] Dr. Rashid, speaking from Tal 'Afar hospital where clashes are under way between a number of gunmen and the U.S. forces, thank you very much for these statements.[end of broadcast]

The Department of Defense decided before the Operation Iraqi Freedom campaign that it would not report civilian casualty counts caused by U.S. action, but it does report civilian casualties attributed to AIF actions. The terrorists in the latter release "indiscriminately" fired a rocket and injured eight. The bomb dropped near Tal 'Afar contained more than 100 times the explosive power of a 107mm rocket. No casualties reported? Or no casualties that we wish to disclose?

Many residents of Tal 'Afar and Mosul believe the U.S. is frequently more indiscriminate than the terrorists. The U.S. government privately spends hundreds of millions of dollars to compensate civilian victims while terrorists do not, but the U.S. does not take public accountability for some of its actions here and many Iraqis are understandably furious. We talk about the peace and stability we bring to innocent civilians yet refuse to discuss that at times we may cause more damage than the terrorists.

I am not questioning the military decisions in Tal 'Afar. I am simply disturbed that our government does not acknowledge the full effect of our actions here. I am not surprised that many Iraqis do not trust us. Our official statements sometimes report casualties as anti-Iraqi forces those who simply want the terrorists and the United States to leave them alone. Occasionally Iraqis have a hard time distinguishing between the two sides based on our actions. When a piece of shrapnel kills someone they love, knowing Americans caused the impact does not help them feel better.

09-10-04 * VILLAGE TRIP

The 100 individually bagged sets of school supplies arrived, unfortunately, after heightened threat levels and fiscal year end budget closures ceased school support trips. I spoke with a Captain who needed to visit three small villages east of Kasroq. He offered to let me tag along.

Our convoy convened at 7:00 am, one hour after I finished a twelve-hour shift. My first duty consisted of inflating a dozen smiley-face volleyballs. I placed one on the hood of our vehicle for a photograph and noticed a sticker on the windshield (*VT 1*). I asked our driver about Trevor Win'E and discovered that he was a 23 year-old gunner who died on a previous mission. Our driver assured me that he had logged 12,000 miles in that HMMWV. The Captain muttered that he often feared the Sergeant's driving more than IED attacks.

Leaving base still requires a convoy of several vehicles and full battle gear (*VT 2*). Some of the convoys for that day were cancelled in anticipation of the events in Tal 'Afar that have since made worldwide news. The Captain decided we would proceed as planned since our destination lie in the opposite direction and since his Colonel was not on base to tell him otherwise. The villages are in the Kurdish area of northeastern Iraq, a region controlled by the Kurdish Peshmerga forces. The Peshmerga, driven from their homes by Saddam, are strong American allies and brave warriors. The terrorists do not have a history of attacks in their area. Not surprising, humanitarian efforts continue in the Kurdish villages while ceasing in more combative areas of Iraq. The terrorists hurt Iraqi communities in multiple ways.

While traveling through Mosul, the most dangerous part of our trip, I realized that no one on the street corners held a "Homeless, will work for food" sign. Instead, men or children (I did not notice any women so employed) at every intersection offer a selection of sundries for passing motorists or pedestrians. In the U.S. we require business licenses for anyone who wants to set up a roadside stand. One can panhandle without a license and perhaps earn more money from passersby than from starting a roadside business. Two of the young salesmen gestured for me to take their photograph (*VT 3*).

After two hours of driving, we turned into a school in Kasroq. I thought we reached our destination but discovered a prearranged guide / translator to take us to the villages. He proved necessary as reaching the villages required navigating a maze of rough roads through the Minor Zab river valley. Even with our guide leading the convoy we needed to turn around a few times after unnecessarily fjording the river. Finally we found the collection of villages, nestled on a rocky hillside overlooking the valley. We drove past two smaller villages, beginning with Bebava at the end of the road.

Bebava contains about 120 houses, all mud huts with thatched roofs and holes for windows and door (*VT 4*). Bebava, as most villages, is governed by a Muktar, a political office similar to a mayor but usually held for life. Only a few homes include an area for visiting with guests. We did not enter any of the residences but toured the village pathways and visited with the Muktar and other leaders in the Muktar's common room, one of the few rooms to have electricity and a swamp cooler. The room also contains one of perhaps three television sets in this village, connected to the outside world by a 70's style satellite receiver. My home contains more television sets, and probably more channel selection than this entire community enjoys. The village has no telephones, no bathroom facilities, only outdoor kitchens and nothing to suggest privacy. I hear that married couples take long walks together at night when they need to get away.

The homes I glanced into did not contain furniture of any kind. The centers of the rooms remain bare while fabric-covered foam pads line the walls. They eat and sleep on these foam mats. I counted only three automobiles in the village, all at least twenty years old. One well provides water for everyone in Bebava. The water flows downhill to a pump house built by UNICEF in the 1970's. The pump delivers water through surface irrigation pipes to the water tanks dotting the village. People draw water from a tank as they need it. The square metal container in VT04 is one of the water tanks.

One 110KW generator provides all of Bebava's electricity. The generator is smaller than the one that runs just our gymnasium. Wires run from house to house about six feet off the ground. I had to duck several times. I do not feel comfortable knowing small children play near accessible 220v lines but that is life in the village.

The Captain came on this trip to ask the Muktars what basic needs we may be able to support. The Muktar of Bebava reported that the generator is too small for the village, an assertion we already believed without his testimony. He also mentioned that the pump needs repairs. The Captain promised help with both issues.

Previous trips to this area resulted in plans submitted to Baghdad for electric lines from Kasroq to service the villages and relieve them of a need for generators. The plans received approval by Baghdad but the local governor squashed the plans to divert the funds to other electrical projects. The Muktar believes they are denied power because they are Peshmerga and fought against Saddam's army. The entire northern area receives less than 50% of its current demand even though it produces most of the electricity for all of Iraq. Rather than prepare another proposal doomed to failure, the Captain hopes to secure several generators from Kuwait and have local contractors install one in each of these villages.

VT04 also shows bricks set aside for new construction. The villagers form these bricks in the riverbed, about a ten-minute walk away. We drove by the brick-making area and I did not see any wood for forms. There is an area near the river they fill with the proper dirt, divert the river flow to form the right consistency, then cut bricks out of the morass and set them aside to dry in the sun. Most of the buildings in the village, with the notable exceptions of the mosque, Muktar's residence and the school, are made with these bricks and finished with a smooth layer of mud.

The women remained distant from us. They did not interact with even the female soldiers on our convoy. VT04 is my closest proximity to any women's group in any of the villages.

The Iraqi government delayed school openings this September for two weeks. The village school was not yet open for classes. The school in Bebava and the neighboring village only offer education through the sixth grade (*VT 5*). A relief agency, Qandil, helped construct both schools in 1997, replacing the open, mud hut facilities with the enclosed, electrical powered and swamp-cooler enhanced structure the villagers here prize and even American inner-city school districts would reject. Most village children do not have an opportunity to advance to the high school in Kasroq because of transportation issues and because the village needs them to work the fields. I asked the Muktar, through the interpreter, how many children attended the school. He estimated at least 150. For a village with less than 120 homes I was at first surprised that Bebava would have so many children in the first through sixth grade age range. I discovered that life expectancy is not on par with American standards for various reasons, including war, and that the village depends on the young labor force for its very survival.

The Captain and I decided in advance how to allocate the five boxes. This village would receive only one, a paltry offering in the face of so great a need. The Captain also informed me that it would be bad form to give bags to 20 children while others stood waiting but received nothing. I decided to present the box to the Muktar and leave its distribution to his discretion. I did not personally distribute any of the school bags as I had anticipated.

The primary crops in the river valley are the thick, long grass they use for their rooftops and baskets, and the skinny trees they harvest as poles for the roof structures (*VT* 6). The village sells excess poles at $3 - $5 depending on length, quality and season. Some of the land within the village is set aside for vegetable gardens. I thought a distant field contained a melon crop but did not confirm my idea with the interpreter.

The village mosque is visible in the upper right corner (*VT* 6). I did not notice a mosque in the two smaller nearby villages so this mosque might serve all three. There are no other churches or missions in the area. I thought the mosque small for just Bebava, but then I do not know how Muslims conduct services or to what extent these villagers practice the Islamic religion. I also did not see any medical clinics or signs of commercial enterprises. No cafes, bank, clothing or shoe stores, no recreation or entertainment facilities. The one street corner does not even have a Starbuck's! No offices for attorneys, accountants, newspapers or government services. Everyone other than the Muktar, school-teacher and cleric appear to have the same job – supporting the community by working in the fields. The village collectively owns the fields it works. Bebava is a nice place to visit but I would not want to live there.

The other two villages we visited are about a 10-minute drive west of Bebava. One school serves both villages, which, together, are smaller than Bebava. I do not know the history of why these two groups of people, only a few minutes walk apart, distinguish themselves as distinct villages each with its own Muktar. I did not see a mosque in either village. I also did not see any connections for satellite reception to homes other than the Muktar's community room or neck-high electrical lines. I could not imagine life more remote than Bebava but we found it.

The remoteness of the villages or the absence of modern technology should not lead us to pity these Kurds or think of them in lowly terms. In the midst of abundance, many Americans express less gratitude than these villagers. We lose a higher percentage of our young people to drugs and alcohol than these villages lose to lack of medicine. We should learn from their communal strength and the family bonds that last even when people move to more populated or modern cities.

I left one box with each Muktar of these two villages and one with the Head Master of the school (*VT 7*). The school serves both villages and is the sole building between them. The eastern village of this pair can be seen almost in its entirety in a shot taken from the school (*VT 8*).

I walked from the school back to the trucks still parked at the second village (*VT 9*) to lead them to a good parking area in the third village. I ran ahead of the trucks and some of the boys decided to race me. Wearing the full body-armor and carrying my M-16 I doubted I could keep up with these kids who walk or run every day but I gave it an all-American try. *VT 10* shows three of the boys after the race, them barely breathing hard, my panting fogging the camera viewer. The kids all wanted to see themselves on my camera screen. I could have filled my memory stick with photographs of village children but I deleted most of them after showing the children their picture on the viewing screen.

The Captain asked each Muktar how we could best help their villages. The Muktars each expressed concerns of access to electricity and water. Their individual generators and wells do not supply enough utilities for even the most basic needs.

All three Muktars served us both water and a sweet tea. By the end of the third visit we needed to relieve ourselves of some of their hospitality but none of the villages incorporated public restrooms into their tourism program. We waited. As we left the community room in the third village, the translator told the four of us meeting with the Muktar that he had written our names in the village register. His house is now our house and if we ever visit again we will be especially welcomed. This trip reinforced a lesson my mother tried to each me years ago; behave in such a manner that we will be welcomed back.

After the meeting with the third Muktar our official party returned to find our convoy personnel enjoying the company of the villages' younger generation (*VT 11*). We attempted a group portrait. I snapped *VT 12* then handed my camera off to another soldier so I could add myself to the disorganized muddle. Other soldiers also passed their cameras to her and ran to the crowd. Unfortunately, she took pictures in reverse order of receiving the cameras. By the time she reached my camera most of the kids had left. In *VT 13* I am one of the two soldiers wearing a hat.

As we packed to leave, we discovered a duffle bag half full with stuffed animals. The Captain started to hand them out. The kids instantly pressed around him, their hands held out, yelling requests in their native language (VT 14). The Muktar from the third village arrived to help keep some order. One of the men

I met in the Muktar official party gestured to me that I interpreted to mean he had a baby girl at home. I told the Captain who then presented the man with a stuffed tiger. He looked extremely happy and thanked me for several minutes. The Captain recognized an outstretched hand as belonging to a kid who had already received a stuffed animal. The Captain teasingly scolded him (VT15).

Climbing into the HMMWV one of the young men that ran with me earlier asked me to take his picture. As I focused for his shot (*VT 16*), I noticed the heads of several women above a wall behind him, the only time I recall seeing any of the women in that village.

Our translator arranged an early dinner in the home of a relative in Kasroq, a town of about 5,000 people approximately 45 minutes west of these villages. Kasroq boasts one paved road, the only high school in the district, running water of dubious quality, electrical service and a few vendor stands in the commercial district.

Parking six military vehicles near our host's modest home drew significant attention from neighborhood children. Two of the twenty soldiers stayed with the trucks and the gathering children. The Captain asked me earlier if we could save one box for our host family. I carried it up the outside stairs and presented it to the owner of the house. It disappeared downstairs. I hoped to finally distribute some bags directly to their intended recipients but even hear cultural mores superseded my plans. The top floor of this home, perhaps the only one in Iraq I will visit, consists of an open patio, a room remarkably similar to the village community rooms and the local version of a bathroom. Still waiting since the village tea services for an appropriate moment, I gratefully accepted their offer. I washed my dusty hands in the freestanding sink on the patio near the door, and then walked in. The bathroom contained a ceramic basin in the floor with a hole in the center, a hose hung on the wall and a small vent near the ceiling. I decided not to peer into the hole to investigate peculiarities of the Kasroq plumbing.

VT 17 is taken from the rooftop patio overlooking their back yard. On the center left of this photograph is another home with a second story similar to the one I stood on; a multi-purpose room and a smaller, almost portable chemical toilet size, bathroom. Most of the homes do not sport an upper room. I wondered if the New Testament upper room resembles these rooms. *VT 18* reveals about one-third of the room. The shelves on the wall, the TV setup, the foam pads on the floor and the size of the room remarkably resemble the rooms in which we met the village Muktars. Only the men of the house ate dinner with us.

I discovered more than thirty people live in this one house about the size of our home that I consider too small for our family of four. The men are from the same family. Asking questions about family life in this house I learned that one of the brothers is married to two wives. He has seven children with one and six with the other. His family accounts for sixteen of the home's thirty residents. I thought about that revelation for several minutes. Same bedroom with both wives or do they all have separate rooms? The house did not seem large enough to give even just the adults their own rooms. I asked the translator how it worked for someone to have two wives. He relayed that a man must demonstrate that he can financially support two wives and that the first wife must approve of the second. That is the extent of my knowledge about marrying two women, an aspect of the Iraqi culture my wife, Philese, told me I will never be allowed to practice.

This family, not rich even by Kasroq standards, prepared an incredible meal for us. A younger male spread a plastic tablecloth between the two sides of the room. One large rice and chicken plate and one vegetable tray per two people plus individual servings of two kinds of soup, a fatty meat that I did not try and a bowl of noodles. Recognizing the generosity this family extended us, and the number of children this home supported, made me feel glad that we reserved one of the boxes for them.

After the same young men that set the dinner cleared it away, the head of the house offered everyone a Turkish cigarette (I declined) and sweet tea. Then two small girls appeared. The translator informed me that the family wished to express their gratitude for the box. The girls gave me a hug and sat on my lap for a few minutes. I could not get both of them to look at the camera at the same time. In *VT 19* I am talking to the girl looking at me, trying to get her to look at the person taking the photograph.

I wish I could travel to different villages every week but this is likely my only trip. Allotments for the next fiscal year, beginning in October, do not yet include a budget of finances or personnel for these humanitarian visits. This work might continue through non-profit organizations such as USAID, Qandil, or UNICEF, although they will not likely resume operations here until the safety level increases.

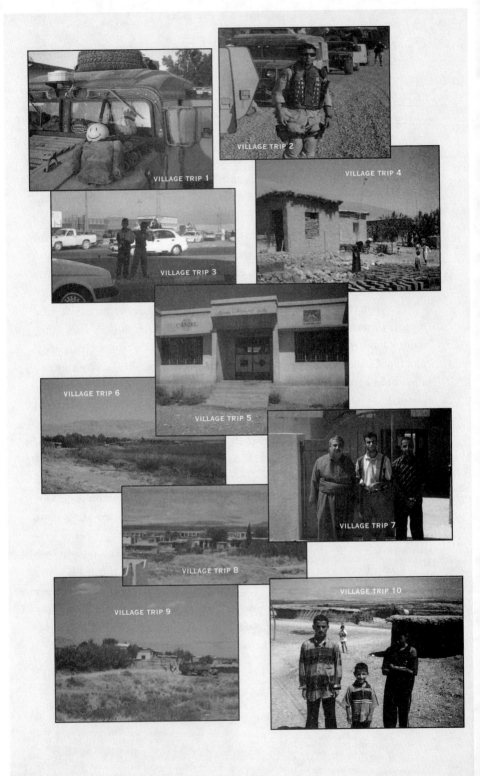

VILLAGE TRIP 1

VILLAGE TRIP 2

VILLAGE TRIP 3

VILLAGE TRIP 4

VILLAGE TRIP 5

VILLAGE TRIP 6

VILLAGE TRIP 7

VILLAGE TRIP 8

VILLAGE TRIP 9

VILLAGE TRIP 10

Life in the Kurdish villages revolves around their Islamic faith. In Bebava the mosque and school are the only buildings not constructed with the bricks that shape their homes. The Kurds exude an intriguing strength and presence.[6] Although the lack of amenities, if not basic necessities, negates any personal desire to live in such surroundings, I admire the faith of the people. They demonstrate the possibility, at least on a village level, to live as a people united under faith, under God. I wonder if harmony would still prevail if one of the village residents converted to Christianity.

Iraq as a nation does not share the unified faith characteristic. The nation is divided along tribal and religious boundaries, the Sunnis and the Shi'ites not trusting each other enough to even form a government together. Although both Muslim sects share the belief that government should listen to God, their differing philosophies of how God speaks to humanity keep them distant rather than united. Watching the development of faith and national identity in Iraq leaves me pondering whether it is possible or advisable for people of diverse theological creeds to live as one nation under God.

Some Americans believe we should remove the words "under God" from the pledge of allegiance. I actually agree with them but not for the reasons they espouse.

At or near the pinnacle of a Top Ten list of things for Christians not to do is taking God's name in vain. It is spiritual suicide, a one-way ticket to hell without passing "GO". More importantly, it is disrespectful to God. Our society flippantly remarks "God damn this" or "with God as my witness" or "God is going to get you for that". What would happen to us if God really did damn everything and everyone just because a Christian said so? To the extent that we do not yearn for God's involvement every time we invoke His name or character we take His name in vain. As a church and nation we invite divine reproach if we incorporate God into our oaths but then do not follow through in our actions.

A better goal for America would be to actually become and act like a nation under God. Although Biblical scholars continue to debate the extent to which a nation other than Israel can claim promises given by God to Israel, America's history clearly demonstrates that we have been blessed by God.[7] Many of God's blessings trickle down to both the just and the unjust. I do not, however, need to live in a Christian nation or a nation under God to be blessed by God. God already furnished the formula for receiving His blessings. (See Matt. 5:1-14). God will bless those who live in concert with His blueprint. Talking about Christian values and characteristics, or posting them on memorial wall, is insufficient.

God remarked of His people in the past that they honored Him with their lips but their hearts were far from Him. How would God judge the hearts of our leaders and our nation today? Our representatives and senators retort that their hearts are in the right place, that God needs only look at their intentions to know they are good people. Does it really matter if they steal to accomplish their intentions, cover their abominations with lies, outcast anyone who does not follow their directives? Yes, righteousness matters. Herod cut off the head of John the Baptist for pointing out Herod's sin before God. The voice of righteousness in our nation is likewise silenced, albeit through media chastisement, civil rights legislation, political correctness and bureaucratic regulation rather than outright execution. Our federal government might display the Ten Commandments and open with prayer for historical, traditional reason but in practice it does not operate under God.

One could argue that the government is different from the people and we the people are the nation under God. We the people elect our government. In the past people demanded a righteous, God-fearing character of their elected officials. Now we demand someone who can manipulate the system to direct the most largesse from the treasury out of the wallets of others into our own pockets. We crave entertainment to the point of addiction, tolerating distasteful productions because of the lack of alternatives rather than saying no. Christianity as a concept of righteous action is greatly diminishing even though a majority of Americans choose the label "Christian" when asked to state a preference. We have the government we deserve. We chose it and it reflects us a nation, a nation not operating under God.

The Bible promises blessings for rulers, judges and people who follow God's laws. America continues to be blessed because God fearing men and women charted a course for our manifest destiny. Some leaders today want to change that course and steer us in a new direction. They believe we will all be better off if we remove God from our courts, schools, legislative bodies and even Christmas. They want to control God rather than submit to Him. They want to create a nation OVER God and celebrate their progress by paying homage to other gods and religions. I do not want to be participating in their programs when God allows them to see the futility of their ways.

I would rather live in a country blessed by God, in a country ruled by righteous people. Yet the truth is that I do not need to live in a country under God in order to live as a Christian. Christians throughout history implemented their faith under unfathomable brutality. Shall we now, surrounded by such a great cloud of witnesses, bemoan our lives of faith today because the United States does not in fact function as a nation under God?

In the attempt to eradicate all religion from the government's thought process, the bureaucracy is creating a new religion. We are asked to bow or pledge allegiance to the power of the law. Our new temple is the courthouse and our priests the judiciary. Woe unto those who challenge the power of the system or point out its flaws. Laws are just and compliance righteousness not because they conform to God's laws but simply because the system created the rules. Once leading the reformation against the divine right of kings, America is on the verge of replacing that tyrannical concept with the equally dangerous divine right of majorities.

Let them remove the words "under God" from our pledge of allegiance. They might discover that many people will no longer volunteer or vocalize their allegiance. Let them try to remove God from courts and schools. They do not realize that I, for one, invite God with to be with me everywhere I go. Students pray, whether the school sets aside time for prayer or not. Some judges, some teachers, some elected officials ask God for wisdom whether the rules allow them to or not. Some Christians increase their spiritual warfare activities in times of adversity.

Christians should allow a national discussion and decision of spiritual allegiance. We should participate by reminding each other, as Joshua did for the nation of Israel on the banks of the Jordan as recorded in Joshua chapter 24, of God's role in our nation's history. Some people believe that it is evil to serve God or to force them to pledge allegiance to God. We should allow them to articulate their concerns and then call for the vote. Choose. Publicly profess. Whom will we serve? God, yourself, the bureaucracy, other gods?

My choice is unconditionally set. Pass laws against belief in God, elevate the power of the majority to divine status, or even ban the discussion of God in public forums. You cannot change my mind or silence my voice. I believe in God.

September 11—Patriot Day; the third anniversary of a day that changed America. Following an uneventful night shift that did not live up to any of the doom and gloom prophecies, I decided to enjoy another run around the airbase. I am training for a 1/2 marathon scheduled here in November. The only other 1/2 marathon I ever participated in was the Capital City Marathon (Olympia, WA) in March 2000. I did not achieve my initial goal of crossing the finishing line in under two hours. I missed my goal by four minutes. This fall I want to beat two hours.

Terrorists altered life as we knew it in on 9-11. Our government used the attacks to justify reaching its cancerous tentacles deeper into our private lives. Rather than giving private citizens an expanded right to protect ourselves and our country, the government restricted our ability to do so and charges us exorbitant amounts of money for systems that, according to the 9-11 commission, still would not have prevented the attacks.

On 9-12-01, three weeks before my second year of law school, I called our unit office and asked to be placed on any available mission rosters. A few months later I received an assignment to assist the Border Patrol's Regional Intelligence Office conduct a survey of 350 miles of the US-Canadian border. Following that mission, I volunteered to work at the Counter-Drug Taskforce. Later I earned certification as an Anti-terrorism Officer and accepted a position at the Washington State Joint Operations Center, a position I held until mobilizing to Iraq.

My life changed significantly on 9/11 more because of the choices I made in response to the attacks than from any direct result of the tragedies endured. Sep. 11 reminds me that I have the freedom to choose whether I will live in fear or respond the challenges life presents. I prefer to call Sep. 11 my "Freedom to Choose" day. Today I chose to run an extra few miles around the perimeter road and fear of terrorists won't stop me.

Some ways of life we have no choice but to change; long lines at airport security check points, additional identification procedures for almost anything, acceptance of Big Brother's eye on society and now no running around clad only in PT clothes. Someone at command levels way above our base decided that we needed to implement a higher threat level. What terrorists could not achieve the government has done for them.

In my off-schedule time I chatted with two Turkish Americans who work on our base to ask their opinion on events in Tal 'Afar. The Turkish government is upset with American action in Tal 'Afar. One member of their government, on their national news, urged Turks to travel to Tal 'Afar and rally with the Turkmen population (Iraqis with Turkish ancestry) against the U.S. forces.

Colin Powell, U.S. Sec. of State, called his counterpart in Turkey to explain that the actions in Tal 'Afar are against the AIF forces only, not the Turkmen, and that we are striving to avoid civilian casualties. The political repercussions from Tal 'Afar could be more serious than those in the Najaf standoff against al-Sadr if Turkey reverses its support for our operations.

I learned this week that one of the family members that hosted us in Kasroq, an uncle to the two girls who sat on my lap, was murdered because his family supports Americans. In addition to providing meals to visiting soldiers the family completed several construction projects for bases in the area. I cannot describe the contempt I feel for the thugs who desecrated that family.

No significant terrorist activities impacted us during our increased threat level. The commander rescinded the extra protection measures this morning (14th). I celebrated with another run. When I neared a location half way around the base, a volley of mortars landed about 600 meters away. Since the mortars dropped in an area where they posed no danger to any troops, I watched the detonations with some fascination, the first time I witnessed live mortar explosions. The fascination disappears when attacks turned devastatingly deadly. One Washington soldier died in Mosul today and we lost more soldiers in other parts of the country. We have lost over 30 soldiers from our state now.

I attended mandatory mental and physical health briefings today. I learned, no big surprise, that I exhibit symptoms of post-traumatic stress disorder. However, diagnosis for PTSD requires that the symptoms persist for a certain period of time *after* the stress has ended. Since we currently remain in the stress and trauma we cannot have, by definition, PTSD. I am glad that the government recognizes service in Iraq as a stressor. I now know what symptoms to display if I feel like claiming PTSD later.

Today I also learned more about Purple Heart awards. A Purple Heart is not a medal of valor or bravery but a recognition that a certain wound occurred during battle. A Purple Heart is an entitlement and is bestowed when conditions are met whether the recipient wants it or not. The discussion of John Kerry's Purple Hearts never interested me for that very reason. I know soldiers here who received a Purple Heart for injuries that didn't even leave a scar. Some did not want the medal but were ordered to report to the hospital and document the injury. They met the qualifications. Others nearly die from their injuries yet received a singular Purple Heart award. A Purple Heart is not a matter of degree but a reflection of the cause of the injury.

One cannot exactly refuse a Purple Heart if it is awarded for an injury, yet one can avoid a Purple Heart by neglecting (failing, forgetting) to seek medical attention for the incident or, if medical attention is necessary, by not mentioning any connection to enemy activity. An enemy connection is rather obvious for some injuries, yet if an individual soldier does not want a Purple Heart for a minor injury he or she can usually find a way to manage the system.

I do not believe it is more honorable or heroic to avoid a Purple Heart than initiate one when applicable. Why then do some soldiers want to avoid Purple Hearts for minor wounds? The answers are as abundant as the soldiers who make that decision. What I do know is that the campaign trail attention on whether John Kerry deserved or didn't deserve a Purple Heart is overemphasized almost to the point of being ridiculous. If he received wounds as a result of enemy operations then he qualifies for a Purple Heart and that should be the end of the discussion.

This week I endured my return visit to the combat dentists. It started out with a statement by the dentist that he wanted to try today's root canal filling procedure without an anesthetic. Lacking proper exploratory or x-ray equipment, he relied on the "patient flinch method" to determine when his files reached the end of my tooth's roots. Using this method, a dentist probes a dental root with a round file until the patient flinches, and then he fills the hole to that depth. I am not a fan of the patient flinch method. I must have flinched incorrectly because we needed to repeat the canal procedure on one of the roots. When he resorted to a cigarette lighter as a heat source to cure the filling I decided to never again question high costs of good dental care back home.

09-24-04 * THE TURKMEN

The Transitional Administrative Law, passed in March 2004, and in force until replaced by the coming elected government, mentions the Turkmen three times:

Article 9: "The Arabic language and the Kurdish language are the two official languages of Iraq. The right of Iraqis to educate their children in their mother tongue, such as Turkmen, Syriac, or Armenian, in government educational institutions in accordance with educational guidelines, or In any other language in private educational institutions, shall be guaranteed."

Article 30: "(C) The National Assembly shall be elected in accordance with an electoral law and a political parties law. The electoral law shall aim to achieve the goal of having women constitute no less than one-quarter of the members of the National Assembly and of having fair representation for all communities in Iraq, including the Turkmen, ChaldoAssyrians, and others."

Article 53: "(D) This Law shall guarantee the administrative, cultural, and political rights of the Turkmen, ChaldoAssyrians, and all other citizens."

On 26 May 04, Iraqi Turkmen political organizations held a conference at the Babel Hotel in Baghdad. The purpose of the conference was to call on the United Nations and the Coalition Provisional Authority to grant the Turkmen full-legal rights and status in the "New Iraq" and bring about the restoration of their land and property seized by the former regime. It is unclear at this time whether the new government will acquiesce.

U.S. clashes with AIF in Tal 'Afar in mid-September reignited the Turkmen – Kurd political conflict. Kurdish soldiers make up a significant proportion of the Iraqi troops fighting with U.S. soldiers. Turkmen in Tal 'Afar complained that the Kurdish soldiers indiscriminately killed numerous Turkmen and were using the U.S. conflict as a mask to wage their own territorial cleansing. Turkmen leaders appealed to Turkey who in turn pressured the U.S. with threats of withdrawing support for Operation Iraqi Freedom. The tribal tension, not currently in headline news, still simmers just beneath the political surface.

The number of Turkmen in Iraq is uncertain and mired in controversy.

While the Turkmen claim they number 2 or even 3 million, US diplomats assess there are 300-500,000, 90% of them outside the Kurd-controlled region. The Kurds estimate only 15,000 Turkmen reside in regions under their control. Ankara estimates 135,000. The truth is probably somewhere in between. I suspect closer to the lower figure. Whatever the actual figure, there is little to dispute that the Turkmen are the third biggest ethnic group within the Iraqi population.

The largest Turkmen urban concentrations are in Kirkuk and Mosul. In Kirkuk, the last reliable census indicated they comprised a slight majority in 1957. The latest census, held in 1997, refused to even acknowledge the Turkmen's existence. In the Kurd-controlled region, most appear in and around Irbil, with some also around Dohuk. Like the Kurds, Saddam's Arabization campaign evicted Turkmen in key, oil-rich areas like Kirkuk and replaced them with Arabs loyal to Saddam. Some 60% of Turkmen are Sunni Muslims, tending to identify with Ankara, while the remaining Shi'a Turkmen are more susceptible to Islamic extremist views.

The Turkmen are probably the descendents of Ottoman administrators and soldiers of Turkic ancestry who settled in northern Iraq over the last few centuries, particularly in the important Ottoman trade center of Kirkuk. However, the Turkmen themselves claim they were invited to the region centuries earlier under the Seljuk Turks. Any international forces interacting with the Turkmen will be regaled with nationalist myths, and a long list of alleged Kurdish wrongs against their people.

Turkmen politics can be divided into two parts: the vast majority who coexist well with the Kurds, and the fringe of nationalists belonging to the small, but influential Iraqi Turkmen Front (ITF). The non-ITF parties include the Iranian backed Turkmen Shi'a Islamic parties, and over a dozen small entities including the Turkmen People's Party, Iraqi Turkmen Union Party, Iraqi Turkmen Unity Front, Turkmen Culture Association, and Turkmen Brotherhood Association. It is a common error, encouraged by Turkey, to see the ITF as the main representative of the Turkmen people.

Mainstream Turkmen participate in the Kurd government. Even under Saddam's regime, those living in Kurdish controlled areas enjoyed rights to education in their own language, Turkmen television stations, newspapers and magazines, and radio stations. By contrast, the other 90% of Turkmen living under Saddam's regime-controlled Iraq were oppressed. His regime denied the existence of a Turkmen minority, insisting that they class themselves as Arabs.

He outlawed their language and forcibly relocated thousands under the same Arabization campaign inflicted on the Kurds. The Iraqi Revolutionary Command Council issued formal decisions to deport the Turkmen to the south, and prohibited them from buying or selling real estate and vehicles as a means of trade.

Non-ITF politicians resent that the ITF has such prominence on the political scene. They question the ITF's credibility, considering it a foreign organization.

The ITF wields far more power than its small numbers would suggest because of Turkey's backing. Turkey works through the ITF to influence political policy in Iraq, while maintaining appearance of non-interference in their domestic affairs. The ITF is actually a coalition of three small parties the Iraqi Turkmen Unity Party (ITBP), Iraqi National Turkmen Party (IMTP), and Movement of Independent Turkmen. Turkey controls it, uses it for intelligence gathering purposes, and as a small military-force-in-waiting in northern Iraq. The Turkish General Staff pays the salaries of ITF leaders and provides them with Turkish citizenship to keep them under control.

Turkey continues to use the Turkmen as a counterbalance to the Kurds, a tool to dilute Kurdish political power and ultimately to frustrate any moves toward independence. Although there is no history of inter-ethnic hatred between the Kurds and Turkmen, there have been a handful of armed clashes and instances of vandalism over the 1990s. In late 2002, tensions were high because the ITF refused to register its guards and weapons with the Kurd authorities, whose authority they do not acknowledge. Turkmen relations are most tense with the Kurdistan Democratic Party (KDP), as there are very few of the minority in Patriotic Union of Kurdistan (PUK) territory.

The ITF has a trained militia, perhaps 1,000 strong, and many more armed members with various degrees of training. Many Turkmen have gained arms and training through stints in the Ankara-run Peace Monitoring Force (PMF, some 90% of the group is Turkmen and 10% Assyrian Christian). Reporting in the past suggested that the PMF's 300-400 troops under Turkish command would join Turkmen fighters during any conflict with the Kurds. Reporting also alleges Turkish Special Forces have trained and armed ITF members, and remain in close liaison with them. The ITF has an NGO front used to organize opposition conferences in Turkey, called the Iraqi Institute for Research.

While comprising less than 2% of Iraqi's population, the Turkmen are a major factor to deal with in the north because of their ethnic ties to, and "Protectorate" relationship with Turkey.

09-24-04 * NEWS FROM THE FRONT

Prompted by stateside supporters to begin writing Christmas wish lists, our unit leadership voted instead to request nothing for ourselves. The Chaplain's office initiated a holiday toy drive for Mosul children. I am inviting anyone who wishes to support our unit for Christmas to consider contributing to the toy drive instead. Iraqi children play with and appreciate anything we give them. The local commerce does not include small batteries so I recommend not sending any battery-operated toys. I also recommend not sending toys that require understanding elaborate English instructions to operate.

Our Gospel service includes a testimony time giving soldiers an opportunity to share their triumphs and blessings, concerns and struggles. Today one soldier shared her frustrations and requested prayerful support before she "resort[ed] to something like killing myself." Something in her mannerisms suggested she intended her comment as a joke. Soldiers responded to her with mild laughter or smiles that indicated they related to how she felt. I take suicidal comments seriously. A few minutes later I reminded the congregation of the importance of supporting each other through tough times. Not referring to the female soldier specifically I expressed my opinion that, when we witness certain behaviors or hear specific phrases, we should not wait for people to ask for help but initiate conversation to express our support.

The incident hardly seems worthy of mention in an e-mail recapping significant events of the week in Mosul, yet my mind instantly thought of this soldier two days later.

Before sunrise another mortar volley landed near the center of our base. Acutely aware of how quickly life can be taken from us, our skeleton night-crew quickly moved into action. Our force protection team responded immediately to the impact sites to search for any injured personnel. Our command and control center, the team I work on, initiated several activities at once including a personnel accountability valuation. The response team reported no injuries; equipment and buildings absorbed all of the shrapnel and flying gravel. I breathed a sigh of relief.

Before I had an opportunity to deal my emotions and thoughts that erupted from our close proximity to another impact the personnel accountability report revealed that during the night a female soldier committed suicide. I immediately remembered Sunday. Was it her? Several members of the deceased soldier's unit attended that service. Could we have known? Did we miss an opportunity to save someone's life? Was it coincidence that I spoke out or was it a warning unheeded and now irrelevant? The questions continued, all of them as disturbing as they were unanswered. Guilt, remorse, self-doubt and grief swirled into my emotional crucible.

Less than an hour later a news flash alerted us to the execution of one of the American hostages. I felt hatred, anger and indignation toward the men who did this. Hate is "not a family value" according to bumper stickers seen around Seattle but I do not care about that right now. I wish them a horrible death and would gladly volunteer to make it happen. I also felt an empty, helpless nausea knowing other kidnappings will follow as the publicity of these events helps bring world attention to the demands of these brutes. I prayed for the hostage's family, wishing I could personally extend my sympathy.

I know people who can open their Franklin Planners and tell me their lunch plans a year from now. A planning junkie myself, I discovered that devout planners often do not possess the skills necessary to deal with extreme emotions in themselves or others. Rather than defining resolution objectively, they consider a matter settled after devoting a specified amount of time. Some days in Iraq we do not have time to deal with intense emotions or repercussions before the next incident pushes us in a different direction. Right now I feel completely inadequate to explain my emotions in experiencing these battlefield events.

An ESPN sports center broadcast from Kuwait, a peaceful haven compared to the frontlines of Mosul, mentioned that soldiers there accomplish more before 9:00 am than many Americans do in a week. I looked at the clock. Almost 6:00 am; the changing of the guard. My daily calendar reminded me to check e-mails and call Philese after work. I logged onto a computer. I felt emotionally overwhelmed and unable to continue with either activity. I noticed a 2kB e-mail from Philese and told myself I could handle reading that one. The e-mail simply stated "I hope you call me today." I did.

"Would you like some good news?" she asked. "Sure," I replied without mentioning any details of my day. She read a letter congratulating me on my direct commission to the JAG Corp. After being turned down for a commission for the fourth time (not enough time in service, not enough college credits, too old) I had appealed directly to the National Guard Bureau (NGB) at the Pentagon. Warned that my proposal would likely not be approved, I persisted, refusing to give up until I exhausted every alternative. NGB made me a First Lieutenant with credit for one-year time in grade. After nine years…

"Are you crying?" she asked.

"No," I replied wiping a tear. I had not finished reacting to the shock of three catastrophes and did not know how to assimilate her announcement.

"I wasn't going to tell you because I wanted to see your face when you read the letter. I wish I could see your reaction! Did I do the right thing by telling you over the phone?"

"Yes, thanks for telling me!" I could not continue the conversation. My emotional circuits overloaded. We remained on the phone in silence for several minutes, not caring about the overseas calling rates . I felt happy, overjoyed, but I still felt all of the other emotions of the morning. I cannot find one single word to describe my feelings in that moment: elation, validation, completion all combined to not seem to describe my feelings. I had struggled to meet the requirements, battled regulation after regulation, and even gave up believing once. I thanked Philese again and left the office to be alone for a while.

Fortunately every day is not as emotionally eventful. Mortars land on average every other day on our base. That day just happened to be the closest I have come to being directly involved in a mortar impact. Suicides, although rare, are a constant concern to those in leadership positions especially as we approach the holidays. Almost every day includes an IED attack against one of our convoys. Another Ft. Lewis soldier died here yesterday as a result of a gunshot received while on patrol. Kidnappings are increasing. News announcers read tragic stories with an expression of sorrow, and then smile instantly as they move to a story with a happier ending. Sometimes the stories in our days change as rapidly as the news broadcasts, but switching emotions is not as easy for those of us living the events.

10-01-04 * AIN SIFNI

Two other soldiers from the 116th, Lt. LaBombard and SPC Lessig, accompanied me on the trip to Ain Sifni. Ain Sifni is the capital of a district in the northern Kurdish region. Our sergeant major, SGM Wilcox, took a candid photo of us loading our vehicle with donations for the school (AS 1) and another featuring our departing adventurer's pose (AS 2). The total convoy consisted of about double the number of trucks and personnel as the Bebava village excursion. The unit that supports missions into the Ain Sifni district is heading home. The district governor invited the commander and a unit contingent to a luncheon in their honor. Although not specifically a school mission trip, the 116th three amigos received permission to participate so we could deliver several boxes of donated school supplies. This expedition marked the first occasion for my companions to see other parts of Iraq.

Within minutes of leaving base, we discovered the air conditioning in our vehicle did not work. The external 110° temperature seemed cool compared to the interior heat of our oven on wheels. About thirty minutes into our trip, we received a radio message that one of our rear tires was flat. The entire convoy stopped in herringbone fashion. The rear vehicles completely block the highway for security reasons. Civilian drivers who refused to wait crossed the median and drove north on the southbound lanes. As the driver of the flat-tired enhanced vehicle, I had the opportunity to change the flat. Our vehicle did not have a spare. While we waited for one from the wrecker, I snapped a photo of a young shepherd watching us (AS 3).

Highways crossing into the Kurdistan region contain a military checkpoint operated by the Kurdish Peshmerga. These checkpoints are one of the reasons that problems in southern Iraq do not plague the northlands. Before this unit started its support operations in the region, the Peshmerga guards stood in the sun all day, their only shelter consisting of a thatched roof on poles. The captain allocated $50,000 to constructing air-conditioned buildings for these guards. The convoy is parked near the checkpoint in AS 4. One of the buildings we provided for them is visible to the left of the guard standing in a white pickup.

The larger building above the other pickup is a grain elevator.

The Kurdish governor arranged for a regional champion soccer team to play the American forces in an exhibition game. We parked in a sand-gravel lot adjacent to the soccer field. *AS 5* shows a portion of Ain Sifni as seen from the parking area. On the center-left of the photo is a flag that marks one corner of the soccer field. The field is covered with the same dirt as the parking area. Sliding into a tackle or block in the game would rip the skin off our shins and I have Army engineers graded this field for the high school and they love it. We also finished the high school with doors, windows, some air-conditioning, upgraded plumbing and improved electrical lines.

AS 6 shows a portion of the high school, the Kurdish soccer team warming up and town residents in attendance to witness the feeble attempts of American soldiers to play soccer. On top of the left building is a satellite dish that brings TV into the classroom. To the right of the dish is a metal tank that is the source of the gravity fed water system for drinking fountains and bathrooms. They still do not have pressurized, treated water available. The tank system might account for some digestive illnesses endured by Americans unaccustomed to the local bacteria. Fresh, sanitized water is something we often take for granted in the U.S. Here it is a luxury and only comes in imported bottles.

I joined the American soccer team and left my camera with someone to take photos of the game. I won't mention the 116th Specialist's name, but he became so absorbed in the excitement of the events he forgot to take any pictures of our meager performance. The Kurdish team controlled the ball at least 90% of the game, which is not to imply that we controlled it the remaining 10%. At best we kicked at and ran after the ball. We tried to disrupt their game but they scored eight goals. Near the end of the game the referee called a penalty against a Kurdish defender within the net minder's area, which gave us a penalty shot. I did not see anything close to a penalty. We finally scored! The game ended a minute later with the final score 8-1. I think they gave us that goal in a manner that saved us the disgrace of a shutout.

The high school was closed for placement testing so we drove into town to have our lunch at the elementary school. *AS 7* depicts residences near the elementary school. The short wall encircles the entire housing area. Ain Sifni construction is a huge improvement on the Bebava village homes, but locals still live at a level of poverty below most Americans.

While waiting for lunch to arrive, the Kurdish soccer team wanted to have their photo taken with some of the US players. *AS 8* is one group photo taken in the school courtyard. Only two American players took part in the photo. Many soldiers remained on the street with our vehicles, preferring to interact with and entertain all of the children that showed up.

I watched someone wiping down a tabletop as lunch arrived. Then I realized he was in fact moving a flat-bread (similar to a tortilla but thicker) around on the table attempting to find the right arrangement. The only plates were the platters containing the food and the only utensils were for serving. AS 9 is the lunch in progress. Some of the soldiers refused to partake of the meal; skittish of rumors that one could contract a series of bacterial infections in these settings. Two days later I did become ill with disgusting symptoms that lasted five days before medication could control the situation.

After lunch, my compadres and I unloaded our donations into the teachers' lounge (AS 10). How many teachers in the U.S. today would remain in the profession if our schools looked like this one? The teachers, students and communities in Iraq appear to place a high emphasis on education, although here the priority is not necessarily equated with the amount of money they spend on education facilities.

AS 11 depicts one of the classrooms. The poorest schools in America provide a better setting than these students receive; yet, education happens here. Some teachers' unions in the U.S. blame poor education results on inadequate classroom sizes, deficient school facilities or low salaries. Iraq's education system turns out some very bright people despite the inadequacies.

AS 12 shows a portion Ain Sifni adjoining the school. The blue ribbon between two poles in the courtyard is their volleyball net. AS 13 gives a perspective of the small size of this school that serves the elementary needs of this town of 10,000. The classrooms are definitely crowded. This photo also includes a basketball backstop. They have no net or rim. Instead, hitting the backstop inside the rectangular area counts as a score.

Although not invited, some of the children managed to sneak into the courtyard. AS 14 includes a couple of young men I caught spying over the second floor railing. One of the electrical lines above them was bare for several feet. I felt nervous for them that their school includes this 220-volt danger. Perhaps, now that the high school is finished, the unit replacing this one can help with the elementary school. Rumors abound, however, that the new unit has a different mission, less involved in communities outside the city of Mosul. AS 15 pictures of some of the school staff, SPC Lessig and our translator.

Upon leaving the school I noticed children flocked around the trucks parked on the street, especially around soldiers who distributed candy or toys (*AS 16*). I witnessed one soldier attempt to hand out a small, plastic American flag on a pencil-sized flagpole. Children soon crowded around, hands outstretched, yelling, pressing closer. Rather than command them to get in line as more seasoned distributors would, he panicked. He retreated into his vehicle after tossing the remaining items into the crowd of children.

The Kurdish people in this region love Americans. They ask little of us, maintain their own security and wish to live in peace. Now if only the rest of Iraq could learn to play this well with others.

AIN SIFNI 1

AIN SIFNI 2

AIN SIFNI 3

AIN SIFNI 4

AIN SIFNI 5

AIN SIFNI 6

AIN SIFNI 7

AIN SIFNI 8

AIN SIFNI 9

AIN SIFNI 10

AIN SIFNI 11

AIN SIFNI 12

AIN SIFNI 13

AIN SIFNI 14

AIN SIFNI 15

AIN SIFNI 16

An officer walked into the end of our service directly off a flight from Baghdad. She informed us that the soldier who attempted suicide last week survived the bullet that pierced her left ventricle. Her family visited her in Baghdad and she will soon be on her way home. Reportedly in good spirits, I hope she cherishes her new opportunity for living.

Duties shared by the battle captain and I include informing the commander of the status of medical casualties. The hospital does not release information over the phone so, when we need updates, one of us walks to the hospital records office. Last week a soldier reported to us that he just came from the hospital and that the soldier in question "did not make it". Walking back to the hospital to confirm his story with a medical staff member seemed redundant. Our source, it turns out, misunderstood or misrepresented the physician assistant's message explaining the reason for the patient's transfer to Baghdad. Solomon wrote "Like the coolness of snow at harvest time is a trustworthy messenger to those who send him; he refreshes the spirit of his masters." I do not feel refreshed. I feel frustrated that my reliance on an incompetent messenger resulted in conveying a significantly inaccurate report to the base commander and to an e-mail audience. I wonder if Dan Rather has days like this.

Someone pointed out that a recent letter to the editor in *The Olympian* quoted me to support the author's viewpoint against allowing a NASCAR stadium in Washington State. I wrote earlier that a soldier dying to defend oil pipelines is a hidden and often unappreciated cost in the price people pay for gasoline at the pump. The letter writer suggested that because soldiers die to protect oil, and NASCAR vehicles burn lots of gasoline, we should not allow the new stadium. I do not mean to offend the author of that letter… actually; I do not care if she takes offense. Does a soldier dying to protect the right to vote mean that people should stop voting? Does my standing guard at a fence-line on the Fourth of July mean that my family should stay home from parades and fireworks to sit in the dark and feel sorry for them? Absolutely not! I am in Iraq precisely because I want my family and friends to continue enjoying the freedoms available in America. I want my wife to take the kids out to dinner if she does not feel like cooking, go to movies, spend time with friends or whatever she needs to do to cope with my absence and enjoy life. I want my community, State and Country to recognize the sacrifices made, honor those who deserve recognition, and find the courage to move full speed ahead. I am not a NASCAR fan and I do not see social or economic benefit coming out of a decision to locate a speedway in Washington. On other grounds I agree with the author, but do not patronize our efforts in Iraq by suggesting Americans honor the fallen by restraining freedoms paid for with the blood of this and previous generations.

Our base continues to change, although not all of it is progress. A Turkish tailor recently opened a shop. After inspecting a few samples of his workmanship and the cloth available, I ordered a suit and two shirts. The suit turned out well but the shirts are a waste of money. He did not display any samples of shirts, only suits. Now I know why. Still, the price I paid, if only for the suit, is still a better deal than similarly priced suits at home. What a war! Wait, this is not a war; the major hostilities are over. But we call it a "war" on terrorism so maybe it is a war. In the midst of this "situation" in Mosul, soldiers can now order suits and shirts custom made by a Turkish tailor in a third-world sweat-shop that only employs adults.

A small group of civilians from the Philippines opened a beauty salon that provides coiffures, manicures, pedicures and massages. I have never received a manicure or pedicure in my life and I am not going to sit through my first one in a combat zone! Custom-made suit? Sure. Manicure? I have my limits. I did try a 30-minute massage after listening to a group of the guys talk about it with no one daring to try it first. The man who provided my massage does not know the art, an opinion I freely expressed to the timid group. I will not be a repeat customer.

Commercial flights into Baghdad recently resumed operation, an event the significance of which does not seem to penetrate the home media. A billboard near the Mosul air terminal still lists a grand opening date of August 20. Commercial flights into Mosul remain delayed for two primary reasons; a shortage of local labor willing to risk assassination to work on the base, and the continued uncovering of ammunition piles during runway excavation. Iraq's sand-covered ammo supply points made headlines a few months ago and the problem literally continues to surface.

The mortars and rockets discovered are all larger than anything launched against our base thus far. Some of them are designed to explode on impact, others when ignited with the proper fuses. We also found a missile of a type not allowed in Iraq by one of the UN resolutions. I think the most dangerous job in Iraq is to work on one of the explosives teams mandated to explode all of these munitions. Last week I heard that a member of an explosive team in Baghdad died in his 69th detonation. Exploding ordnance here is more complicated and dangerous than most controlled blasts back home for two reasons. First, the age of the explosives can make them react in unpredictable fashion. Second, EOD must sometimes detonate the munitions in place and the explosion can trigger other ordinance buried near the detonated rounds.

The IEDs used against American and Iraqi convoys are typically these mortars and rockets buried around the country. Former Ba'ath party members know the locations, and we keep stumbling upon them. A loud explosion shook our office this morning. After several phone calls, we discovered that an IED detonated against an Iraqi National Guard (ING) patrol. Three ING and several civilian bystanders died. This afternoon an even louder blast sent several soldiers ducking into concrete shelters; EOD detonated rounds discovered the previous day. Same type of munitions, same loud blast, totally different purpose. They aim to kill; we strive to make this country a safer place. Hopefully, we will soon even open the airport to commercial traffic.

10-15-04 * News From the Home Front

Last night Philese and I took Tori and Layne to watch the premier of "Remembering Saddam", a documentary featuring six businessmen who had their right hands cut off at Saddam's instruction. The film's creator, journalist Don North, uses their stories to highlight the atrocities committed by Saddam's regime in extinguishing an estimated 2 million people mostly of his own country. We purchased a copy of the documentary and highly recommend it. One of them men interviewed exclaimed:

> "We do not need to find WMD to justify taking down Saddam. The WMD is in Saddam's own brain."[8]

Leaving home a second time is emotionally more difficult for me than the first. Many soldiers share stories of their struggles returning to Iraq after a short stay at home. Younger children often cry louder than the first time, loving spouses cling more tightly, anxiety diminishes the former sense of anticipation and adventure. Some soldiers in Iraq decided not to return home for two weeks just to avoid the emotional crisis. I would never trade a minute of my two weeks in San Antonio and home to avoid boarding to return to my volunteered duty.

Sometimes we do not know how to let go. We do not want to, we are afraid to, we feel pain at the thought of letting go, yet despite all of this contrary evidence sometimes letting go is the very best thing we can do.

For some the first time we learn to let go of someone is when we face our first day of school, our parents no longer around to protect or love us. A high-school student may need to let go of a sweetheart who changes schools; a parent lets go of a child going off to college. Letting go is often accompanied by emotional pain, usually proportional to the love we feel for the one we release or the fear of how much we anticipate loneliness.

Some people reason that life is safer, less painful if we do not love. Separation from a loved one is not a pain easily dealt with by reciting trite expressions such as "It is better to have loved and lost than not to have loved at all" or "If you truly love someone, set him free." Living in the pain of letting go requires courage to continue alone, allowing ourselves moments when we do not even realize they are gone.

When I think of Philese and my children I feel a sorrowful longing. I want them to be happy even in my presence, but am I more fretful for them or for myself? Do I feel their pain, or do I feel my own? If I do not feel my own pain and understand how life can be lived in the midst of it, then I will never truly be able to empathize with others in similar emotional experiences.

Faith does not take away the heart-felt hurt in times like these. Faith allows me to bear the pain of letting go. Faith gives me the hope to think about life on the other side of my distress, life in reunion, life in fellowship. Although I do not believe that faith gives me a definite promise we will be together again in this life, I will, however, live in concert with the hope of our reunion.

"Now faith is being sure of what we hope for and certain of what we do not see" (Heb. 11:1). I first learned about this kind of faith from my mother. In my early childhood years our cupboards lacked enough food to prepare a meal. My mother prayed like our survival depended on God and worked like it depended on her. She often quoted David's observation "I have never seen the righteous forsaken or their children begging bread" (Ps. 37:25). She transmitted her certainty God would provide even though we could not see how or when. When money or bags of groceries arrived from anonymous sources we prayerfully thanked God.

Today I remember her certainty. She never doubted God. I hope to return home safely yet I am not certain that God promises a safe return. My mother based her certainty on Bible verses that directly addressed our need. I do not know any Bible verses that state all Christians fighting in a war for specific reasons are guaranteed to return home safely. Some soldiers quote Psalm 91 and believe with unshakable conviction that God will protect them from harm. I never debate soldiers on this issue even though I do not believe that Psalm applies to Christian soldiers serving in Iraq. Perhaps their assurance is the only thing that keeps them going one more day.

My hope and faith are based on a relationship with God. I do hope to return home in good health. I pray to God for protection not only for me but also for my family and friends at home. I sensed God's protection during the IED explosion and several other times. I do not know what I will do if I return home critically injured. I pray that I will be courageous, valiant, even heroic, but I do not know for sure. Sometimes I complain, get angry over things that don't matter, criticize or tune out the world. Mercifully my salvation and eternal security are in God's hands rather than mine.

God is always faithful, always true, always watching over and out for His children. God is always on the throne, flawlessly executing His duties as Commander in chief, Supreme Judge of the Universe, Redeemer, and Counselor. In God all things are possible. In God all things have meaning. In God my faith and hope are anchored to a solid rock that withstood every tempest throughout time immemorial. Whether I live or die I want my life and death to honor Him.

My wife, Philese, met me in Dallas and we enjoyed a week together exploring the San Antonio region. Then I spent a week with my children, met a few friends, gave a few speeches and found six of the twenty-six pounds I lost in Iraq. We have a physical fitness test in a month and I am now seven pounds over my limit. Still, I would not trade away one minute of spending time with my wife instead of exercising, or indulging in foods I missed, or Starbuck's lattes with whip-cream. I wear these six pounds as cherished memories, although I hope to keep the memories and discard the evidence before next month.

A crew-member of our military flight into Mosul announced that, due to recent events which he did not explain, our approach to the airstrip would be "fast, steep and evasive". I did not think of his comment again until I felt the plane drop out of the sky faster than the Freefall ride at Magic Mountain. The windows were all covered so I had no exterior perspective with which to control my vertigo problem, although I doubt it would have helped in those circumstances. Within seconds I started sweating, large droplets rolling off my face. Lacking an airsick bag and even a few inches of space not taken up by soldiers or baggage, I removed my helmet. I did not enjoy returning to Mosul as my dizziness lasted for several hours.

I later discovered that the events referred to by our airman included mortars and rockets launched at arriving planes. The Islamic Holy month of Ramadan started a few days before my return. Historically a month of peace, most Muslims observe Ramadan's spiritual reflections taught. Terrorists seem to think Ramadan stands for "Real Arabs must annihilate devilish Americans now" and that Ramadan is double stamp month on their entrance to the Garden of Allah punch card. The day I returned to Mosul set a new record for indirect fire (mortar and rocket) attacks against our airfield and helped October already surpass the entire month of September, our previous record month.

A member of our unit picked me up at the terminal. Noting my lack of color, wobbly legs and distinctive just-threw-up-on-myself odor, he dropped me off at my room rather than take me back to the office for our return briefings. At one point I heard several mortars impact near the trailers but could not muster the strength to move. For a few seconds I entertained the thought of one landing on my room and putting me out of my misery, but I quickly verbalized an objection to that thought on the grounds that it was a really stupid idea. I sustained my own objection, and prayed for a less lethal resolve to my overwhelming nausea. The 8 rounds did not hurt anyone and I eventually recovered from the airsickness.

The civil affairs team in charge of my trips to Bebava and Ain Sifni was scheduled to return home shortly before I left for leave. I heard they decided to stay and continue their mission. The Army allowed them two weeks of leave before attaching them to the incoming civil affairs unit. The day after I returned to Mosul I learned that a civil affairs convoy, returning from one of their humanitarian missions to a local hospital, was hit by an IED blast. Two soldiers died and five others were wounded in the attack. I knew one of the deceased. He was a guest of honor at the celebration in Ain Sifni.

I believe that he is a true hero of Operation Iraqi Freedom. He helped small Iraqi businesses start up or recover through a small-business loan program. His unit also supported over 100 villages and schools with donations from U.S. civilians and contracts from military funds. He found ways to support Iraqis even when the military did not provide him all the funds he requested. He was killed just three days after returning from a two-week leave with his wife and family. Hundreds of Iraqis attended a ceremony to honor this man. Several remarked that they will never forget his efforts. His work here helped thousands more, yet one terrorist who claims all Americans are evil, killed him in a New York minute. I am angry, very angry, yet I do not know who to be angry at or what I can do about it.

This week also holds some good news. Chaplain Timothy Vakoc remains in critical condition but has returned home to Minnesota for further treatment. The 44-year-old Army chaplain and Roman Catholic priest grew up in Robbinsdale (MN) and served parishes in Minneapolis before becoming an Army chaplain based at Fort Lewis. Father Tim, as we all called him, was transferred from Walter Reed hospital to the Minneapolis Veteran's Administration hospital to recover closer to his family. The report we received did not indicate to what degree Father Tim has regained consciousness but I feel strengthened by the news. We continue to pray for him here. His sister created a website to keep everyone who is interested updated on his condition.[9]

My Iraqi friend, Ahmed, received a well-deserved Bronze Star and a Purple Heart. While it is difficult for non-Americans to receive these honors, Ahmed's dedication to our efforts, and direct involvement in numerous explosions resulting in several shrapnel wounds, warrant this recognition.

We experienced a windstorm this week after which the temperature dropped over 10 degrees. Our highs are now in the low 80s and lows in the mid 50s. Still no rain since the beginning of May but we expect that to change soon.

Communities of Christians inhabited modern-day Mesopotamia virtually since the dawn of Christianity 2,000 years ago. The Iraqi Christian population includes two primary groups; the Chaldeans, Eastern-rite Catholics whose native tongue is Aramaic, and the Assyrians who belong to different denominations, including the Ancient Church of the East, the Syrian Orthodox Church, and several Protestant denominations. The remainder consists primarily of Syrian, Armenian, and Greek Catholics; Armenian and Greek Orthodox; and, Mandaeans, who are followers of John the Baptist.

Historically, the Chaldeans and Assyrians lived in the Mosul area, although many left seeking economic opportunities in other regions. During successive periods of "Arabization" in the post-colonial era, and particularly under Ba'ath rule, some Christian communities, like other non-Arab groups such as the Kurds, were displaced in order to make way for Arabs from the southern Iraq.

1.4 million Christians lived in Iraq in 1987 according to the last national census. Today, some leaders estimate that 800,000 Christians remain in this country of 23 million. Most of the emigration took place after Iraq's invasion of Kuwait in 1990, when UN sanctions began. As Saddam's reaction to sanctions weakened the middle class during the 1990s, tens of thousands of Christians emigrated to Syria, Lebanon, Europe and North America.

Under Saddam Hussein, Christians, particularly Assyrians, suffered from forced relocations in the north, and, like Kurds and Shi'ite Muslims, were banned from organizing political parties. They were welcomed into the Ba'ath Party (co-founded by a Christian) and permitted to rise to senior posts if they followed party rules. Originally the regime did not interfere with their religious practices and even provided subsidies to cooperative churches. Later, popular pressure induced the Saddam government to adopt Islamic slogans, build mosques and even introduce a ban on alcohol, which hit Christian business owners particularly hard. Anonymous thugs attacked or killed several Christian liquor-store and restaurant owners and their families in predominantly Muslim towns and cities including Mosul.

With the recent rise of Islamist sentiment, Christians grow increasingly concerned about their fate in Iraq. In August, five churches in Baghdad and Mosul were blown up in a co-coordinated series of bombings. Criminal gangs target wealthier Christian families for kidnappings. Non-Kurdish Christians have reportedly come under attack by Kurdish militias in the north as Kurds push to extend their control to "Arabized" areas they consider traditionally Kurdish. Four Christian Iraqi workers on our base were gunned down on their way home and Christian university students receive death threats warning them to adopt Islamic practices or else. The conflict in Iraq decreasingly resembles Extreme Islam v. America and increasing plays out as Extreme Islam v. Christianity.

Most clerics in Iraq, both Sunni and Shi'ite, condemn the attacks against Christians. Christians and Muslims do not want to repeat the bloodshed of the Crusades. I believe that the terrorist masterminds are not fundamentalist Muslims. Rather, they use the historic friction of Muslim v. Christian to motivate people to violence. While we are busy fighting each other they grow stronger. One day they hope to be strong enough that even if we work together we will not be able to defeat them and then their true anti-religious nature will surface as they move to annihilate all faith.

The extent to which the new Iraq government accepts and protects Christians is watched closely by Christian minority populations in neighboring countries such as the Maronites in Lebanon, the Copts of Egypt, and the Chaldo-Assyrians in Turkey. The Coalition Provisional Authority proposed the concept of a Christian security zone. The Interim Council has not moved on this idea and is not likely to before the January elections. There is one Christian on the Iraqi Interim Council who advocates religious liberty in the council meetings but he is not effective at appealing to terrorists to stop their violence. The new Iraqi Constitution might guarantee Christians freedom of worship and association, but exercising their freedom could cost them their lives.

The Book of Acts tells the story of a vehement persecutor of the church named Saul who met Jesus while riding to Damascus and became Paul, one of the church's strongest advocates. (See Acts 9:1–18). The Iraqi church needs such an advocate today. I pray that a terrorist on the road to Mosul, or any city where Christians dwell, will come face to face with the One he is really persecuting and become a spokesman for the dwindling body of believers. I also pray that this new Paul arises before the Church in Iraq suffers any more calamities.

Sunday morning, shortly after 5:00 am, we heard a blast from across the river. We checked our maps to discern what non-residential buildings are near the explosion. We could only find a church. I feared another attack against the local Christians. We later learned insurgents targeted one of our patrols with an IED. Everyone returned safely. Most of the car bombs and many of the IEDs are now targeting Iraqis. Christians, easy to distinguish because they do not wear the headdresses required under Islamic law, are increasingly targeted, as are their places of worship. One local news story highlighted social progress in Iraq as demonstrated by female university students adopting a business casual wardrobe. Another story mentioned that females received threats stating that they will be killed if they do not wear Islamic required clothing. Christians did not need to don the headdresses under Saddam's regime, allegiance to the Ba'ath party measured in other ways, but they were still isolated for persecution at times.

During our pre-deployment stage I hoped to visit at least one Christian service here. Christianity here is different than in the U.S., honoring traditions that date as far back as the 5th century. Since the churches are already targeted, and a visiting American would make any church even more subject, that goal will not likely materialize. What I learned about the church in Iraq comes from reading and talking to a few local citizens.

The military chaplains on our base hold Protestant, Catholic, Contemporary Christian and Jewish services. They also sanction a few ordained ministers to conduct additional services. An LDS elder sponsors a service for members of that faith and three gospel ministers from Mississippi started a Gospel service shortly before our arrival. A Satanist in the British Navy on his way to the Persian Gulf recently received permission to worship according to his faith. We do not have any strong Satanists on our base to my knowledge. As an ordained minister, in addition to being a lawyer (an odd juxtaposition perhaps), the gospel ministers asked me to join their team in March. Since then I have preached once per month. Their unit is scheduled to leave in a few days and will take all three other ministers, most of the choir and a majority of the congregation with them. Shortly before I left on leave, the lead pastor asked me to continue the Gospel service after their departure. I told him I would think and pray about it. I doubted my ability and time availability. I decided during leave to end the program and direct the remaining attendees to the chaplain programs. Our unit's potential transfer reinforced that decision. This Sunday, in a service dedicated to the departing units, soldiers related stories about how much the Gospel service means to them. The head pastor called me to the front of the church, where I accepted the mantle of leadership. I am still more nervous about this than about the mortars and rockets.

Mosul continues to make stateside news almost daily for the car bombs and IED attacks. Mortar and rocket attacks continue at a Ramadan heightened pace. Iraqis bear the brunt of the car bombs and drive-by shootings while the IEDs target American patrols and the mortars and rockets are aimed at our bases. American news venues recently mentioned a poll of Iraqis and how they feel (strongly negative, understandably) about the security problems. I found the actual poll and discovered that, even with the security issues, Iraqis are optimistic about their future and the future of Iraq.[10]

Another Iraqi pro-troop statement missing from most news accounts is from Prime Minister Allawi's "State of the Union" conference. In our office we watched the broadcast with interest. Prime Minister Allawi summed up his sentiments regarding our presence with these words:

"The day will come, God willing, when the Iraqi Army will protect our borders while the National Guard will provide security for cities, and the police will maintain order and security, and ensure the supremacy of law. Until this is achieved, we will require the assistance of the multinational forces. Those who are attacking these forces are in fact working on prolonging their presence in our country because they realize that ending violence and having our forces control security will speed up the departure of these forces."

Seattle talk-show host Mike Siegel invited me to call his show this week. I worked with the official channels to obtain permission. The day before the show, and the day after the previous issue surfaced, I was informed that I could call the show if I printed the talking points from the public affairs site and had an officer next to me during the call to verify that I stayed within the points. I found the website only to uncover that the talking points, not updated since March, no longer contained relevant information. I wrote Mike to decline his offer, compounding my frustration with the military information system.

All 18 of the 343rd Quartermaster Company's soldiers involved in the refusal to obey a convoy order returned to duty. According to lawyers involved in the case, up to five of them are pending a criminal investigation. The most likely criminal charge is "failure to obey an order" which carries a maximum penalty of two years confinement, a dishonorable discharge and a forfeiture of pay and allowances. On the lenient side, the soldiers could receive a letter of reprimand.

11-12-04 * VETERAN'S DAY

Growing up in a family and church with strong Dutch connections, I remember many veterans of World War II who fought for the Netherlands or Canada. Some of the veterans shared stories to help us understand history or just because they loved to tell stories. I thought of veterans as "older". My own father, the oldest of his siblings, was a young teenager during the War. His family emigrated from the Netherlands to New Jersey shortly thereafter.

As I aged, my concept of veterans aged ahead of me. They still belonged to the "older" crowd even though the austere group included Korean War veterans, Vietnam, Gulf I. Veteran's Day parades brings memories of someone picking up a veteran, wearing an aged uniform that didn't fit as well, taking them to a parade to sit in the grandstand or ride in a seat of honor. Today it hit me that the people I work with and I are now members of this group I know as "Veterans".

I don't know what to do with this new designation. The almost eight months of nights in this windowless room, time spent writing, e-mailing, eating almost every meal in a modern dining facility, sleeping in my own room, and working out at a decent gym does not fit my concept of veterans. This does not match the stories I grew up with, the incredible sacrifices made by the soldiers on the front and an entire country at home that went without or recycled metal and rubber so the soldiers could have the tools they needed to win the war.

Now eligible for admission to the Veterans of Foreign Wars (VFW) organization, I feel more than a little hesitant to sit on a stool next to someone who fits my image of a veteran and swap stories about earning our right to drink a double shot of Johnny Walker Black Label for $4 in a VFW establishment. I also feel reticent to accept the fact that, to many young people, I am now part of the older crowd that comprises their view of veterans. My dress uniform still fits fine, thank you very much.

A sincere salute to all veterans from someone who is honored and proud to join your ranks. Even though history will never fully reveal how the world would look today without your service, I know that your sacrifices helped preserve freedom and liberty in our often chaotic world.

The action in Fallujah dominates the television news reports, yet Mosul increasingly makes headlines in the on-line and print media. Although we do have problems to address in the city, I personally do not see us becoming the next Fallujah as some news reports suggest.

One Task Force Olympia soldier was killed and a second service member later died of wounds following a mortar attack on a Multi-National Base in Mosul at approximately 10 a.m. The names of the service members killed in the attack are withheld pending notification of next of kin. A civilian contractor also wounded in the attack was evacuated to the military hospital in Baghdad.

Two terrorists attacked soldiers from the 73rd Engineer Battalion from a vehicle with small arms fire as soldiers swept local roadways for roadside bombs in southern Mosul. Soldiers quickly engaged the terrorists killing one and detaining the other. No MNF soldiers were injured during the attack on their patrol. SBCT detained one additional person for anti-Iraqi activities.

In other news, our perpetual sunshine ended with the turning of the calendar to November. We have been blessed with rain on a daily basis since. Our once dust covered ground is now slick mud and large puddles. The Mosul 1/2 marathon is now history. Advertised as "The Most Dangerous Marathon in the World", it is the only race I have seen where course security required gun trucks. Even though I trained for several months I could not participate as a contestant. My ability to breathe became severely limited about a week before the run, shortly after the weather changed. With guidance from some incredible combat medics on our base and strength from their supply of appropriate medication I am progressing to a solid recovery if for no other reason than I am too stubborn to be sent home for an illness. I helped with security but could not convince the sponsors to give me a finisher's t-shirt despite my history of promoting the run, training and race-day volunteer activities. Nuts.

The ING and SBCT detained eight people for anti-Iraqi activities and collected a variety of munitions today. ING and MNF soldiers from 3rd Battalion, 21st Infantry Regiment (3-21) conducted a joint cordon and search in the northern Mosul neighborhood of Al Arabe and detained five people suspected of planning and conducting attacks against Iraqi Security forces and MNF. The suspects are in custody with no injuries reported during the operation. 3-21 soldiers also conducted a cordon and search just south of Palestine neighborhood in Mosul and detained an associate of a known terrorist network. The suspect is in custody undergoing questioning with no injuries reported during the operation.

In response to a request by Nineveh Provincial Governor, Duraid Kashmoula, Iraqi National Guard (ING) soldiers and Multi-National Forces (MNF) from the 1st Brigade, 25th Infantry Division Stryker Brigade Combat Team (SBCT) initiated offensive operations in southeastern and southwestern Mosul at approximately 1 p.m. against known concentrations of insurgents. The Governor's request resulted from a series of attacks on Iraqi Security Forces yesterday and overnight in Mosul. Insurgent forces attacked several police stations and other targets within the city. In several cases, Anti-Iraqi Forces exceeded the capabilities of the police on site, ransacking the stations of their weapons and uniforms. Reports that terrorists control several police stations, specific neighborhoods or large areas of the city are exaggerated. A few hundred people with a death wish and weapons stockpiles can cause considerable damage in this large city but they will not win. We outnumber them. We are better trained. We have more and bigger guns and we do not like to lose. Personally, I think we have a win-win situation developing. They want to die for their beliefs and we want to live for ours.

Mosul definitely made the news this week with headlines ranging from a quelled resistance to complete city-wide anarchy lasting several days. At the height of the conflict I volunteered to maintain a position on the fence-line but met an insistence that the military needed me most in the operation center. So I listened to radio communication and analyzed reports, confined to a windowless room, unable to witness for myself the activities that made top headlines around the world.

Terrorists attacked several police stations in areas more supportive to their ethnicity or message. They brought only death and destruction to these neighborhoods, a lesson many residents will vividly recall the next time someone has a grand scheme to teach the American puppet government a lesson. The police in at least six stations fled without firing a single shot, a despicable record that quickly prompted the governor to replace the police chief with someone who will enforce the law. The terrorists stole weapons, uniforms and vehicles, destroying some of the buildings in their wake. Some of the terrorists then attempted two foolhardy campaigns. One group attacked the Peshmerga (Kurdish) headquarters (PDK), the same ethnic group that repelled the Iraqi Republican Guard in 1991. The PDK adamantly held their ground. Another small group attempted to take on some American forces. The terrorists that survived these skirmishes appear to have fled into whatever cave they crawled out of.

At no time did the terrorists or anarchy control the city. Most of the police maintained their stations. The Iraqi government dispatched troops to the city, exercising the leadership that is its responsibility since the transfer of authority. The people of Iraq are learning that they need to stand up to their countrymen who foment violence as a means to achieve anything worthwhile. The people of Iraq are collectively growing stronger as the recent events in Mosul and Fallujah demonstrate.

To grow strong, one needs to be challenged, to toughen up and face harder challenges. A tree that grows without wind against it may grow, but never has it strengthened because it did not have to. When wind does come, the tree then breaks under the strength of the wind. The trees life is lost because it never faces a challenge before and did not grow for wind to come. Iraq is facing a wind like it has never faced since its inception; a sale force wind of terrorism blowing against the fledgling society of freedom and democracy. Because of the fall of Saddam, the Iraqi people need to toughen up a little. Saddam performed unspeakable evil, tortured people, gave to those that he liked and oppressed the people he did not like. Saddam and his family lived in palaces when his people starved. Under all of his tyranny the people of Iraq survived. The tough character the people of Iraq developed under Saddam's rule is different than the character they need now to thwart terrorism and seize their freedom. Because of the way Saddam ruled no one could stop him. Terrorism can be stopped. The situation is different now and the challenge is difficult for many Iraqis to understand and fight.

Under Saddam's regime no one had freedom but there was no terrorism. Under his regime, people did not have access to material goods but they were relatively safe as long as they did not complain about Saddam. It is now up to the people to stand up for their security. It is up to the people, not a tyrant, to decide what happens to their country. Some Iraqis say that they would rather have the security and tyranny than to have freedom and determine their own destiny. I believe time will demonstrate to the world that freedom and democracy is better than tyranny. Iraqis have the choice to live the life they want. If they want to live free from terrorism, they need only to realize that they posses the power to change Iraq.

Under Saddam Iraqis did not need to die if they chose to acquiesce. With terrorism even the innocent, some argue especially the innocent, are murdered, beheaded, blown into pieces. Terrorists will not exchange security for submission or participate in a legitimate electoral system. Terrorists thrive on chaos, manipulate discrepancies between groups of people, and cause these groups to fight each other. Iraqi is finally waking up to realize that placating terrorists does not generate security in the same way that conciliating Saddam brought safety.

Iraqi citizens will not break because they are used to the wind of life. They are a tough people. But the wind comes from a different direction than what they are use to. They need to remain firmly planted in their culture and link their common roots together to survive this wind. The Iraqi government is doing a better job every day to bring security to Iraq. It needs help though. In democracy and freedom, the system needs help from the people in order for it to work. People need to stand up against terrorism and not hide and bend when terrorists are in the neighborhood. These terrorists are the reason why Iraq grows so slowly.

Terrorism is like a strong wind, and also like bad water given to a tree. If the tree does not get good clean water, it will not grow so strong and may die. Why would anyone choose to put bad water on a tree that they love, a special tree that produces good fruit? Freedom demands a sacrifice from everyone who would live free. The result is a nation where people do not have to fear, and the people do not have to depend on one man to give them mediocre security at his whim while he steals their birthright.

Our six months of solid sunshine converted to rain when we flipped the calendar to November. Heavy rain quickly transformed our dusty roads into mud bogs and parking areas into slippery pits. The temperatures, a few months ago were doubling the highs in Seattle, now approach freezing levels.

We walk to work, meals and bathrooms in miserable weather, endure mortars and rockets from people who do not want us here, and rarely receive an encouraging word through the major media about the work we do.

Today, Thanksgiving Day, I am not grateful to be in Iraq. The decorative attempts to re-create traditional settings only reinforce my desire to celebrate Thanksgiving at home with my family. Still, my life is full of reasons to remain thankful.

I am thankful for the soldiers who initiated Operation Iraqi Freedom and set the foundation for our success. The 101st Airborne comprised the first American soldiers into the Mosul area. I am blessed with a hard structure room, phone and Internet access, laundry facilities and even a gym. They had none of these luxuries. They slept in tents or on the ground, ate packaged meals, did not have air conditioning for the hot summers or adequate heaters for the winter, lived the stereotypical life of an Army soldier yet went beyond their basic duties to prepare a better life for the soldiers who would follow them.

I am thankful for the support we receive from people back home. A stranger, now good friend, sent an e-mail to me asking what kind of candy I like. I mentioned Haberno Gummi Bears and Bassets licorice. Two weeks later I received a box from her with a bag of each inside.

People who know nothing more about me than that I am an American soldier who occasionally writes newspaper columns have sent a plethora of supplies, most of which I give away to other American and Iraqi soldiers. Even people who do not support Operation Iraqi Freedom itself still pass along wishes for our safe return home. I am thankful for every package, every letter, especially those from my wife and children.

American generosity extends to the Iraqi people as well. I accompanied two convoys to villages in northern Iraq where we dispensed dozens of boxes of items donated to the schools and children. Thousands of toys are now beginning to arrive for our Mosul Toys for Tots program, an outreach where we will deliver toys around Christmas time to local children. I am thankful for this support because these moments of personally interacting with Iraqi people who want and need our help are the most cherished memories of my time spent here.

I am thankful for the ability to communicate with those I love. I cannot imagine for the levels of anxiety or anticipation felt by soldiers or their families enduring wars where correspondence was limited to censored letters that took months to arrive. When my family hears news reports of soldiers killed in our area, I can reassure them within 24-hours via e-mail or a phone call that I am OK. Although I may sometimes feel lonely, with modern communication I never feel alone.

I am thankful for the state-of-the-art weapon and protective systems available to the U.S. military. The sound of an approaching Blackhawk, Apache or F-18 is sometimes enough to ensure a victory for our soldiers in an intense firefight. Our troops are the best trained in the world on the best weapon systems available.

We also protect our troops as much as possible. The military has spent over $150 million just on armoring vehicles. The extra steel plate saved my life when a bomb exploded on my HWMMV door June 18.

Not all of us, though, will be returning home. Some soldiers, including a few who became my friends on our short service together, are not with us to celebrate this Thanksgiving. As well-trained and equipped as we are, we will likely lose even more soldiers before Christmas.

My most solemn and heartfelt thanks are reserved for the families of those soldiers who paid the ultimate price for America's security and Iraq's liberty. God bless you all.

12-03-04 * OUR NEW BASE

Our unit spent most of Thanksgiving finalizing our move to the base I labeled Gilligan's Island because it is as primitive as can be. South and slightly west of Mosul is an expanse of desert nothingness and this base. This base sets the standard for "the middle of nowhere", a title I formerly bestowed on Death Valley, California. There are geographical and ecological reasons that the local people choose not to live here. The one well on the base delivers large quantities of undrinkable water, at times so bad last summer that soldiers showered by pouring bottled water over their heads.

Most of the soldiers on the base live in Sealand shipping containers refurbished with aluminum paneling and two or three overhead lights depending on the length of the container. Each container includes a heater / air conditioning unit, two beds, two wall lockers, a table of the card playing size and four chairs. Not as nice as the former residence but better than living in a tent.

Our job in this new location is to build it up to a fully functioning base. My position includes surveying buildings for potential tenant use. Since the local labor pool is almost non-existent the soldiers need to do most of construction. In the time the airfield base received nearly 400 rounds of mortars and rockets this base received six. Some of the time spent protecting ourselves from local bad guys as we did in Mosul can be diverted here to more positive pursuits. Since very few people live in the area, we have a 360° view of the horizon and can return fire without fear of hitting civilians or destroying property we later need to pay for. Earlier this evening I heard, for the first time since arriving, some loud explosions that my days at the airfield would have led me to interpret as incoming mortars. However, the noise came from a field artillery unit sending 155mm rounds on targets many kilometers down range. We did not have gun systems this large on the airbase. At first I wished they could move their weapon systems farther away to reduce my chances of my going deaf from friendly fire, but the realization that they are one of the reasons bad guys don't drop by for a visit helped me appreciate their noisy barrage.

This base does not have a PX or any shops run by Iraqis. No Internet café or

AT&T phone center. No short walks either as this base contains more than four times the area of the Mosul airfield. Unlike the Mosul airbase, however, we have no mud. The Mosul airfield's grounds, on the banks of the Tigris River, turned to mud when the first rains arrived at the end of October. We trudged through mud to the restrooms, the gym, the dining facility, our office, and the chapel. I stomped through a lake of mud on my way to breakfast while others attempted to avoid splattering themselves by circumventing through shallow muck on the fringes. Someone questioned my sanity at walking shin deep in liquid dirt. I replied, "My mother wouldn't let me when I was a kid." Within seconds a few others joined me, making up for lost childhood experiences.

Gilligan's Island is a former Iraqi Air Force base, home at one time to their Mirage aircraft. Two of them are still here, unfortunately inoperable. I tried. One of our officers builds airplanes for a living. He thinks we could salvage enough parts from the two planes to make one that will fly. While he and I discussed plans to become the Sanford & Son scrap yard of Iraqi planes, an eavesdropping commander reminded us of the legal action the military would undertake if we proceeded. Nuts.

At the beginning of the 1991 invasion, our fighters expertly took out one of the two runways, isolating the Iraqi planes and rendering them useless for that war. The Iraqi military did not repair the battered runways or buildings. Last year, the 101st Airborne took over the airfield here as they did in Mosul, but the military decision makers did not sustain the operation after their departure here as in Mosul. That decision is now changing for reasons that may translate into news in a few months.

After every rocket and mortar attack in Mosul members of our unit conduct crater analysis (an examination of the impact sight to recover fragments of the round used, direction of travel, and blast pattern). The largest rocket launched at us in Mosul left a crater no more than a couple of feet across, although the fragments could injure someone 50 – 75 meters away. The craters in the runway here, made by 2,000 lb. American bombs, left holes large enough to lose a HWMMV in. The Iraqi Air Force possessed a few bombs that large but we never allowed them the opportunity to send any our direction.

The placement of the bombs prevented the Iraqis from launching their Mirages if they wanted to, yet still allowed future American troops, such as the 101st Airborne, use of the other runway for their operations. Complete annihilation is not always the best long-term option even for the military. If I was an Iraqi pilot in 1991, witnessing the precision firepower of American fighter jets,

I think I would have called in sick the rest of the war. The OIF planners did not originally envision much of a presence here after the 101st vacated the area and we find ourselves needing to quickly build an infrastructure that could have been created by now. The Army would not be the institution we know and love without frequent changes such as relocating our unit here.

We spent our first week remodeling an open courtyard into office space. A day after creating a false ceiling in the courtyard a pair of bats decided to move in to the office space rather than continue hanging under the higher rafters. Another soldier and I captured the 3" bats and set them free outside. We also discovered the hole they used to fly into the office and plugged it with toilet paper rolls. Other wildlife on this base includes vipers, snakes, coyotes and jackrabbits. So far no scorpions or camel spiders.

Someone asked me today why he is unable to pray his wife's cancer away. After witnessing testimonies of healings and miracles, he wondered if perhaps his wife is not healed because of his lack of faith. He quoted Matthew 17:20: "He replied, "Because you have so little faith. I tell you the truth, if you have faith as small as a mustard seed, you can say to this mountain, 'Move from here to there' and it will move. Nothing will be impossible for you.'"

My heart ached as I listened to this child of God question his faith, his relationship with God, even his salvation and eternal security all because his wife is enduring what for many is a fact of life. We talked about faith, about what we believe God can do compared to what we see God actually do. We talked about our relationship with God as the most important part of life and that nothing, not even cancer, can separate us from God's love. Then I shared with him a lesson many prominent faith teachers today do not discuss.

To answer the disciples' question on why they could not cast out a demon, Jesus told them in Matthew they did not have enough faith. In the book of Luke, Jesus told his disciples something similar during a lesson on forgiveness. The disciples asked Jesus to increase their faith. He replied, "If you have faith as small as a mustard seed, you can say to this mulberry tree, 'Be uprooted and planted in the sea,' and it will obey you" (Luke 17:6).

One of the interesting things about these two verses is that there is no account in the Bible that Jesus Himself ever did the two deeds He mentions. Jesus did not go about moving mountains or casting bushes into the sea to prove that He had faith.

Some people speak of a mountain as a symbol of anything that blocks us in life. They speak of the mountains in their path; or being faced with a mountain; or the mountain they must climb. Then they apply Matthew 17:20 and conclude that they should be able to move that mountain with a verbal phrase. When the mountain does not move they conclude something must be wrong with their faith. I think there is something wrong with their conclusion!

God did not design this world in a way that we would always overcome obstacles in our lives with verbal commands. What if the dishes pile up for a few days because I am sick? In the midst of curing the sickness can I also call upon the scrub brush to automatically clean all of the dishes? Can I command the broom or vacuum to sweep the floor? How about clothes flying through the air into color segregated piles, the laundry machines washing and drying them, followed by automatic ironing, folding and storage?

Okay, that scene sounds more like something out of *Harry Potter* than what most people expect their faith to do for them. What if I consume poison in a daily basis and expect not to get sick because of my faith? Most people I talk with have a problem with that as a spiritual, proper exercise of faith. What about poisons or toxins that I don't know about but are killing me anyways? Now it gets less clear. What about toxins in the water we drink, air we breathe and food we eat that we know about but are at levels we consider, or our government considers, acceptable? What if we don't exercise as we know we should, reward ourselves for the occasional good choice we make with food that is bad for us, or overload our liver with cigarette smoke or alcohol?

Now I have definitely crossed the line into bad things we do to ourselves rather than bad things that happen to us. People seem to be uncomfortable using faith as a tool to remove "mountains" that they cause themselves; slightly comfortable with allowing faith to heal "mountains" they may have caused but didn't know it at the time; and, fully comfortable with using faith when they are innocent victims.

Perhaps God's message to us when our prayer of faith is not answered is "My child, you are not a helpless, innocent victim who needs to be rescued. There are things you can do to triumph over this situation. Ask me for the wisdom and the courage to overcome!"

Most Christians (at least in the U.S.) do not want to go through any kind of suffering. They want, in order, 1) an instant healing miracle, or 2) something to happen to them such as a drug treatment where they don't need to do anything. Very few Christians pray a way for them to work out their own healing without realizing what they might be missing by avoiding this approach!

For example, a woman in her late forties acquiresd cancer. She prays, her family prays, her church prays, but no healing. Then I pray the prayer I typically pray with people who ask for healing. I pray that she will be healed AND that God will give her the wisdom to participate in that healing AND that whatever the results she is at peace in her relationship with God. She starts studying cancer. Perhaps she even contacts the Weimar Institute or similar organization. She learns how to deal with cancer through natural means and receives both a healing and an education. The education helps her to stay in remission rather than return to a lifestyle that would allow the cancer to return.

Do people ever receive miraculous healings? Sure. But who are we to demand that we deserve a miracle just because someone else received one? We end up sounding worse than spoiled children at Christmas. My point is not to stop praying for miracles. My point is that if we do not receive a miracle, don't start questioning our faith. God may very well have something for our faith to do. We should instead find a way to work out your faith by participating in moving our mountain.

12-10-04 * NEWS FROM THE FRONT

We lost a few more Americans in Mosul this week due to suicide bombings and improvised explosive devices. Three of them were stationed in Washington. Our unit is safer on our new base. I did not come to Iraq to be safe while other soldiers continue the fight for a secure Iraq. I would prefer to work in Mosul but that is not my decision. I feel detached from my life lately, as if I am merely marionette acting at the direction of a puppeteer thousands of miles away. I realize that many people view soldiers as nothing more than actors blindly following stage directions, yet in Mosul I felt that I at least played an important role in the international drama. Here I am a stagehand, cleaning the set and preparing backdrops for the next troupe.

My job includes surveying all of the buildings on base to ascertain their availability for American use. Two others work with me. We explored underground bunker complexes, hangars, and maintenance, power and communication facilities. I first hoped we might stumble across something interesting or important hiding behind a panel or buried in a cement vault. Nothing. Anywhere. Iraqis stripped the entire base clean before the first wave of Americans occupied the field. They took all of the electrical and plumbing fixtures, the floor tiles, even the wiring to use in their own homes. Most of the base is like walking into a ghost town in the Arizona desert, some signs of life in the not too distant past but only jackrabbits, pigeons and vipers remain.

No illegal missile silos, no weapons of mass destruction labs, no Ba'ath secrets revealed or devilish plots unveiled. At the apex of activity this base at most assembled air-launched missiles for the MIGs and Mirages stationed here and housed 1,000 – 1,200 soldiers.

Last week a soldier told me he found a black mamba snake in a manhole while surveying underground conduits. This week we decided to clear them of snakes. I doubted that black mambas live in Iraq but reported it to the chain of command since the soldier appeared very certain ("I researched it on the internet and it's the same snake"). We found the snake this week; a black viper roughly 18" long. Still poisonous but not as deadly as the embellished story I heard last week. We also found a tan and brown viper, about the same length, that fell into a different manhole. My two colleagues and I set them both free. Ten years from now if I see a headline that a soldier on this base died from the bite of a huge, black viper I might regret our compassion but this week it felt like the right thing to do.

I visited with an interpreter here who has a bachelor's degree from Baghdad College in economic administration and a Master's in English. The Master's degree is different than an American degree of the same name in that the emphasis under the Ba'ath party was not mastery of the language but translating documents in that language into Arabic for the government. I learned that the College was one of two colleges started in the Baghdad area by the Jesuits in the later 1930s. The Ba'ath party nationalized both schools in 1968 and kicked the Jesuits out of Iraq. A Muslim, born in Mosul, she told me that she refused to join the Ba'ath party. They questioned her repeatedly about why she wanted to study English and whom she knew in English speaking countries, predominantly the United States. She confirmed that the government did not charge tuition but she did need to pay for books and living expenses. After her bachelor's degree she worked for the Health Department. She made $2 (U.S. equivalent) per month. The doctors who worked for the department made $4 per month. Since the ousting of Saddam wages continue to climb. The doctors now earn $500 per month. To employ more people, many government jobs, her admin position included, required only 30 hours per week. She studied for her Master's degree after work. Now she works for the U.S. government translating Arabic into English. I did not inquire into her present salary.

I asked her thoughts on the upcoming election. She replied that she does not trust any of the candidates running for national offices. She is familiar with many from her previous position and others at least by reputation. She told me several times that she is going to write in "George Bush" for the position of President, not as a joke or to imply that the new government is a puppet of the Bush administration but because she fully believes Pres. Bush would do a better job for Iraq that any of the current candidates. She claims to have convinced the rest of her family to write his name in as well.

She shuddered as she told me a story of someone she knew whose tongue was cut off for questioning one of Saddam's decisions. Even those who joined the Ba'ath party lived in fear although they were favored in some ways such as job placement and travel. Our interpreter was not allowed out of the country. Her travel between cities in Iraq was often criticized and always scrutinized. Once the new government is installed, she hopes to obtain a passport and start traveling. I asked her several questions: Is she glad Saddam is no longer in power? Definitely. Feelings about the American presence in Iraq? Our military offers the only solid, short-term hope for success. Possibility of Democracy working in Iraq? Maybe in 10 years.

Our interpreter's views obviously do not represent all Iraqis, yet I find in them a theme consistent with others I talk with. They are glad Saddam is gone, they want the Americans to stay, and they are not optimistic about a viable democracy in Iraq within the coming few years. Their pessimism does not stem from ill feelings about what the Coalition Provisional Authority created, other than they wished we could have continued it longer, but because they do not trust the politically connected Iraqis running for office. Resembles how some Americans feel about politics in our country: results will be the same no matter who wins so why bother getting excited about voting.

Someone recently sent me a copy of an e-mail that another soldier wrote about the height of attacks in Mosul. Since the incidents he described happened at a time when our unit was in charge of the area under discussion, I knew with certainty that about half of the stories were either magnified or complete fabrications. I wish I could state that all stories written by soldiers on the front lines are true. I hope mine are at least objective. Some soldiers make themselves look heroic by exaggerating their involvement in certain conflicts, others report stories told by their buddies as fact (like I reported a black mamba on our base last week), and some downplay or skip parts of the action so their loved ones won't worry.

12-17-04 * News From the Front

This week American news services reported more murdered bodies discovered in Mosul, a health ministry official assassinated, and continued IED and indirect fire attacks on coalition forces. Some of the violence is now thought to be Kurdish faction against Kurdish faction, questioning the presumed stability and unity of the Kurdish region. This type of violence will not cease with national elections. Some Iraqi leaders even question whether democracy is the most appropriate form of government to create in Iraq at this time. If Iraq is to survive as a nation something strong alliance needs to surface, some identity that motivates people to act. The other possibility is an authoritarian system with the power and will to govern in the face of violent opposition without becoming violent itself. The Iraqi people may be so disgusted with the current state of affairs that they will vote away their potential democracy to create one or more sheikdoms or Islamic states. The democratic drama continues to unfold.

The chapel on our base held a memorial service for two Apache pilots, stationed here, who died in a tragic accident in Mosul. I find it easier to accept the death of our soldiers if they occur in the line of duty than if the result of senseless American error. The initial report is that an Apache and a Blackhawk, both in blackout conditions, collided on the airfield. We pray for the families, find ways to cope or deal with the questions, and continue the mission.

At our new base we experience none of Mosul's conflict or political theorizing, just frustrations of a distant bureaucracy changing local decisions. Even though I often find work mundane or different than I would chose if given the opportunity, every day I find ways to do the work as required and mark the day one successful step toward getting home. Years ago, then Sergeant Major of the Army Woodridge remarked: "In our Army, every soldier must care about his job. Often if the duty seems menial or humdrum, it is hard to cultivate this attitude. But it must be done. What you do in your job each day you do for the Army." The same can be said of, I imagine, every vocation or pastime. Every day people all across America (and maybe a few Canadians) daydream briefly but fondly about a different life, fume over decisions that negatively impact their life, rant at injustice inherent in the system, then set about their own tasks and make their world a little bit better than the day before. Soldiering is no different, other than the stakes are higher.

This week also witnessed the passing of a wedding date of one of our soldiers, a ceremony postponed by our deployment. We marked the occasion by giving him marital advice for when he does get married after our return. Male soldiers, isolated in Iraq for 10 months, giving marital advice to a young man about to embark on this sacred voyage is not the most useful collection of wisdom. Although we started with the tough guy concepts (How many men does it take to open a beer? None... it should be open by time she brings it to you), mature insight prevailed. One remarked that, in a marriage, the wife is really in charge and gives the husband permission to say he is to his friends. Another stated that the worst statement he ever made to his wife occurred as he looked out the car window at a pedestrian; "Some people should not wear Spandex, but she can get away with it." A third passed on tips to survive questions such as "Does this dress make me look fat?" Hint: two incorrect answers are "Yes" and "It's not the dress, dear."

Some spouses worry about the changes their mates go through in a deployment, whether upon returning home, for example, a once well-trained, housebroken husband might turn into a wild, potty-mouthed, restless, imbiber. If this week is any indication of at least the soldiers I am fortunate to serve with, professionalism will prevail and even our engaged soldier will build a foundation to live happily ever after.

The unit finally administered an Army Physical Fitness Test (APFT) this week. As National Guard units, we are required to record an APFT to Army standards at least annually. Our last APFT occurred prior to deployment in Nov. '03. I scored 215 last year and topped the scales at 242. The test consists of performing as many correct push-ups as possible in two minutes, then as many correct sit-ups as possible in two minutes, then running two miles. Each event is scored out of 100 and their sum equals the total score out of 300 possible points. The Army weight standards require a body-fat analysis for people over a certain height/weight ratio. For my height, if I weigh 214 or less I do not need a body-fat test. When I arrived in Iraq I set a goal that, when our next test occurred, I would weigh less than my limit and score significantly higher on the APFT. The new results are in: 213 lbs. and an APFT score of 274. Consuming Christmas cookies and candy sent from hundreds of supporters is not helping maintain the weight loss. However, I have not set a post-APFT maintenance goal yet so I am enjoying a sample of every package other than the Christmas stockings. My official story is that we are saving all of our Christmas stockings to open Christmas Day as requested by the donors.

Christmas is just over a week away. Christmas is a different, not entirely pleasant, feeling this year. Christmas in Iraq is vastly different than at home. I do not miss the crowded malls, mailboxes stuffed with ads, merchandisers telling me that I can find the Spirit of Christmas by spending money at their shops. I do not miss the political turf wars that secularize, if not eliminate, any reality of Christmas so certain groups will not feel offended.

I do miss my immediate and extended families. I miss waking up next to the love of my life, thanking God for the gift He gave me when we met. I miss time with my children on Christmas, sharing something of ourselves with each other in the gifts we bring. Sending presents will not replace the lack of presence I feel. I miss our large family gathering. Even though I see some of my relatives once or twice a year, and know them less than I know some of my friends, the annual invitation to our Christmas gathering reminds me of the important role they played in my life and of the vital role all families play in a strong society.

Two weeks ago I started wondering if a Christmas miracle would occur this year. Miraculous things can happen when people believe. One sad aspect of miracles is that so few people ever notice them. The Christmas story occurred and, out of the millions of people alive at that time, only a handful of shepherds, a small group of astronomers and a priest in the Jerusalem temple knew about it. A miracle could happen this Christmas and most of us would never know. What captures our attention instead, and especially makes the national news, concerns death, destruction or deception even at this time of year.

Some people question why I use Christmas as a time to remind myself and family of miracles. I would rather reinforce believing in miracles than believing in, for example, flying reindeer helping an old man in a red suit deliver toys made by elves in a secret sweat shop at the north pole to children all over the world in a sleigh about the same size as a carriage but able to carry everything in one trip so you better be good this year or I will tell him otherwise.

Other people question the entire concept of miracles since numerous bad things happen in the world that miracles could but do not prevent. Our joy this Christmas is celebrated in the shadows of the most tragic, fatal incident to befall American troops in Iraq since the start of Operation Iraqi Freedom. Even a scant perusing of the news this week would include reports of what some reporters call the Massacre in Mosul. 22 deaths, over 70 injured, all the result of an explosion in the dining facility on Marez during lunch. Soldiers from our base interact daily with Marez and MAF. Some of the soldiers killed and injured this week were stationed here at Endurance, working at Marez that day for various reasons.

The explosion is under investigation. Current findings suggest a local national worker who worked on the base long enough to have access to the area turned suicide bomber. Marez and MAF have a similar dining facility, both frequent targets of mortar and rocket fire. MAF has the only military hospital and aircraft landing facility in the city. The office we occupied on MAF was located about halfway between the dining hall and the hospital. The dining halls have high concrete barriers around the outside. The only way a typical mortar or rocket would do any damage is a direct drop inside the barriers, a difficult feat considering the imprecise equipment they use. Since the bad guys failed to hit us indirectly, this time they used a more direct and deadly approach.

During our stint at MAF we received almost 400 rounds of indirect fire and several direct attacks including a suicide bomber driving a large explosive charge into our main gate. Yet we experienced no US fatalities on our base. Why? Providence? Miracles? Better force protection measures? Bad guys less dedicated back then? I have no better answers to those questions than why people continue to send fruitcake as Christmas gifts.

According to American military statistics compiled after the invasion of Fallujah in November, nearly 500 of approximately 700 terrorists in Iraq aligned with or sympathetic to Zarqawi and Al Qaeda live in or around Mosul. One conclusion I draw from this is that the Fallujah insurgents who then came to Mosul were really returning home and not coming to Mosul because Mosul is the next safe haven on a list. Military officials estimate that about 11,000 to 20,000 insurgents are spread throughout Iraq.

Fewer anti-American Iraqis exist or appear willing to do battle. It used to cost $50 to hire an Iraqi to fire a rocket-propelled grenade at American troops; it now costs $100 to $200. Important captures have been made recently, including a top Zarqawi lieutenant, Abu Saeed. More than 200 insurgents have been killed in Mosul in the last month as the military is taking a more operationally aggressive stance than first taken at the transfer of authority to the interim government, a move I wholeheartedly applaud.

CHRISTMAS EVE * NEWS FROM THE FRONT

All bases in northern Iraq are on high alert. In addition to our normal duties some of us have guard duty as well. For many of us Christmas is a 10 – 12 hour work day but not because of last minute shopping or presents to wrap or food to bake or children to placate. Tomorrow we plan to enjoy a meal together as a unit thanks to organizations that donated boxes of food. One of our officers cooked most of the food using a large toaster oven and a propane camping stove. Another officer somehow acquired two turkeys. We didn't ask. The commander decided to deep-fry them – generally my least favorite way of preparing food but I am told I will thoroughly enjoy deep-fried turkey or receive a full refund.

We also received boxes of presents and stockings from family and other supporters. No one in our unit is left out. In fact, the support is so overwhelming we decided to share our bounty with soldiers of other units and some interpreters that work for us.

If there is a miracle this Christmas, perhaps it is the love we share with each other that can even reach half-way around the world to people we barely know.

12-25-04 * CHRISTMAS IN IRAQ

The Christmas message of "peace on Earth and good will to all mankind" rings hollow this year for soldiers engaging enemy targets in a predominantly Muslim country. Detached from my family and dearest friends, part of me rebuffs the mediocre decorations and dispassionate celebrations available to help soldiers cope with the loneliness of separation at this family-focused time of year. Yet I also know that, for peace to survive, we must live the Christmas message in these less than hospitable circumstances.

In Iraq we do not have, nor do I wish to recreate, overcrowded malls, mailboxes stuffed with superfluous advertisements, or merchandisers pontificating that I can best demonstrate the Spirit of Christmas by purchasing their wares, on credit if necessary. I do not want to import the political diatribes that secularize or eliminate any reality of the original Christmas story. I do not miss the smog of stress strong enough, at times, to choke the spirit of charity and joy out of the Christmas air. Christmas, our season of peace, too often materializes as an emotional, economic or legal battleground. Lonely individuals walk deserted streets, their only potential company another disenfranchised, wandering soul. People measure love with dollar signs and disrespect the thoughtfulness of others if a gift does not meet their exorbitant expectations. We do not need these ignominious aspects of Christmas in Iraq or in America.

One Muslim, English-speaking Iraqi expressed to me that he does not see hope for peace in Iraq. Despite our heroic efforts and generosity, he fully believes the new government will fail to end IED explosions, ethnic and sectarian violence, or the vitriolic assassination of Iraqis who simply help someone of a different nationality or religion. I shared with him my hope based on our determination and commitment to create security in Iraq. "It is not enough," he replied.

To produce peace in Iraq we need a miracle of supernatural, Christmas proportions. We need wisdom to interpret the stars sent to guide us, and humility to ponder solutions as inconceivable as a baby in a manger.

Presents under an 18" tree adorned our conference table at the office Christmas Day. Although a workday, we leisurely consumed a lunch on Christmas as grand as any back home. By time I reached the break room, only a skeleton remained of the deep-fried turkeys. I still do not know how it tastes, other than listening to the "This is the best turkey I've ever tasted" comments by those with better timing. I am so happy for them.

I argued that, born in Canada, I should get Boxing Day off. The Major laughed. Not only did I get to work a full day, I posted guard duty on a perimeter tower that night from 10 pm – 2 am and needed to return to the office by 8 am for another full day. That's life in the Army. We remain at a heightened security level following the Mosul incident. Most enlisted soldiers in our unit have additional guard tower duties until the security level stabilizes. Officers, higher ranking enlisted soldiers and females of any rank are not on the guard tower duty roster. We perform guard duty with an Iraqi soldier, a combination that often does not work well if our soldier is a female. Their male-dominated culture views females so differently that their biases force us to bend our equality standards. Many Iraqi soldiers refuse to work with or take any amount of direction from a female. A few times in the past sexual harassment incidents arose resulting in the firing of the Iraqi soldiers involved. We are not likely to change their centuries-old traditions and, with our new status as guests in their country (not exactly, but closer to guests than, for example, occupiers) the simplest solution to the problem entails restricting female soldiers from working directly with Iraqis in any isolated duty.

The towers are open on three sides, allowing a full view of and direct fire access toward a long segment of the perimeter fence. The open stance also means that the tower stays cold at night. Temperatures drop into the low 30s every night and that night was no exception. The tower I occupied contains a kerosene heater similar to and slightly larger than a Coleman lantern. Since lights in a tower make them an instant target, the heater is maintained at a level producing only a dull red glow. Dressed in polypropylene underwear under my uniform,

a Gortex jacket and gloves, I shivered most of the night, often walking a tight
circle in the tower to keep my blood circulating.

The Iraqi guards work a 24-hour shift followed by two days off. Two Iraqi
guards stay in a tower on shift although one is allowed to sleep on a cot in the corner. I climbed the stairs into the tower and discovered one guard sleeping under a
single blanket, the other sitting on a stool and warming his hands over the heater.
The latter stood and invited me to sit in the only chair. I checked the radio and
night-vision goggles, and then joined him in the small circle of warmth.

The first guard I worked with spoke very little English, though still infinitesimally more than my Arabic. I learned that he is in his early 30s, is married
and has two children, ages 9 and 12. He lives in Qayarrah and began working
with Americans since the 101st Airborne arrived. He cleaned helicopters for
them. When the 101st left, the helicopter population dwindled on this base so
he started working as a tower guard. I sensed that he possessed an aircraft background and probably worked on the base in or for the Iraqi Air Force in some
capacity though he did not directly communicate either of these assumptions.

Two meals arrived shortly before midnight. The guard ate a few bites of a
pastry but ignored the boxed meals. He placed a tortilla looking flat bread on
top of the heater. Soon the smell of warm bread with a hint of kerosene filled
the tower. He broke the bread into several pieces, chewing each piece slowly. I
alternated between watching him and scanning the horizon. He finished, rubbed
his hands over the heater, politely woke up the guard sleeping on the cot and
curled under the blanket.

The second Iraqi stretched, muttered a few phrases in Arabic, scanned the
landscape and sat on the stool. After warming his hands for several minutes he
picked up the two Styrofoam containers and handed one to me. Not accustomed
to eating at night, I did not expect to receive, or necessarily want, any of the
guard's food. I lifted the lid. In the darkness I could not see more than an outline
of the food yet the enticing aroma informed me the food did not come from
our "If it's bland, it's grand" mess hall. Basmati rice covered with something that
tasted like chicken, meaning it could have been almost anything; squirrel, snake,
but not camel. I have heard from someone claiming to know through experience
that camel does not taste like chicken. After a quick midnight snack I opened
a bag of sour gummy worms and offered one to my companion. He took it,
although I did not stop to think what it might have looked like to him in the
dimness. I offered him another one after he finished but he refused, pointing to
a tooth and muttering that it hurt.

He pulled out a tattered book and attempted to read it in the red glow of the heater. After several minutes of watching him squint at the pages I turned my flashlight on. He held a well-used Arabic-English phrase book. He flipped through the book, stopping at phrases such as "You are nice"… "My name is Abdullah"… "I am 25"… "I live in…" followed by the name of his nearby village. He pointed out several common sentences, teaching me to say them in Arabic.

Stopping at a page of religious terms, Abdullah asked me "Are you a Christian?" I replied affirmatively. "Christian good. I am a Muslim. Muslim good." Then he made a gesture of holding out the index finger of both hands and moving them together, side-by-side. "Muslim and Christian should be like this," he added, tapping his fingers together. I agreed.

He then turned to a page of occupational titles. "I am a carpenter," he announced proudly. He told me that his father worked at the airfield as an electrical engineer. Well-educated, hard working yet paid very little by Saddam's government. The family lived in poverty and scrutiny. Abdullah referred to Osama as "bad", the terrorists as "bad", his teeth as "bad" but he did not label Saddam that way. He appeared to be searching for a word far worse than "bad". His face showing deep disgust. Finally he held an invisible AK-47 and said, "I shoot Saddam… I shoot him." His anger against Saddam did not pass as quickly as the pages turning in the phrase book.

He asked me what I do in the States. I told him that I am an attorney, without going into details of just passing the bar and not having a full-time job in over five years. "Good," he replied. "Attorney good. Are you Rick?" he asked. Rick? I looked puzzled. He pointed to a word in his book. Rick, written with a "k" and pronounced in that manner by Abdullah. The word directly beneath Rick was translated "Poor" so I concluded he meant to ask me if I am rich. I do not consider myself rich according to American standards, but after listening to him describe his poverty, I do not feel poor either. I am married to someone I adore, we have a combined family of six great kids, I am blessed with hundreds of friends and acquaintances, inside our home we do not need to be concerned about 30 degree temperatures in the winter, and I am not likely to get tortured in the U.S. for speaking my mind in political circles.

The bulb in my mini-mag flashlight burned out with about 20 minutes left in my shift. We warmed ourselves, monitored the perimeter, and chatted without the benefit of the phrase book. When I departed I said good-bye to him in Arabic. He beamed. One question continued to preoccupy my thoughts. Am I rich? If Abdullah could have in Iraq what I have back home he would consider himself rich. Some wealthy people do not possess, and cannot buy with all of their money, blessings in my life I sometimes take for granted; love, health, friendship, respect, opportunity, peace, joy. Yes, I am rich in the truest sense of the word. I am blessed. And I am grateful.

As I reflected on the four hours I spent in that tower, I wonder if I did find a miracle this Christmas after all. Like two shepherds watching for danger while hundreds of troops lay sleeping, we shared a meal in the darkness, communicated with the help of a worn translation tome, looked at bright stars in the clear night sky, and huddled around a small heater for warmth. His one simple question reminded me to be content in all circumstances, to be grateful for what I have rather than waste any amount of time or energy in regret over what I do not have, to live in peace, to remember that I am indeed rich no matter what my bank account tells me.

The extra security measures in place because of the recent dining hall explosion in Mosul and the upcoming elections created a plethora of additional activities even for soldiers on our remote base. I accompanied two external patrols this week, glad for an opportunity to get off the base for a while. Not much to look at around this base; buildings completely leveled in previous campaigns, abandoned fighting positions, dirt roads leading to an empty horizon. All of the signs are in Arabic. At one intersection we looked to the right, following a dirt road with our eyes until it disappeared into the Al Jazari desert. From the driver's seat I asked the other guys, "Do you think if we followed this road we might find a Dairy Queen?" They both expressed a strong belief that we would not so I continued along our preassigned route. No AAA from which we could request maps or travel advice, no mapquest.com, not even a young goat-herder. Staying near the base we did not run a risk of getting lost, but I wanted to go on a little adventure.

One adventure did, unfortunately, materialize this week. An Air Force plane crashed. No fatalities. A few serious injuries but most of the passengers will be fine. The crash will not likely make the news and is under investigation. One of the search and rescue team members asked me, "First live crash site?" I nodded. I guess I had the same bewilderment in my eyes other first-timers display, revealing their novice ranking in the airplane crash site community.

A C-130, the same type of plane that carried me here from Kuwait and will likely return us to Kuwait when it is our time to depart. Looking inside the plane at a HWMMV strapped to the rear of the plane, I commented that the passengers were fortunate the straps held. The inspection team member told me that the straps had broken under the forward thrust of the HWMMV on impact. A pallet between the vehicle and the passengers stopped the HWMMV from catapulting into the passenger area. The inspector commented that the passengers are lucky to be alive.

Violence continues in Mosul, perhaps the second most dangerous area of the country now. The targets include American troops, Iraqi elected officials, voting areas, places where voting materials are stored, and people registering to vote. News of 18 bodies found in a field, all Iraqis whose only crime was getting on a bus to find jobs at our base. The bus was hijacked and all 18 job-seekers executed. Democracy will not come easy for Iraq. The terrorists are not working to create a Muslim state; they want instability, which gives them freedom to operate. They want destruction, death, intimidation. They want the U.S. to look bad in the eyes of the world and especially in the eyes of the Iraqi people.

During the creation of Iraq and some Arab states following WWI, the U.S. took a strong position of self-determination. I think we backpedaled from that stance. I wonder whether we are imposing on Iraq our view of what is best for their country, a view tainted by what is best in their country for U.S. security, U.S. economic interests, perhaps even a U.S. self-image. I do not mean to suggest that our course of action is wrong or worse for Iraq than what another other country would create here. I do mean that solving Iraq's security issues, repairing the infrastructure damage and managing the oil proceeds for all Iraqis might require a different form of government than a government that would be the best for U.S. security. But now I am speculating about political intricacies far beyond my circumference of visibility.

Amidst the seriousness of our work we do try to laugh, tell jokes, and even pull an occasional minor prank. The *M.A.S.H.* show would never need to fear a rivalry from us as the majority of what we spout forth as humorous anecdotes either would make Jerry Springer cringe or contains more flops than Roger Ebert's book *"I Hate, Hate, HATE This Movie!"*

I was sent to our medical clinic on a particularly difficult breathing day. I waited in the exam area with one other patient, his malady a sprained ankle. A female doctor and assistant started with the ankle injury. The doctor described how he needed to continue taking care of his sprain because many people damage their ankles by placing weight on sprains too soon. "It would be better for you if it was broken," she remarked.

I suggested, "Then why don't we just break it for him?" All three of them looked at me, astonished expressions rendering them speechless for several seconds. No one laughed.

The x-rays showed a spot on my lung the same size as in the November x-rays. At least it isn't growing. When I returned to our office, someone asked me "Well, are you dying?"

"Yes," I gloomily replied. Noticing their horrified faces, I added, "The doctor said that even with proper exercise and nutrition I have only about 40–50 years." I smiled. No laughter. I stopped smiling.

Our first sergeant frequently remarks, "A red-headed monkey could do that job!" to people he thinks capable of working harder. Our son Layne, 9 years old, sports a fuzz of flaming red hair that makes him the envy of older ladies who would do anything to have hair that color. We started calling him our red-headed monkey when he decided to entertain house guests with chimpanzee antics. We laughed, even though we tried not to, and our laughter encouraged him to do sillier and louder primate tricks. The day after my medic visit, our first sergeant stomped into our office, bellowing his famous line. I stood up, announced, "I don't know about that, but I know a red-headed monkey can do this!" and proceeded to imitate Layne imitating a monkey. More blank stares. I struck out worse than the Seattle Mariner's starting line-up.

This week I did, indirectly, finally bring raucous laughter to our office. I picked up my laundry and discovered that the poly-propylene pants I wore on the night of the guard tower duty had shrunk so much a red-headed monkey could not fit into them. I showed my roommate first, as I uncovered the shrunken skivvies while stowing my laundry in neat military fashion in our container. He laughed so hard his side ached. I did not feel sympathetic. The first sergeant became hysterical, in the hilarious sense, and took possession of the paltry poly-pros to show everyone. With unintended visual humor I succeeded with my goal of getting people to laugh this week. Now if I could only bottle those results and take a sip before telling a joke.

I am glad the Seattle Seahawks are in the first round of the NFL finals. I am the only one in the office who believes they have a chance to beat the Rams. Optimistic to the end, I think it is about time a major league Seattle sports team won a championship. After a 25-year absence since the Sonics victory in the NBA we are due a major league title. My wife, and a few others, might want to remind me that the Seattle Storm won the Women's National Basketball Association title last year. I would like to point out that I was discussing major league sports. (pause for dramatic affect) I wish I could tell if anyone is laughing.

01-07-05 * "NEWS FROM THE FRONT" COMES TO AN ABRUPT AND PAINFUL END

January 7 * I injured my back moving furniture during preparations to return home. I later went to the gym to stretch and bend my way out of pain. Nothing helped. The pain is so intense, perhaps the most pain I have ever felt in my life. Given the number of accidents and injuries I experienced doing high risk activities I cannot fathom how this much pain can result from such a trivial incident. I took a Motrin, okay a few Motrin, and went to bed.

January 8 * This morning I woke up around 2 am in the most excruciating pain of my life. I could not get back to sleep. When Beau woke up I told him I needed to see the medics. Our base only has a battalion aid station staffed by physician's assistants (PA). I felt like asking if there is a doctor in the house but it hurts too much to laugh. The PA gave me more ibuprofen and pain killers, told me to relax and come back Monday. I am unable to walk to meals and must rely on buddies to bring me something, but usually I do not feel hungry enough to eat.

The pain is so unbearable! I can't move. I can't sit up, roll over, and take one single step without wanting to scream. Some people say I must have a high threshold for pain given how seldom I cry out. They do not understand. I have spent most of my life in some sort of physical pain. Add spiritual or emotional pain and I don't think I could find a week of my life without one of the three.

When I was in pain as a child I would cry. My dad would often hit me and say something stupid like, "Let me give you something to really cry about." I learned not to cry. That was a shame really because later I wouldn't even cry when I was sad. I had trouble expressing emotions in any real way, whether love or anger or joy. One of the worst ways to screw up a kid's life is to not let them feel what they are feeling.

"Shh… don't cry!" parents often tell a child. What is wrong with crying when we feel sad? We laugh when we feel happy. And when we love someone, we should find a way to tell him or her how we really feel rather than having to prove how tough we are by not needing them so much. Would it really be such a bad thing to say, "I love you" a little more often?

Sometimes… and every time it happens I remind myself this is not a nice thing … sometimes I wish that everyone who does not believe I am in pain could experience this pain for just one hour. Sometimes I wish that everyone who complains I am not as nice these days could live like this for just one day and see how nice they feel afterward.

My pain isn't just one hour, or just one day. This is every hour of every day with no end in sight! Then add the plans I have with my wife and children that this changes, the desire I had to return home with my unit now unrealized, my goal to become a JAG officer diminishing before my eyes, potential employment with a law firm decreasing the longer this continues.

The reason I am not complaining all the time or screaming out every time I move is that I am spending most of my mental energy on reducing the pain and controlling my anger. Some teachers of what we commonly call eastern traditions can slow their heart rates to levels thought in the west too low to sustain life. We can, with enough practice, learn to control every physical function. I am one of the lucky ones to have plenty of practice opportunities to learn to control pain. Turning anger into patience is not a strong trait of mine and I would really prefer not to practice it in this manner.

Actually, I don't wish this pain on anyone, not even myself. I am angry, I am in intense pain, and I don't want either characteristic to be true for another minute. But a minute passes, then another, then an hour, then two. All I can do is lie on my back, hoping the painkillers will put me to sleep. So far the pain is winning. I am still awake. Normally I welcome every day, rejoicing to be awake and part of this game of life. Not today. Not yesterday, and probably not tomorrow.

Most people are actually very thoughtful – with the exception of two battle buddies who promised to bring meals and forgot, may they feel guilty forever. I am blessed to have such support. I really am grateful! It just that, compared to the possibility that my life as I dreamed it is about to disintegrate, I do not vocalize my gratitude any more than I cry out in pain.

January 10 * My birthday. Monday morning. Stretching, relaxing and pills have not helped ease the pain. I am exhausted even though I spend almost every moment in bed. Every time I roll over in bed the pain wakes me up. Walking hurts so much. This morning I also noticed tingling sensations in my left leg below my knee, muscle spasms in my left thigh and quad that added to the pain. Even with Vicodin the pain level is a 9 – 10. The X-rays revealed a disc problem in the L4/5 area. I am being referred to the hospital at MAF for further evaluation.

Ever since arriving in Mosul I have been asking for a ride in a Blackhawk. Today I got my wish but I would rather have avoided the necessity of this trip. For my birthday, but not at all because of it (the military is not that charitable unless one is deemed especially important); I receive a half-hour ride in a Blackhawk. I disembark at MAF in the evening, shortly after some ING soldiers who received direct RPG fire arrived at the emergency wing. 3 KIA, 6 injured and all of them needing immediate medical assistance. I waited. The PA on duty gave me more pain medication but no exam of any kind. I walked back to my room across the flight line in agony.

January 11 * I returned to the hospital with my referral for an evaluation. I finally found someone who could help. An intake sergeant set an appointment with an osteopath at 1300. I walked to lunch at the food court, glad to be back at MAF but not enjoying the experience. Less than half-way to the food court I stopped at the chapel, unable to walk any further. I met one of the chaplains who updated me on the gospel service. He prayed for me and I continue on. I ordered fajitas for lunch, the first meal I consumed since the injury. I returned to the hospital for my appointment.

A physical therapist evaluated me first. He noted the severity and location of the pain and referred me to the osteopath. The osteopath ordered a CT scan. The scan showed a possible herniated protrusion in L4/5 area, but the doctor wants an MRI to be sure. He began paperwork to send me to Germany.

I wanted to visit Germany during leave and now I am on my way. Once again something I really wanted to happen materializes but for all the wrong reasons. Do I need to be more specific when I wish for something? Do I really need to say "I want to go to Germany between these dates and in good health and not at other times for stupid, asinine reasons such as intense back pain when I won't be able to enjoy the trip?" Walk back to my room and await the flight.

Jan 12* At 0340 the CQ woke me up, although I had not slept. My flight left at 0420. He drove me to the hospital. The paperwork necessary to send me to Germany is complete. The shift crew is new; they do not know the answers to even basic questions such as what kind of plane is coming. A C-130 arrived several hours late but finally we departed MAF destined for Balad and Kuwait. One more noisy, painful, ride but this time hopefully to someone with answers.

The Balad staff welcome me to a CASF (contingency aeromedical staging facility), a medical holding area for patients from all over Iraq destined for either Germany or Kuwait. No, they tell me, I am not headed to Germany today. This is the process. Based on my injury, I am assigned to the litter ward. The other ward is for ambulatory patients. My other companions are a soldier who tore some tendons in his ankle while walking and one who accidentally shot the back of this own leg.

Three days of narcotics starting to take affect. Pain is less severe and negligible when I am lying on my back. It still hurts when I move in my sleep, which wakes me up. I hurt when lying on my side. The numbing sensation in my left shin is increasing. This could mean, according to one nurse, that the reason my pain is decreasing has more to do with nerve blockage than the medications. My frustration level is increasing significantly. A fear that my life might be crumbling consumed me for several hours. Would Philese still love me if this proved permanent? How would we cope financially? How could I play with my kids or do the hundreds of other activities I enjoy?

I diverted my depressive thoughts by adopting one of the best therapies for situations like this: help someone else. My bed is the closest one to the ward's TV. We can watch DVD's or VHS movies. The library contains over 100 VHS tapes but no DVD's, an aside I mention in case anyone wants to know a way to support the CASF. The TV is also connected to AFN but none of the staff can figure out how to display the TV channels. I decide to devote my attention away from my self-pity and to fixing this problem for them and the soldiers who will come to this ward in the future.

After an hour of listening to nurses asking "Shouldn't you be in bed?" examining connections and changing remote batteries, I finally figured out the problem. The TV channel input selector on the TV was set to AUTO. I changed it to CABLE, queued an auto find of stations, and Voila! We had TV reception. Triumphantly I watched the news, although the increased pain from my efforts soon replaced the triumph of my ingenuity.

Jan 13 * I did not sleep at all. Originally told we would be leaving around 0200, I stayed up all night watching news. No plane. A prep team arrived around 0400 with the litter (stretcher) I would be strapped to for the flight. This did not look enjoyable at all! Still no plane. Finally, around 0630, we began preparations. The plane departed around 0830. Between the prep time and flight, I would be strapped to that litter for over 9 hours. Nine hours of lying on my back. Nine hours of my mind trying to put things into perspective. Nine hours of questions, worry, reliving moments of the deployment.

Will Philese be less interested in me? How would any potential long-term injury affect us? Will I still qualify for the JAG commission? Will I be able to find employment? How will I support my family? What law firm is going to hire someone who can't walk into the interview? A firm wanting to check a diversity box for disabled Vets perhaps. This could work out after all. My drug infused brain will not shut up!

01-14-05 * THE LAST FAREWELL

There is a world of alternate reality unfortunately shared across all age groups, economic strata, religions, and education levels. Soldiers, or perhaps their adversaries, enter this parallel universe with greater per capita than any other due to the violent nature of our activities. Intense pain for an extended period of time changes perceptions, creates dependencies, even alters relationships. I touched the edge of that world this week, fortunate not to venture too far. Last Friday, just after sending my weekly e-mail, I injured my back moving some equipment. I spent the next two days fluctuating between intense pain and a drugged stupor.

Sitting in a chair against a pale yellow wall, between a fire extinguisher and a canister vacuum for "infectious medical waste", I waited in agony while soldiers in even worse condition wheeled by on trolley stretchers. A truck of Iraqi soldiers received an RPG round directly into the rear compartment killing three and severely injuring six. Hospital staff wheeled one soldier past my position. His face, what remained of it, was covered with blood. Another, led by a nurse, hobbled past on crutches and one good foot, his other mostly missing.

A radio message reported a Stryker vehicle received direct fire. American wounded on their way. More intense than any stateside ER, this hospital specializes in life saving operations. A herniated disk may be intensely painful but not life threatening. I gladly waited while the staff attended to more urgent care needs.

One CT scan later and the doctors began paperwork to send me to Germany. It seems the fluid in my L4 disc did not like its placement in life and embarked on a nerve-racking excursion. Fortunately, doctors have been working on a spinal lube job that should return me to civilian life soon. In the meantime steroids, Flexoril and Vicodin are helping me stay out of the pain vortex.

I am still having trouble with dependency, nurses constantly reminding me to ask for help when I want something. They explain that I should not look at this situation as a loss of independence but as a method to prevent further injury.

"Let us do our job and you do yours, which is to get better." While the medications keep the pain threshold down, they also prevent my body from telling me when I might exacerbate the damage. One weird aspect of this injury, at least as one not experiencing this before, is a loss of function in my lower left leg while the only pain is in the L5 disc area.

Doctors in Germany will perform an MRI and use the results to determine if I need surgery (a foregone conclusion according to the doctors here) and whether to perform it in Germany or return me to the States. Based on surgery and rehab I may be allowed to stay in the military or I might be discharged. My direct commission to JAG requires a no-deficiency health condition so even if I stay in the Guard I will likely lose my commission. I intend to concern myself with none of these questions, do what I can to regain my health and let the results fall where they may.

As this is my last week in Iraq, this e-mail is my final weekly update. My mission is cut short. The last chapter in a novel should answer remaining questions or dilemmas and leave the reader with a sense of closure and satisfaction. Only fairy tales conclude with "And they lived happily ever after." If viewed from outside the fabric of life, I expect we would not see a tartan plaid, squares of segregated colors, as if flying high above Iowa crop fields in late summer. Rather, I find life a tapestry where joy and sorrow, faith and fear, pain and health weave our life together into a pattern symbolizing our circumstances and how we face them.

A member of our unit revealed to me that he could not see any reason for our transfer to FOB Endurance. For him, God ordained everything that happens to us. He struggled with the reason why so much it affected his countenance in the office. I shared with him my belief that God does not cause all things, rather, God causes all things to work for the good of those who believe. He understood instantly, a smile spreading across his face, eager to cooperate in the plan that would make the transfer work for his good.

This is not the way I wanted my experience in Iraq to end. I joined my unit late, missing the departing ceremony and most of the training. Now I am leaving early, missing the election I wanted to watch from inside the country. Maybe I will be home in time to join the welcoming ceremony for the unit's arrival. After 5 days in three hospitals in Iraq I finally scheduled to fly to Germany. I feel like I just walked through the door in the end of the background canvas on my own *Truman Show*. Due to the uncertainty of the operation, rehab time and what the military will decide to do with me after that, I can't see very far through this door but I do sense possibilities. Two weeks of rehab in the Bahamas paid for by the Army is not one of them. So far the four doctors I asked about relocating to the Bahamas do not think that will happen. Not even my unit commander is backing me on that one.

02-14-05 * FAITH AND LOVE

The hospital staff chose to place me in a Landstuhl barracks rather than at the hospital because I could get myself around, painfully, with a cane, and because they needed every bed for soldiers who need constant medical attention. I met a few soldiers injured in VBIED explosions, mortar attacks or accidents. Some of the soldiers with minor injuries will return to Iraq after treatment. Others will never recover. Every day I am grateful that I can at least get out of bed in the morning.

My third day in the barracks I heard singing from a library room. I hobbled into a worship service already in progress. A Marine chaplain and two assistants ministered to injured Marines. They allowed me to join their group. I desperately needed the rejuvenation.

On my way back to the home one of the meeting attendees stopped me in the hall. He was a visiting osteopath surgeon and wanted to ask me questions about my injury. He believed, based on some simple observations, that he could develop a program to help me walk again without surgery. I listened to him because, to that point, no doctor at the hospital offered such hope. He proscribed a physical therapy program different from what the therapists outlined and his ideas made sense. Within a week I started seeing some progress, although I still needed the narcotic pain medications to help me cope with the pain level.

After an MRI and a plethora of muscular-skeletal tests the Army decided not to treat me in Germany but return me to Fort Lewis for further evaluation. I waited several weeks for the movement orders to materialize confined to quarters for medical safety. Every day I wanted to explore Germany on my first visit to that beautiful country but sorrowfully felt blocked by restricted mobility, high levels of pain, and the barracks staff under orders to ensure all patients followed their treatment programs.

One day I noticed a sign-up sheet with the heading "Marines Only" on the door of the Marine liaison. Of course, the curious Army NCO that I am, I stopped to read it. Some Marines in the U.S. raised money so wounded Marines in Germany could experience a Rhine River cruise and meals at some of the finest local restaurants. The trip leader and primary sponsor was a retired Marine living in Manheim. I wanted to accompany them on the trip but needed a medical release which, the orderly told me, would not be approved for my injury, and approval from the Marine Liaison, also predicted to be denied since more Marines wanted to attend than the tour allowed.

The chaplain's assistant and I became friends as I volunteered to do what I could in their bi-weekly evening services. He tried to secure a place for me on the excursion but reported that the trip was full. The morning of their departure I watched with a sad puppy-dog face as they loaded into three vans. My friend related my story to the trip leader who asked me to accompany them. I literally jumped for joy, felt a stab of pain shoot through my body, stopped jumping, but remained joyful. The desk sergeant didn't even ask for my medical release as he typed my pass. Some people suggest that if God really loves me He would have prevented my injury. People conclude that God does not love them based on what they think God did not do in a certain situation. What about what God DOES do? Terrorists planted IEDs to kill soldiers. The enemy seeks to kill and destroy. Sometimes he accomplishes his evil intentions. God works through people to reconnect, rebuild, restore, regain. People say that if God really did love the world the world would not look like this with wars, murder, hatred, racial and ethnic strife, poverty, hunger. I ask them what the world would look like if everyone committed themselves to God's plan and asked God every day what He wanted them to do. Would we have war? Would we have hatred? Would we have mothers abandoning their children or governments slaughtering their own people? Would people steal from each other, rape, and abuse or kill one another? No. The issue is not whether God fails to perform according to our demented logic of His responsibilities, but what people actually do while failing to uphold our own.

God created people with the power to create and destroy. We can, if we choose, surround each other with love, and encourage each other in faith. Even though I am not experiencing the relief I want from the Army medical system, I am daily surrounded by love. Even though God has not healed me, I am healed in other regards. No matter what my physical condition I can daily participate in God's plan for this world. God has not placed any burdens for participation on me that I am not able to bear. On days when it hurts too much to do anything at all he sends people in my life to lift me up and help me get through the day.

One year ago I wanted to go to Iraq and accomplish great things. Today I wonder if I will ever accomplish anything significant again. This much I do know: God loves me, my wife loves me and numerous people spend hours every day taking care of me because they truly care. I am inundated with loving support from people I hold very dear. I am blessed.

One lesson I am learning living with pain and near immobility is love's power to reach through pain. I believe we win more people to God through loving action that articulate argument. When we see a sister in pain we can chastise her for her stupidity or love her into a stronger recovery. If we see a brother sin we can judge him and, with a righteous finality, never deal with him again, or we can work together with him toward restoration.

Love is not an easy option. Sometimes the results do not justify the effort. Other times we make mistakes and sabotage the outreach. Yet, we continue to love because God first loved us. "If anyone says, 'I love God,' yet hates his brother, he is a liar. For anyone who does not love his brother, whom he has seen, cannot love God, whom he has not seen. And he has given us this command: Whoever loves God must also love his brother" (1 John 4:20, 21). We have our orders.

Our Washington Guard unit just returned from Iraq, some of us experiencing our initial foray into a combat environment. Facing hostile fire for the first time is a rite of passage that sears its induction rituals into graphic, lifelong memories, creating a fraternity often more reluctant to share their stories with outsiders than any ancient lodge. Our year in Iraq, however, taught us some lessons we need to share despite our aversion to discourse.

One is our need to redefine the concept of whom or what comprises an enemy. America's modern enemies do not identify themselves by a specific uniform, national distinctiveness, particular weaponry or other overt symbols. Our enemy specializes in utilizing guerilla tactics, maximizing casualties, and purposefully targeting noncombatants or civilian targets. The leaders behind the international terrorist movements, masters of persuasion and psychological operations, will recruit from and manipulate any religion, ethnicity or ideology that will further their purposes.

The enemy could currently be our friend or co-worker, as we discovered in a Mosul dining facility explosion before Christmas. Lest we embark on a hunt reminiscent of Sen. McCarthy or the Salem witch trials, we may need to redesign our concept of military and law-enforcement operations. I am not generally a proponent of broader government powers and it does seem to me that we are trading some of our civil liberties for a dubious promise of increased security. In this instance, however, the trade-off may prove worthwhile. The police in northern Iraq either could or would not do anything to stop the terrorists. Unless we provide our domestic law enforcement the necessary tools to track sophisticated terrorists and terrorist acts, we could find ourselves combating terrorism on our own soil, a realistic potential I fear worse than abuse of the Patriot Act.

I also realized in Iraq the fallacy of the adage "There are no atheists in a foxhole". A staff volunteer with our chapel, I spoke with hundreds of American and some Iraqi soldiers about their beliefs. Most soldiers who arrived in Iraq without religious values did not suddenly acquire a new belief in God just because of the life-threatening danger level. Some soldiers who came to Iraq believing in God struggled with and, in a few cases, abandoned their faith.

Shortly after my arrival in Mosul, Chaplain H. Tim Vakoc from Missouri received a piece of shrapnel through his skull. If this spiritual leader, this hero to hundreds of soldiers, did not receive the protection for which he prayed, could anyone expect that God would hear their prayers? Many of the soldiers sent home in body bags had families that depended on them, acted as leaders in their church, prayed for the safety of their fellow soldiers in Iraq. Why become a person of faith in Iraq if God's people fare no better that the atheists? Are promises for protection really hollow sentiments meant only to inspire us to bravery? I learned that academic answers for why bad things happen even to believers are not as convincing on the battlefield as when discussed in a safe, calm environment.

The third lesson could prove the most important. In the aftermath of 9/11, our nation moved quickly to restore communication, travel, finance and government systems. We raised a national awareness that if we could not resume living as Americans do, the terrorists would have succeeded in destroying us. Our nation lost over 3,000 lives, our economy billions of dollars, yet we persevered. But something more sinister may be developing.

I witnessed several soldiers become bitter with hatred, willing to apply overkill to a situation, such as annihilating the entire country of Iraq with a nuclear weapon, as if hating someone automatically gives us the right to use deadly force. Others endorsed a hatred for Saudi Arabia, Muslims in general or Shi'ites in particular. While understandable as a reaction to deep pain, soldiers, communities and nations consumed with hatred carry a burden that the actions carried out as a result will not heal. If we live every waking moment in hatred, we are no different than the terrorists we despise. We will not heal our pain but only add fuel to our internal fire.

Epilogue * One Year Later, No Regrets

I love happy endings to well written stories, endings where the good guys win, the hero and heroine live harmoniously ever after, and our sense of suspense and incompletion transform into anticipated satisfaction as the masterful plot designer finally reveals the completed tapestry. With a turning of the final page on such stories I feel closure and, after a reflective pause, a renewed desire to fully engage my own life with the passions that remain long after the book returns to my library shelf.

This story does not have such an ending, but then this tale is years from its conclusion. Although a full year has passed since the incident that prompted my hasty departure from Iraq, none of the major themes are fully settled. Hours of every day are consumed in my role as dance instructor and choreographer for the clumsy coupling of pain management and personal desire; parts of Iraq remain mired in deadly conflict; and answers to the questions that challenged my faith trigger more questions than they settle.

There is enough improvement with each theme, however, to offer hope that continued involvement will create a better ending than the alternative of despondent isolation.

Personal—Walk Tall and Carry a Big Cane

I sometimes imagine a Richard Bach styled parallel existence where the frustration of pain and temporary immobility drive my alter-self to bitterness and resentment. That surreal soldier lashes out at the war, the government, his God, and eventually his family and friends who fail to solve his problems for him. Years later we see him on the streets of Pioneer Square swapping tales of misery with other homeless destitutes and any passerby who might pity him enough to part with some spare change.

When I am tempted to feel bitter I remind myself than if that soldier is a victim of anything, he was first a victim of his own inability to adapt and improvise. I then remind myself that blessings surround me, that God watches over me, and that small progressive steps, repeated often enough, result in incredible journeys.

One year ago I felt invigorated at the thought of heading home. I packed boxes, rearranged living areas, moved lockers, and then my life changed. In less time than it takes to say, "I am not invincible," I went from vivacious, tenacious citizen-soldier to frustrated, pain-racked hospital patient. In Iraq the adrenaline of infusing more than one minute's worth of effort into every minute of the day suppressed any fear that might have surfaced in the pervasive danger of the environment. Confined to bed by the sheer inability to do anything else, fear often seemed overwhelming.

On month later, when the Army finally transferred me from Landstuhl Regional Medical Center to Madigan Hospital at Fort Lewis, Washington, I understood the nature of my injury which calmed most of my fears. I left Germany aboard a civilian flight with a CD copy of my MRI scan, the physical therapy plan created by my osteopath physician guardian angel, and a determination that no matter how many pain pills I needed to take or how much it hurt my wife would see me walk off the plane. Our reunion, and every day since then, positively demonstrates that my adorable wife Philese continues to be my biggest supporter and best friend. Her faith and devotion helped calm my soul to bravely face the incessant, spooky maze called "medical hold".

Med-hold is a detachment or company injured Guard and Reserve soldiers are assigned to while the military sorts out their medical requirements, disability status, benefits and other administrative details. When I arrived the med-hold company included over 180 soldiers. Some of them needed medical treatment identified in their deployment screening. After the treatment they would join their units in Iraq. A few of these deploying soldiers seemed to know how to work the system to continue receiving medical treatment and stay in country. The majority of the unit consisted of returning soldiers requiring some level of medical attention before being released to civilian life. While in med-hold soldiers continue to receive their pay, most soldiers did not want to be there. Not exactly the positive environment I wanted for my recovery period.

As in Landstuhl, soldiers with the most serious conditions received rooms at the hospital itself. I was assigned to a barracks in the vicinity. The med-hold company at Fort Lewis filled a company area in one of the older sections of the base. A van shuttled soldiers to the hospital or elsewhere around the base. By the time I arrived at Ft. Lewis, the med-hold system allowed soldiers who met strict guidelines to recover at home. I desperately desired to receive approval for that program even though it meant termination of my military pay. The staff informed me that based on my injury I would likely remain in med-hold for 12–18 months.

A few weeks later, during my surgery consultation appointment, a doctor informed me that surgery would probably not resolve my pain. According to one reading of the MRI, the discs in my back deteriorated to a degree that negated the feasibility of surgery to relieve my pain. He wrote a temporary 3-month "L3" profile, scribbled a few prescriptions for pain-killers and muscle relaxers in a language I prayed the pharmacist could comprehend, and arranged for daily physical therapy sessions. I did not realize at the time how the MRI reading would complicate the already burdensome, bureaucratic labyrinth of determining military liability for my injury.

According to the med-hold procedures, the length of time stated in a temporary profile indicates when the next medical review should take place. The end date of the profile can also indicate when the soldier will be fit for duty. The profile then simply expires unless the soldier seeks further medical treatment. When my profile neared its expiration date I announced, to the surprise of everyone at med-hold, that I had recovered and was fit to return to duty. In my case, since I had no orders other than med-hold, "duty" meant returning to National Guard status and civilian life. The Army processed my paperwork to end my active duty tour.

From my first visit to the physician assistant in Q-West to my release from Fort Lewis I experienced professional, top-quality health care. I am very impressed with the quality of our medical and support staff in both the military and the veteran's administration system. I am not as impressed with the bureaucratic boondoggle of administrative rules we force them to work under. We, as a country, are perhaps doing more today to take care of veterans than at any time in our history. I am grateful for all of the support.

The National Guard processed me back into a new unit and position reflecting my direct commission. Remaining hurdles included surviving an officer review board and passing Officer Basic Course (OBC). Outside the room reserved for the hearing board, an officer recruiter informed me that the review board never asked any tough questions and only served to weed out the obviously disqualified. That comment did nothing to sooth my concerns. I knocked, approached the three-member panel, saluted, and sat when directed to do so. Without any preliminary conversation one board member tapped on a thick file and requested, or ordered, (depending on your point of view), "Tell us about your back injury." I answered with an honest synopsis of the events and diagnoses. Based on my promise that my injuries would in no way interfere with the duties I owed to the Guard and my country as an officer in the JAG Corps, the review board welcomed me into the fraternity of military officers. I passed the physical fitness test in JAG OBC with my worst PT score ever, but I passed.

Returning from JAG OBC in the fall of 2005 marked nearly two and one-half years of military assignments that started winter quarter of my third year in law school. I submitted over a dozen resumes to various attorney positions in the Seattle area. I decided that if I received 10 negative responses I would open my own practice. In some sense the letters I received were not negative. The Seattle culture is so polite, or lawsuit adverse and afraid of confrontation, depending on your point of view, that none of the letters actually used any synonym of the word "No." Each rejection letter, as if the various firms all hired the same consultant, highlighted my wonderful accomplishments and prophesied that with my stellar credentials I should have no problem securing an appropriate position. The law firm in question, in the opinion of the letter's author, sadly could not offer such an appropriate position. After receiving seven such requiems I decided I could not face any more polite rejection and opened my own practice ahead of schedule.

Some people tell me that my life over the past ten years reminds them of Job, in the Old Testament. They witnessed the events that devastated my life, the years of frustration and searching, followed by the blessings that now surround me on a daily basis, and noted some parallels. One person told me that my life represents the biggest turnaround he ever witnessed. Another said my life is like a Horatio Alger story, just longer. The truth is that, while I lived for years with frustration as my daily companion, I played a significant role in creating my own demise. One day I decided to partner with God and turn my life around.

I first needed to give up my victim mentality. Living as a victim has certain advantages, such as demanding compensation or charity and participating in group therapy pity parties. Overall, though, I do not recommend cultivating the idea that life or people or God treated us unfairly and therefore we have an excuse for our misery. Switching from the victim mentality habit (VMH) to habits that promote success is not an easy step. I replaced VMH with the thought that only one person in the entire world held responsibility for my life and that is the person looking back at me in the mirror. Yes, bad things happened to me, and yes, many times I did not deserve them nor directly cause them. I released my claim that life, people or God owed me because of my misfortune and, instead, focused on what I can do to create the life I want to live.

Fortunately I learned how to relinquish and, later, avoid VMH years before my back injury. I feel a deep empathy for soldiers who return home from Iraq or Afghanistan with devastating injuries. Some of them move on with their lives with heroic courage and perseverance. A few fall into the VMH trap. I do not blame them since I spent several years of my life sinking in VMH quicksand until bitterness and despair clouded my life like a thick London fog. Yet I firmly believe that if I succumbed to VMH one year ago I would not have the mobility I enjoy today, my JAG commission, or my legal practice. More importantly, caustic emotions accompanying VMH would have substantially inhibited the love of my family and friends that plays such a vital role in my continuing recovery and success.

The message I have for soldiers caught in victim mentality (and anyone else with the ears to hear) is "You are right. The lack of fairness, poor leadership, and all of the reasons you express for how your situation happened are not your fault. So stop spending every waking moment trying to convince people. We believe you! Given that all of this is true, the question is, what are you going to do about it?" I recommend you replace any thought or expression of a victim mentality with the realization that you are responsible. I am not suggesting that we are responsible for everything that happens to us, but we are responsibe for what we do about what happened.

Second, I learned the power of incremental steps. Sometimes when I challenge personal responsibility someone vehemently responds, "There is NOTHING I can do!" In this they are not right. Fully ensconced in VMH I uttered and believed those fateful words. Years ago I could not envision how to achieve my dreams and therefore stopped trying. Eventually I learned that every "impossible" goal includes a plethora of possible phases. The key is to continue breaking down all of the phases into smaller components until you look at one part and say, "I can do that one."

At least I thought I learned that lesson years ago. In the medical center in Germany, battling pain and the effects of the drugs, I could not visualize a plan to achieve my goal of walking without pain or drugs. Fortunately, and I believe divinely engineered, an osteopathic surgeon with incredible insight spotted me in the barracks and took the initiative to offer a few suggestions. He explained his philosophy of using pain as an indicator of movements to avoid. We discovered a large range of motions either I could not perform at all (structural or nerve impediment) or could only perform with intense pain. After several hours we discovered a movement I could perform relatively pain free; laying flat on my back with my knees elevated, I pulled one knee toward my chest. He smiled a broad smile that radiated hope. Based on my ability to perform that simple, albeit restricted range, task, he developed a plan.

Under a panoply of changing doctors, including surgeons, physical therapists, chiropractors, and even a dietician, the original-single component plan grew to a daily regiment of stretches and exercises. I needed to relearn how to get out of bed, drive, walk down stairs or pick objects off the floor to avoid injury. Sometimes pain lets me know I attempted more than I can physically handle. Is that not the purpose of pain after all?

Although I no longer need a cane, I keep one in my bedroom. Every day that cane reminds me that somewhere a soldier did not return home, somewhere a soldier cannot get out of bed today, somewhere a soldier needs a wheelchair or cane to help him walk, somewhere a soldier is learning to work with a replacement for a part of himself he left behind. The pain I deal with seems insignificant by comparison. That cane helps me avoid developing a victim mentality and motivates me to keep going, step by step.

IRAQ—SIGNIFICANT PROGRESS MADE AND A LONG WAY TO GO

People ask me how they can follow the progress in Iraq since our national media does such a poor job of reporting any good news from that part of the world. Many soldiers and imbedded reporters wrote memoirs or accounts of campaigns in Iraq. The last time I checked, one on-line bookseller listed over 2,400 titles related to the war in Iraq. Although many of them tell amazing stories, once published, a book turns into history. To learn more about operations in Iraq and stay current with the constant changes I recommend the following resources:

- The USAID Mission in Iraq carries out programs in education, health care, food security, infrastructure reconstruction, airport and seaport management, economic growth, community development, local governance, and transition initiatives. USAID produces weekly updates on the entire scope of their work. Their website includes an archive of their weekly updates that dates back to March, 2003. You can also subscribe to e-mail updates and discover ways to help without signing up for military service.[11]

- For a historical perspective on the transition period under the guidance of The Coalition Provisional Authority, visit their archive of press releases including their final release entitled "An Historic Review of CPA Accomplishments".[12]

- The United States Department of State publishes weekly reports on the progress in Iraq. The update archive dates back to July, 2005. This resource also includes Section 2207 Reports on Iraq Relief and Reconstruction and links to other major reports.[13]

- The Special Inspector General for Iraq Reconstruction (SIGIR) publishes Quarterly and semi-annual reports to Congress including audit reports, congressional testimonies and lessons learned. These reports summarize key findings on the progress of Iraq reconstruction efforts and provide recommendations for corrective action.[14]

- If you want information about traveling to or from Iraq, along with information about various exchange programs, visit the U.S. Embassy in Baghdad on-line before you show up in person.[15]

- In Iraq we monitored Al-Jazeera on a daily basis. The Arabic version provided more interesting information than the English site, but for those who do not know Arabic or do not have the benefit of a government provided translator, I recommend reviewing their English website.[16]

- Finally, a shameless plug for helping others learn stories behind the Iraq headlines - buy a copy of this book for them.

FAITH—TRAINING A FEW GOOD FAITH WARRIORS

One of the most emotionally and spiritually challenging experiences for me in Iraq occurred in discussions following Father Tim's injuries and the assassination of the four missionaries. I originally feared that nothing I said could help soldiers who questioned the validity of faith. What could I add to the observation that faith did not prevent tragedies to some of faith's greatest proponents? Some people believe that there are no atheists in the foxholes of war. I found that there are no easy answers.

In addition to dealing with the horrors of war, soldiers needed counseling or advice for coping with a failing marriage, handling stressful work relationships or praying for illness in a beloved family member. Problems from home intensified under the stress of a battle environment. We needed answers, hope, and a plan of what to do next to keep people actively engaged. We found some of the answers in a discussion of what it really means to ask in faith.

Even though I do not possess a neuroscientist's understanding of glucose metabolism concentrations, I remain fascinated by positron emission tomography (PET) scans and neuroimaging human functions. Glucose is virtually the only energy source for the brain. PET images of glucose concentrations provide a signature or map of brain function. We can see differences in regional activity of the human brain in response to stimuli such as looking, listening, and remembering. We can also distinguish patterns created by various emotions such as joy, peace and anger. I have a theory that if we could isolate faith as a distinct experience, PET scans would reveal a complex and unique snapshot unlike any other human activity.

Faith operates similar to electricity. Whether electricity flows through a particular location in a circuit depends on only three variables; the power source, a proper ground or ultimate connection and the validity of the circuit between the two. If we could isolate a faith experience and map it with a PET scan like an electrical engineer monitors current, I believe the results will show that faith is more than an intrapersonal experience.

We do not, however, need to understand the physiological components of faith (or electricity) to experience its power. Fully immersing ourselves in a present faith connection can bring spiritual energy and hope into any situation. One of the greatest missions of the church today, and sadly one of the most neglected, is to teach members of the body how to live by faith.

A soldier walks into your office thousands of miles from home. He received a phone call days earlier informing him that his wife or child are suffering with a serious illness. He feels helpless, isolated, powerless to do anything, guilty for being absent at a time of great need, angry at the military for not allowing him to go home. His constant prayers produced zero results. The Bible is not giving him the answers he wants. He is quoting all the right Scriptures. Yet a few minutes ago, on another call home, he learned the situation remain unchanged. What do you do or say?

Pray? He's done that, as have dozens of others. Read a Bible verse? He read them all repeatedly. Pull out your copy of "Miracles for Dummies"?

Every situation is unique yet teaching someone to ask in and live by faith worked in every one of them. I do not mean that the results the soldier wanted instantly materialized. By stating that this technique worked I mean a position in which the soldier could respond "I know what I need to do next." We rarely see the entire path before us but it really helps if we can at least see the next step.

The two-pronged technique first asks from a position of faith, "God, what would you have me do?"

Some people object, "I tried that and it didn't work. I didn't get an answer." Sure, they tried asking God what to do, but not from a position of faith. If they could PET scan their soul they would see that they asked in fear, timidity, anger, resentment, anxiety, a plethora of spiritual, emotional or physiological conditions but not in faith.

Adding the words "I ask this in faith" at the end of a prayer does not suffice. We either approach God from a position of faith or something else. The Bible is not a book of magic spells. Connecting with or getting answers from God is not like using an Ouija board or reading a crystal ball. We might convince an entire local congregation of our sincerity or our stupendous faith but God is not deceived.

God invites us to develop a genuine relationship with Him. Faith is both a mechanism for creating that relationship and evidence that it exists. Faith walks, talks, lives, and breathes. Faith becomes an encompassing spiritual, mental and emotional experience. Someone who lives by faith does not wait for God to show up in a time place or manner that others experienced Him hundreds of years ago. Faith is current, dynamic, and as alive as God Himself. When we choose to live by faith and communicate with God through faith He directs our paths in ways we never experienced Him before.

Second, ask everyone involved in the situation to add their faith. Imagine the power of a doctor asking in faith "God, how can I best help this patient?" Imagine what might happen if parents, children, siblings, friends all asked in faith, "God, what would you have me do about this situation?" This approach is radically different than the usual prayer where everyone gets together to tell God what he or she wants Him to do. This format allows God to lead and accesses His wisdom and direction.

A civilian contractor asked to meet with me away from church. He needed prayer for his wife. I sensed that he also needed prayer for himself since he struggled with his lack of connection to God about his wife's illness. He felt powerless to help, guilty for not being home with her and frustrated with the lack of results. He told me that he wanted to see me specifically because he wanted the kind of faith he witnessed in my sermons and prayers. We discussed this faith technique and what it means to ask in faith. Then we prayed. When he opened his eyes his face displayed an incredible sense of peace.

He shook my hand enthusiastically and exclaimed, "I know what I need to do!" Two weeks later he shared the story of his wife's miraculous recovery.

Faith does not guarantee us the results we want. Faith does allow us to feel at peace with God and ourselves no matter what results we experience. Faith eliminates the fear and anxiety entangled in unwanted situations which allows us to focus on the essence of the solution beginning with our relationship with God.

These words of St. Paul encompass every moment of our lives: "And we know that in all things God works for the good of those who love him, who have been called according to his purpose" (Rom. 8:28). No matter the situation, even when I mess up my life seemingly beyond repair, God works for my good. God's plans always work out better than my own plans even when I do not receive the results I want.

I challenge you to live by faith. Pray in walk. Walk according to faith. Then get ready for the most incredible experiences and results imaginable.

NOTES

1. I feel stronger about this message after serving in Iraq. It should take more than willingness to fight for a cause to earn hero status. Terrorists willing to kill thousands of innocent people to promote their cause want people to consider them as heroes. The definitions of hero and terrorist should not depend on cultural objectives. I abhor the rhetoric that one person's (or nation's) terrorist is another's freedom fighter.

2. Dr. Karl Menninger, *Whatever Became of Sin?* (New York: Hawthorne Books, 1973).

3. www.prisonexp.org

4. Seymour M. Hersch, "Torture At Abu Ghraib," The New Yorker (10 May 2004), www.newyorker.com/fact/content/?040510fa_fact.

5. Now Joni Eareckson-Tada, Joni founded an incredible ministry in 1979. You can learn more about Joni and Friends at http://www.joniandfriends.org/

6. See also Christiane Bird, *A Thousand Sighs, A Thousand Revolts: Journeys in Kurdistan*, (New York: Random House Publishing, 2004). The first few pages of this fascinating look at life in the Kurdish region tell a story of our translator's family. I find him an honor and privilege to work with, a credit to the Kurdish people.

7. For example, see: Edwin S. Gaustad and Leigh Schmidt, *The Religious History of America: The Heart of the American Story from Colonial Times to Today*, (New York: HarperCollins, 2002).

8. Don North, *Remembering Saddam*, (DVD, December, 2005) available at
   http://www.rememberingsaddam.com/

9. www.caringbridge.org/mn/timvakoc

10. International Republican Institute, Survey *of Iraqi Public Opinion,*
    September 24 - October 4, 2004, http://www.iri.org/10-22-04-iraq.asp.
    This website includes a written summary and a link to a slide presentation
    of the results.

11. http://www.usaid.gov/iraq/

12. http://www.cpa-iraq.org/pressreleases

13. http://www.state.gov/p/nea/rls/rpt/

14. http://www.sigir.mil/reports/Default.aspx

15. http://iraq.usembassy.gov/

16. http://english.aljazeera.net